KARL PENTA

A Mercenary's Tale

JOHN BLAKE

Published by John Blake Publishing Ltd, 3 Bramber Court, 2
Bramber Road, London W14 9PB, England

First published in hardback in 2002

ISBN 1 903402 59 X

British Library Cataloguing-in-Publication Data: A catalogue
record for this book is available from the British Library.

Designed by GDADesign

Typeset by Mac Style Ltd, Scarborough, N. Yorkshire

Printed in Great Britain by Creative Print and Design (Wales),
Ebbw Vale, Gwent

1 3 5 7 9 10 8 6 4 2

Papers used by John Blake Publishing Ltd are natural, recyclable
products made from wood grown in sustainable forests. The
manufacturing processes conform to the environmental regulations
of the country of origin.

Acknowledgements

Thanks to my co-writer Mike Ridley, to Sue Preston for the many hours she spent transcribing my story and to publisher John Blake. Also many thanks to Dean Shelley for getting the whole thing going.

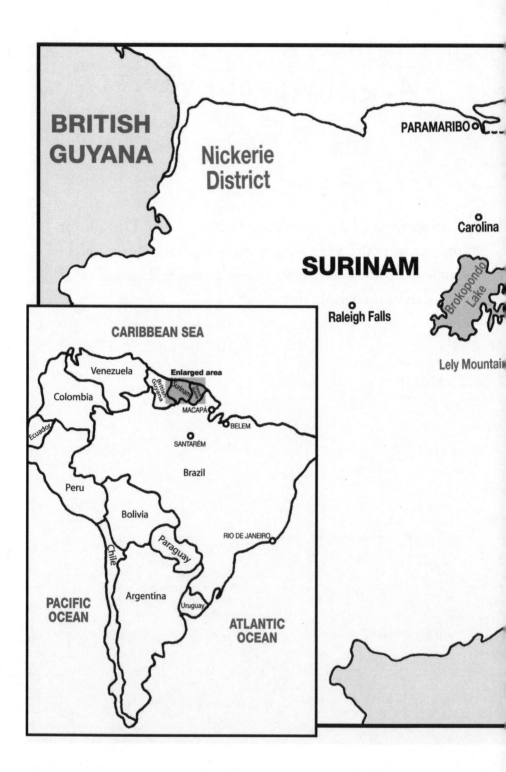

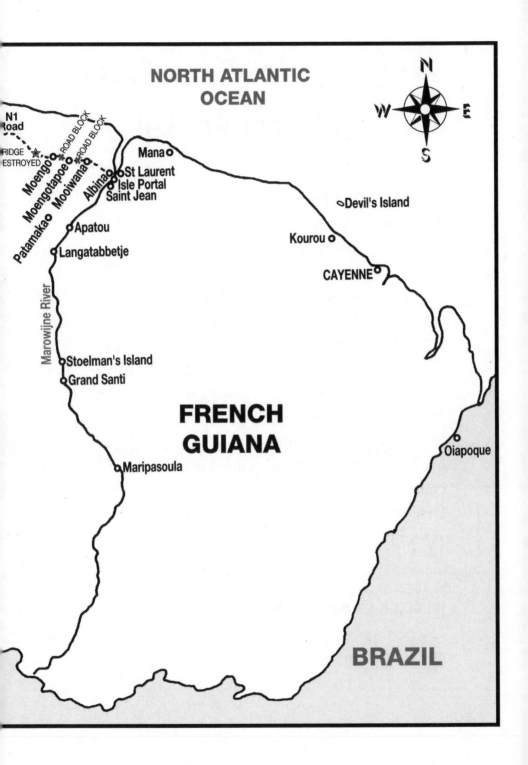

How the Two Sides Matched Up

ARMED FORCES OF SURINAM

2,500 personnel (approx)

Cascavel – Brazilian-made six-wheel armoured car with 90mm gun and laser range finder

Urutu – Brazilian-made six-wheel armoured personnel carrier armed with .50-calibre machine gun

YP – Dutch-manufactured DAF two-man scout car

S-class boat – Dutch-built coastal patrol boat (approximately thirty metres long) with 2 x 40mm Bofors cannons plus machine guns

MAG – 7.62mm machine gun

FN-FAL – 7.62 rifle manufactured in Belgium, or Brazilian copies

Defender – Britten-Norman Islander aircraft (military version)

JUNGLE COMMANDO

250 personnel (max)

40 fire extinguishers and 250 sticks.

PROLOGUE

I rose to my knees behind the cover of a giant tree, brought up the barrel of my FAL assault rifle, flicked the weapon to automatic, and took aim at the truck full of troops. They were all staring down the road ahead. One of them was leaning with his left arm over the edge of the truck, a rifle clutched in his right hand.

As I lifted the FAL and took aim, the man in the sights stared straight at me. He couldn't fail to see me – I was just eight yards away under cover of the dense, steaming rainforest. I let rip. Rat-tat! The first burst of automatic fire hit the soldiers sat at the side of the truck. Over the haze from the muzzle blast, I saw men bouncing and jumping. I fired straight into them. Stop – the mag was empty.

I ducked quickly behind the cover of the tree. John popped up behind me and opened up with one burst as I changed the mag. I rose again from behind the cover of the tree. Click. Nothing. Bastard! I cocked the rifle again. Still nothing. I could see a brass cartridge jammed in the breech. As I changed the next mag, the sound of loud, rapid firing drowned out all other noise. Bam! Bam! Bam!

This was direct firing at one target – me. Dirt spat from the ground. Leaves showered from the tree I was hiding behind. I fell to my knees to clear the weapon. Bam! Bam! Bam! Bam! Bark ripped through the air. I stayed there for a couple of seconds and the firing stopped. My mind whirled; I had to get out of there.

The engine of a Brazilian-made Urutu armoured personnel carrier revved up; then came another loud burst of fire. Leaves and branches fell on top of me. I scrambled round the other side of the tree and watched the Urutu scream back up the narrow jungle road and crash into the bullet-riddled lorry.

Bang! Bang! Bang! Bullets from the Urutu's fifty-cal machine gun just missed me again. Jesus Christ! This guy definitely had a bead on me. I got down on my stomach behind the tree. Another loud burst of fire. I rolled to my right and looked up. Bang! Bang! Bang! He carried on stitching rounds into the ground; the fifty-cal spat out a dozen bullets in a second. I felt one of the rounds touch my trousers and for a sickening moment thought he had taken my leg off. Miraculously, he'd missed.

I rolled over to my left behind the tree. Bam! Bam! Bam! I could feel the heat of the muzzle blast. I rolled backwards and forwards. I knew this guy had a hundred rounds in an eleven-foot belt and that he was going to have me. Then I tried to steady myself: don't worry Karl, any second now this guy is going to be shot by one of the Jungle Commandos on the other side of the road. Any second now they'll get him.

For what seemed like an eternity, I rolled backwards and forwards as bullets ripped into the ground. By now I was convinced I'd catch one at any minute. I cursed myself. I'd only been in Surinam a couple of days and I was already staring death in the face. What a twat.

There was a lull as he changed the belt. I hissed: 'Cover me John.'

Nothing. Where the bloody hell was John?

No time to worry about that now. This is it. Let's go. I ran four or five long paces and threw myself into a thorn bush that almost ripped me to bits. Bosh! I landed on a French cameraman and scrambled out of his way. I was under fire again....

CHAPTER
1

John Richards first spotted the advert in the *International Herald Tribune*:

MEN WANTED
Ex-military personnel to work abroad.

If John hadn't seen it he might be alive today – and I would not have set out on the most amazing job of my life as a mercenary. I wrote off straight away to the address in Holland on the ad. The reply came quickly. It looked like something from *Soldier of Fortune* magazine. 'Please can you help rid our country of this Communist murderer?' screamed a headline above a drawing of a black dictator, blood dripping from a knife in his hand.

I threw it in the bin.

A few days later, more mail arrived, this time begging, 'Can you please help us? We urgently need men, weapons and finance.' 'Jesus Christ,' I thought, 'this lot think I'm a registered charity.'

Instead, I went to India and for six weeks I thought no more about the black dictator. But when I got home, a stack of mail was waiting from an organisation called the

Ansus Foundation, c/o Amro Bank, Amsterdam. This time they'd included a telephone number in the Netherlands and instructions to speak to 'Mr. John'.

I rang him. To my surprise, he said straight away, 'Can you travel in a week's time and bring seven men?'

'Seven men? How are we going to travel? As tourists?' I asked.

'Yes, as tourists. We're going to French Guiana with Air France,' came the reply.

'Seven blokes on Air France – that's going to look suspicious. I think we'll take four.'

'OK, four is fine. I'll call back tomorrow.'

The next day, Mr. John phoned back and told me, 'We need an officer.' I didn't know any officers, but Mr. John was adamant on that point. 'We must have an officer, otherwise it's not really worth going. We need an officer to advise the guerrilla leader you will be working for.'

I put the phone down and rang an old friend, Colin Newman. As far as I knew, he used to be a cook in the British Army and had taken part in Angola with Colonel Callan, so I promoted him to major. I rang back Mr. John. He was delighted. 'A major's fantastic. Can you come over to Amsterdam in three days' time?'

'No problem. I'll bring three men with me, including the officer.'

I rang up former French Legionnaire John Richards, former Cheshire regiment sergeant Keith Kenton and, of course, 'Major' Newman. We'd meet John in Amsterdam. The rest of us travelled together from Manchester airport.

It was cold, raining and we weren't in the best of moods. Keith was carrying an old battered bergen packed to the hilt; it was so tatty that it should have been thrown straight in the bin. In the coffee lounge at Ringway airport, Keith put his hand in his pocket and pulled out a flick knife with an eight-inch blade!

'Keith, look,' I told him, 'I don't know how many planes you've travelled on, but after we've had this cup of coffee we have to show our passports to Immigration and go through Security to get on the plane. They're gonna take that flick knife off you. They'll pull you and us to one side and it's going to cause a bit of a problem, so you'd better get rid of the blade.'

Keith didn't want to. Apparently, he'd had the knife for years. Finally we told him, 'It's you or the flick knife, 'cos you ain't coming otherwise.' After more moaning, he dumped the knife. 'Fucking hell,' I thought to myself, 'I reckoned Keith would be a bit more lively than that.' After all, this was an experienced military guy.

There was no sign of my green nylon rucksack on the conveyor at Amsterdam's Schiphol Airport. I was a bit nervous in case anyone opened it and started asking awkward questions about all the military gear packed inside it. Ten minutes later Keith turned up with my bag – he'd found it mixed up with luggage from a Chicago flight.

Once we reached the hotel in central Amsterdam, Major Newman took over and made contact with Mr. John who arrived a while later with three guys – one was half-caste, the other two were black. The half-caste guy was young – between twenty-five and twenty-eight – tall, thin, lithe, looked fit, with short hair. Quite well dressed, he was wearing an expensive watch, gold chain and pricey-looking rings. The other guy was a slimy-looking son of a bitch. Short, stocky and very black, he wore sunglasses. The third guy looked totally innocent, one of those blacks with a nice, smiling face – cheerful, happy go lucky. They introduced themselves. The half-caste's name was Raymond, the slimy-looking son of a bitch was Keith and little smiler was called Tony.

'Mr. John' turned out to be George Baker. He looked about sixty and had a Mediterranean complexion. He owned a bar just off Amsterdam's red-light district and also ran the Ansus Foundation. He had a huge rolled-up map, the sort that used to hang on the wall at school, tucked under his arm. After shaking our hands he went over to the reception desk, pulled a large wad of money from his pocket and handed it over. He wanted to leave a deposit in case we decided to go on a drinking binge. Things were looking up. Then he turned to us. 'Right boys, how much did it cost for your tickets?' Major Newman had it all written down. We also got fifty quid each in Dutch guilders – enough for a wander around town.

By now, John Richards had arrived. John had served five years in the Deuxième Rep, the French Foreign Legion's parachute regiment. He and I had worked abroad together before. We all sat around a table in the hotel's tiny restaurant as George unrolled the four-foot square map. Imagine four English blokes, two blacks and a half-caste sat around a huge map trying not to look suspicious. The map showed Surinam – a tiny country perched at the top of South America. It's north of Brazil, sandwiched between French Guiana and the former British colony of Guyana.

Bit by bit, George explained that Surinam had once been Dutch Guyana but became independent eleven years earlier in 1975. In 1980, Desi Bouterse, then an NCO PT instructor in the Surinam army, had launched a military coup with just sixteen men, successfully overthrowing the civilian government.

Bouterse declared martial law and claimed the People's Republic of Surinam would take its inspiration from Cuba. Prime Minister Chin-a-sen fled to Amsterdam and launched a Committee of Liberation. Bouterse's next step was to cold-bloodedly execute fifteen of his political opponents – two former cabinet ministers, the dean of the local university, four prominent lawyers and four journalists were among the dead.

Libya's Colonel Muammar Gaddafi paid Bouterse $100 million to open a 'cultural mission' in Surinam's capital, Paramaribo. The Libyans were also running a military training camp near a remote village on the Brazilian border.

In July 1986, six years after Bouterse seized power, one of the dictator's own bodyguards led an uprising of bush negroes – the descendants of black slaves who lived in the jungle along the Marowijne (pronounced Marowayne) River that divides Surinam from its neighbour French Guiana. The former bodyguard, Ronnie Brunswijk, and his rebel force captured twelve government soldiers in their first attack against an army post. On the same day another attack against the garrison town of Albina failed because the rebels – known as the Jungle Commando (or JC) – lacked enough weapons.

A few days later, in New Orleans, FBI officers arrested fourteen U.S. mercenaries who had been hired to fight with the Jungle Commando – they had been recruited by Ansus Foundation director George Baker. We would be fighting with the JC. George showed us the areas the guerrillas held – it didn't amount to much. He also pointed out the rebels' two island bases on the Marowijne River. We fired questions at him: how many troops would we have? What weapons do the enemy have? How much equipment have they got? Apart from being low on weapons, George didn't know too much. In fact, he'd never met any of the guerrillas. He was backing them because he was originally from Surinam and wanted to help. We'd find it all out when we got there. And we were flying out in two days.

The next day, George arrived in a BMW to take us to buy some kit. We pulled up at an army surplus store with a second-hand sentry box outside. Inside, it was full of tents and camping equipment. Keith bought himself a knife and I got a compass; otherwise, the shop was useless.

The following day we drove in a minibus, in the pissing rain, from Amsterdam to Paris. George came with us and on the way we picked up Tony, Raymond and Keith, the guys we'd met that first night. With Air France you can drink as much as you like for nothing – a nice little perk – so Kenton and I got stuck into the wine, while John had a couple of beers – he wasn't much of a drinker. On that seven-hour flight to French Guiana, Newman talked about nothing but getting back to the U.K., so we christened him 'Major Getback'.

Towards the end of the flight, the captain came on the Tannoy: 'Ladies and gentlemen, we are now starting our descent towards Cayenne. If you would care to look out of your left window, you will see Devil's Island.'

After the rain in Amsterdam, the humid heat of the Caribbean was welcome. Apparently, Raymond had been to the French Guianan capital of Cayenne many times before, and he organised a large Mercedes estate taxi to meet us. Cayenne is a mixture of old wooden houses and even older wooden huts. The place looks rough and so did our hotel. It was owned by the Chinese and Hotel Splendido it was not.

Now, Raymond was a bit of a Jack the Lad. He was full of himself, always bouncing up and down – 'I've been here there and everywhere, I know everything.' So I asked him, 'Can you buy weapons here?'

'Yeah yeah, what do you want? A machine gun, a shotgun or a pistol? What you looking for?'

'Actually, three submachine guns would be very nice. Or better still, an automatic rifle each. And pistols. Any chance of any grenades?'

'No problem, leave it with me.'

So we hired a white Datsun saloon, handed it over to Raymond and he went off to make his contact. He returned four hours later with a very worn-out-looking, middle-aged white woman in the car.

'It's all in hand,' he assured me. 'I can manage three pistols.'

Three pistols? For fuck's sake!

Little Tony had hardly spoken a word. It turned out he lived in a place called Albina, on Surinam's border with French Guiana, and knew some of these Jungle Commando guerrillas. So we decided to send John with Tony to St Laurent – the French Guianan town opposite Albina – about seventy miles from Cayenne, to try and make contact with the rebels. Raymond turned up again, stoned out of his mind, and started rowing with Kenton. I was furious, and let him have it: 'If you start fighting we're all going to get arrested and we'll look right fucking wallies. We'll be put back on the next flight to Europe – end of story. You, Raymond, forget it! If you go near the car again you'll get a few smacks in the gob – that's you blown out.'

His friend Kenny, the black man, then revealed that Raymond had got a bit of a drug problem. Oh, fucking great. I headed with Keith Kenton and the Major for a part of Cayenne that was optimistically called Chicago. Only half a mile from our hotel, it was a stinking open sewer full of drug addicts and prostitutes. We went into the seediest bar we could find. As I ordered drinks, I told the barman we were tourists who'd come to see Devil's Island, the hell-hole prison from which the famous Papillon had escaped.

'Listen,' I said to him after a while, 'any chance I can buy a small pistol, because we'd like to travel up to the jungle. I've got the cash here, how much is it gonna cost?' He came up with a totally crazy price. 'Forget it,' I told him. 'We'll go without.'

John called the hotel. He'd made contact with the rebels, someone would be in touch with us tomorrow. Terrific.

Next morning I was sat under an awning on the pavement outside the hotel, drinking beer, when a scruffy-looking guy in crumpled T-shirt turned up. He spoke excellent English. He said he was from British Guyana, the country next-door but one on the western side of Surinam. He asked me where I was from. It told him I was from Liverpool and gave him the old Devil's Island story.

'I've been to Liverpool,' he said, 'do you know Upper Parliament Street?'

Of course I knew Upper Parliament Street. He reckoned he'd been there on a ship. Casually at first, he started pumping me for information. 'Why are you here? Why have so many of you come to see Papillon's jail?' I became very suspicious. This guy was more than just an inquisitive bum. Eventually, I got stroppy with him and snarled, 'Listen, mate, fuck off and mind your own business.' He disappeared.

A couple of hours later, a large white Peugeot taxi pulled up A big black man with a beard wound down the window and pointed at Baker. Georgie Boy went over to the car and hopped in. The taxi did a sharp right before roaring off. Shit, there goes our bank! It was pointless trying to follow. At least we still had our return tickets and £150 each – not what I'd call a job, but at least we could get home if George disappeared. This was frigging ludicrous!

An hour and a half later the taxi returned. George jumped out and the cab roared off.

'What the fucking hell have you been doing, George?' I demanded.

'Don't worry boys, don't worry,' he said, 'Everything's arranged. The guy we needed to see actually lives here in Cayenne.'

'George, don't you ever, ever jump in a car again without letting us know what you're doing. We're getting a bit pissed off now. This thing's getting a little bit amateur.' Amateur? We didn't realise how amateur and foolish things would look very soon.

With John still stuck in St Laurent, we spent another night waiting for Jan – the name of the guy who'd picked up George in the car – to return.

Next day a car arrived. The driver wasn't Jan, but a little guy with a row of shining gold teeth. This was Bonanza. He drove George, the Major, Keith Kenton and me out of town to Jan's home, a bungalow off the beaten track, where four black men, all wearing smart suits despite the jungle heat, were waiting. They were all politicians from Surinam and they were on their way to meet the Jungle Commando. They spoke good English, but Baker did most of the talking, in the local pidgin language – Taki Taki, a mixture of English, Dutch and West African. West Africa had been the original home of these guys' slave ancestors.

Jan was already at the house and Baker handed him a large wad of money. He came across to us, and announced, 'I understand you're looking for guns. Bonanza here is a resident in Cayenne and has a shotgun licence.' If you have a shotgun licence over there, you can own 500 shotguns if you like. 'How about a couple of pump-action shotguns?'

'Is that the best you can do? Pistols?'

'Pistols, no chance. Two shotguns,' Jan replied. 'And by the way, if you want to do a big favour for the Jungle Commando leader, could you possibly buy a Barnet crossbow?' The leader – Ronnie Brunswijk himself – had seen one of these crossbows in a film and now he wanted one. I was beginning wonder about the kind of man we were working for.

A couple of hours later, Bonanza returned with two Italian pump-action shotguns, 500 rounds of 'oo' buckshot and solid slugs, some tear gas canisters, plus a box with a Barnet commando crossbow inside, complete with telescopic sight. We assembled the guns and sawed the barrels down so they were nice and handy to use.

That afternoon, George insisted on wandering off on his own around the back streets of Cayenne, so we left him to it and went downtown for a drink. When we got back to the hotel, a little Chinese guy came running out, waving his arms, screaming, 'Get out of here! Get out! Quick, quick. The police have been here!'

The cops had arrested Baker plus two black guys, Raymond and Kenny. Oh shit. We grabbed our gear from the hotel and threw it in the hire car. We had to get to Jan's house. But where was it? The route was complicated and I hadn't been paying proper attention when Bonanza took us there. But Keith Kenton clearly had, and we soon arrived at Jan's.

Jan phoned the hotel and quickly got the full story. George had suspected that the two black guys were working for the enemy, and wanted nothing more to do with them, but when he tried to get rid of them, they'd phoned the French Guiana police and told them Baker had arrived in Cayenne with a team of mercenaries who hoped to overthrow the government of neighbouring Surinam. The police had come down in force and arrested Baker. Jan looked a bit worried about Baker's arrest, but was keen to stick to our original objective. 'In the early hours of the morning, we're going to Surinam.'

With the politicians in tow, we were going to go to St Laurent, join up with John and Tony, then cross the border into Surinam. The Major was asking no questions whatsoever. He was getting increasingly nervous because it was nearly time to leave to and start the job. He didn't like guns or bombs themselves – he just liked to talk about them.

As the politicians sat talking on the veranda with Jan, we assembled our webbing nearby. As I was attaching the six-inch long, two-inch thick 'Big Boy' tear gas canisters to the yoke on the webbing, I decided to give one a tiny test squirt. A few seconds later, as the gas drifted off, the politicians started jumping over the small railing on the veranda, coughing and spluttering, tears falling down their faces. I was left trying to hide the tear gas canister and act like nothing had happened. You played a blinder there, Karl.

However, all was forgiven and the politicians left with Bonanza. We crashed out at Jan's place for a couple of hours before Bonanza arrived back in a minibus. Jan climbed in the driver's seat and, with reggae music blasting from the cassette player, he took Major Getback, Keith Kenton and myself along the main road in French Guiana. They call it the main road, but it's just like a two-lane B road that runs 150 miles from Cayenne to St Laurent. It was two o'clock in the morning and there was nothing on it, but that didn't prevent Jan from stopping at every crossroads, looking up and down the road, left and right, before moving on.

After about fifty kilometres, we turned off the road into Kourou, the nearest town to the Arianne rocket base, and pulled up outside a smart hotel. Five minutes later, the politicians sneaked out of the hotel and onto the minibus. They looked nervous. It turned out the scruffy guy who'd been pumping me for information about Liverpool just happened to be the military attaché from the Surinam Embassy in Cayenne.

Keith and I poked some slugs up the mag on our shotguns. Not a lot was said for the next two and a half hours, but Keith and I exchanged glances and the odd grin that said, 'What's the matter with these guys? Anybody comes near us, we'll blow their frigging heads off with a shotgun.' I know it sounds a little cavalier, but that was the attitude: we've started, we're armed, we're on the job. It was still pitch-black as we drove into St Laurent, but I could make out a church and a few wooden buildings as the minibus rolled slowly down the main street to a shanty town down by the river. It was a lively place, with a party going on at one house. The non-stop beat of salsa music thumped the air as we stepped out of the minibus, parked out of the way between two buildings.

Jan spoke, his voice barely audible above the din: 'We've sent for a boat to take us to the guerrillas' first island base.'

I hissed, 'Never mind the boat, where's John and Tony?'

'Somebody's gone to get them,' he replied.

The stench on the riverbank was overpowering; the whole shanty town used the Marowijne River as a lavatory. I must have been bitten by thousands of mosquitoes as I stood there. Mozzies actually think the world of me – they can't keep away from me, the little bastards! Across the river, lights twinkled in the blackness. As I surveyed them, one of the politicians came up to me. 'There you are,' he said, 'enemy territory. That is Surinam.'

'Yeah, yeah,' I replied, 'no sweat, we'll be there soon.'

'I don't know about that,' he countered. 'There's a very strong garrison there. Hopefully, please to God, something will happen. Maybe you boys can do it for us.'

'Do you mind if we change into our working kit?' I asked him.

'No, not a problem – in fact, we'd prefer that. There's a little hut over there, you can use that.'

Newman stood there, waffling on about, 'The quicker I get back, the better it'll be.' Kenton and I changed into our uniforms. I swapped my T-shirt and jeans for Portuguese camouflage; Kenton had a green shirt and green pants and we were both wearing canvas jungle boots. We put our webbing on, filled the ammo pouches up with shotgun cartridges and took a quick look at the shotguns. We plastered on cammo cream by the light of an oil lamp.

'Where's Major Getback?' Kenton asked.

'Don't worry about him,' I told him, 'he's down there crapping his pants.' What we didn't know was that he'd stripped off in front of the politicians. I had to give it to Major Getback: in his olive greens, jungle boots and beret with Sandhurst flash, he looked the part.

A strange feeling came over me just then, as I thought back to those first letters from the Ansus Foundation. Now we were thousands of miles from home, sitting in a hut in a shanty town in South America, being attacked by mosquitoes and dressed up ready to do the business.

The silence was broken, the quiet moment of reflection gone. Thump! Thump! Thump! up the hut steps, followed by a burst of Cockney: 'All right mate? Fuckin' 'ell. Glad to see you lot. Fuckin' 'ell, you two you look like you're ready to start a bleeding war!'

'We will be shortly, John, 'cos we're getting on the boat.'

'What, are we going now?'

'Fucking right we are.'

John had only had time to take his training shoes off before somebody shouted, 'Right let's go!' Back on with the training shoes.

A forty-foot long wooden canoe with a sixty horsepower Evinrude outboard engine on the back waited on the bank. As we all clambered into the boat, I noticed they'd actually hoisted a French flag on a little pole at the back of the canoe. Kenton and I pushed the boat out. We didn't mind getting up to our thighs in mud and shit – but we didn't want the politicians getting wet. We hopped in and the damn thing roared off up the river like a Porsche! At that point the river is nearly two miles wide and we stayed on the French side. After an hour, dawn broke to reveal a thick mist on the river. It was frigging cold, but I wasn't letting on. Because I'm right-handed, I had my shotgun pointed out to the left. Kenton was sitting next to me, his gun pointing out to the other side, because he's a left-hander. John Richards and Major Getback were behind us and behind them sat Jan and two politicians. Right at the back was the guy driving the boat. Three politicians and a couple of blacks sat in front of us. The mist lifted after an hour and it became scorching hot. Every now and then, a sound like a circular power saw came from the jungle, and I asked Jan whether there were guys working in the area. The source of the sound turned out to be an insect half an inch long, which makes this incredible saw-like sound.

Just then, the canoe wobbled. I look around to see
Major Getback standing up undoing the belt on his pants.
In a low voice, I said, 'What are you doing Col?'

'If you've got to go, you've got to go... I'm dying for a
crap... I've got to do it.'

Down came the pants, arse over the side, and suddenly
everybody's looking at a British army 'officer' having a
crap. I think nerves had finally got the better of him and
he simply had to do it. As it turned out, that was the only
contribution Colin Newman actually made to Surinam.

Approaching the French Infantry Marine garrison at
Apatou, I pulled a tarpaulin off the cargo and we hid under
it until the canoe was safely past the military base. The
river narrowed as we approached a set of rapids. I spotted
a little figure hiding behind a rock outcrop half a mile
away on the Surinam shore. He ducked back down.

I nudged Keith. 'There's a little guy up there with a gun,
looks like a rifle... behind the rocks, over on the right-
hand side.'

'OK, got it. It's a shotgun,' he replied.

Jan tapped me on the shoulder. 'Hey, relax.'

'No you relax,' I replied. 'That's what we're here for – to
make you relax.'

As we powered towards the rapids, we realised that
there were, in fact, six guys hiding behind the rocks. And
you've never seen such a bunch of ragamuffins in your life.
One was armed with a Brazilian-made FN-FAL automatic
rifle, the others had shotguns. Jabba, jabba, jabba... they
were walking along talking to the politicians as the boat

moved through the water. I have to say, the politicians didn't look too happy about things, and neither did Jan. The canoe stopped in a lagoon at the foot of the rapids and we all got out.

The politicians started shaking hands with these scruffbags. It all seemed friendly enough. Keith sloped off to my right and stood with his back against a rock, shotgun 'casually' resting in his hands. I moved a little bit ahead of him and did the same.

Because the Major hadn't been doing his job, i.e. finding out the plan, we didn't have a clue what was happening. Pleasantries over, the politicians started clambering over rocks, following the ragamuffin river guards towards the jungle. There was a camp in a small clearing not far from the river's edge. I have never seen such filth and degradation in all my life. The men there were crapping literally ten yards from the hut they were sleeping in – and not burying it. Millions of flies swarmed everywhere. They drank out of old empty coffee jars. Most of their weapons were rusted to hell. A couple of the guns were so old I could have auctioned them at Christie's and made a few bob.

About fifteen yards away, the politicians and a group of River Guards were stood in a circle, chanting. When the chanting stopped, they moved away to reveal a voodoo shrine. One of the politicians, a guy called Eddie Dapp asked, 'Boys, what do you think about our little camp?'

'Very nice, Eddie. Very professional indeed,' I replied, sarcastically.

Fucking Jesus!

CHAPTER
2

As the canoe passed close to the Surinam border on our journey upstream, I spotted some tangled wreckage lying on the river bank. It was the remains of a helicopter loaned to President Desi Bouterse as a counter-insurgency aircraft. It had been on the job for just half an hour when it passed over the heads of twenty Jungle Commandos. A couple of them were armed with FAL rifles, the rest had shotguns, and they peppered the chopper full of holes. The engine started screaming, the helicopter wobbled in the sky, flew for about a mile, landed awkwardly on the river bank and toppled over onto its side. By the time Ronnie's boys reached the stricken aircraft, the crew had fled into the bush.

Four hours after leaving the rebel camp, I spotted a 150-foot high radio mast sticking out of the middle of the jungle. At last, this was the rebel's island base at Langatabbetje. Jan had been looking nervous for the last few miles; now he started to go pale. I couldn't work it out. We were approaching friendly territory and he seemed more edgy than ever. We rounded a bend and half a mile ahead a village appeared. Clean, bright, neat houses ran down to a huge jetty standing twenty feet higher than the level of the river. The closer we got, the scruffier the place started to look. Word of our arrival had spread. A hundred ragamuffins, all armed, stood at the top of a mud embankment. Jan and the politicians climbed out. This is where the Major was supposed to take over, but he was still in the boat, his arse frozen to the seat.

'Look boys,' said Jan, 'bring everything else but please leave your shotguns in the boat. Nobody's going to steal them.'

It was pointless taking them with us anyway. If anything went wrong we'd be shot to bits. We left the guns and climbed a set of steep steps carved in the embankment. The sea of faces parted, every one of them scrutinising us as we walked past. A thin Hindustani guy in a combat jacket and camouflage cap, a rusty old Smith & Wesson revolver in a holster above tatty shorts, came up. 'Come on over boys,' he said, 'Sit yourselves down.' Chairs appeared for us to sit on. I don't know where the hell he got them from, because in the months after I never saw another chair. We sat on the floor or on a wooden box. All these black guys gathered round to look at the strange sight of four white soldiers with a bunch of politicians.

The Hindustani introduced himself as Radjin. We told him our names; he instantly forgot them.

'Where's the leader, Ronnie Brunswijk?' I asked. 'We want to talk to him.'

'Ronnie's not here at the moment. He's somewhere up the road,' came the reply. 'He'll be here shortly in a couple of hours, you'll see him then.' The meeting then continued in Taki Taki.

Radjin stepped in to explain. 'Listen ,boys, what's being spoken about now has got nothing to do with you, it's about politics. So how would you like to have a tour of our little island?'

Langatabbetje had been built by the Dutch when they ran Surinam. There were two schools, one for the local blacks and The Internat – an international exchange school where they'd send white kids from Holland to sample life the jungle. The Internat hadn't been used for years. What had once been nice houses built on stilts lined the dusty road to a clinic that was in use but had no medical facilities. In fact, they had frig all. The clinic doubled as the guerrillas' radio station, but the mast I'd seen from the river hadn't been connected for years.

An airstrip overgrown with grass stood at the top of the lane. Virtually the only piece of equipment inside the rundown airport building was a weighing machine for baggage, which obviously hadn't been used for years. But beside the terminal, hidden under a pile of palm branches, sat a Cessna 206 light aircraft.

'Does it work, Radjin?' I asked. 'Oh yeah,' came the reply. Now, I can fly a bit, and I was looking forward to gunning the Cessna along the strip to get the feel of the controls.

We wandered down to the native village on the island. Black women and children stared at the 'weirdos' wearing webbing and cammo cream. The headmaster's house next to the native village school was to be our home. It had been stripped almost bare. A couple of old cane chairs, a coffee table and three iron-framed beds with grim-looking mattresses were the only things left in the whole place. What had been the main classroom was filled with Jungle Commandos, stoned out of their brains, sleeping on hammocks. The stench of marijuana fugged the air.

We'd already gone two days without sleep, so John, Keith and myself kipped on the beds. The Major was too nervous to relax, so he sat on guard. We'd only been asleep for an hour and a half when he woke us up. By now he was looking quite pleased with himself, 'Wake up! Wake up! He's here.'

While we'd been sleeping, Ronnie Brunswijk had popped his head in the door, given us the thumbs up and told Major Getback, 'Excellent, this is what I need, professional soldiers. I am very, very pleased. Thank you for coming.'

Outside the bedroom stood a big, fit black guy, wearing full combat gear and a red beret. A broad smile lit up his amiable face as he shook our hands and slapped us all on the back. He was full of himself. 'Hello, my name's Ronnie,' he announced, beaming. He looked at our sorry arsenal of two shotguns, 'Get rid of those, I give you weapons.'

We put the 500 rounds we'd brought with us on the table and the present from our boss George Baker. Ronnie's eyes lit up as he unwrapped the Barnet Commando crossbow. As Ronnie, whom we christened

Ronbo, started to assemble the bow, Major Getback announced that he really had to be getting back. The politicians' discussions with Ronnie were over and the canoe would be returning in the next few minutes. Thank fuck for that, we could now get rid of a Major headache.

I had a quiet word with the Major. 'Look, Baker will most probably have been expelled from French Guiana, so when you get back to Europe, track him down. Don't worry about getting more men, find out first if the money that's been promised to us has been deposited in our accounts.'

We were supposed to have received a grand each before we even started work. 'Phone Jan in Cayenne and say Keith's wife has had a baby,' I told the Major. 'If the money's in the bank, say it's a boy. If it's bad news, say it's a girl and we'll get the message.'

Colin promised he would, then stripped off, put on his civvies and gave us all his kit. It wasn't like Colin Newman to give away yesterday's newspaper, never mind combat gear – that's how happy he was to get away. We watched him disappear in the canoe, then heaved a collective sigh of relief.

When we were in Cayenne, George Baker had bought us about 5,000 cigarettes. I quickly discovered none of the Jungle Commandos at Langatabbetje had any fags. So – diplomacy first – I wandered round like Father Christmas, handing out 2,000 cigs as a goodwill gesture. Then we got our first taste of Jungle Commando food: a plate of rice, with a piece of foul-smelling meat on top covered in a sauce that tasted like Castrol GTX motor oil. There was obviously not going to be anything else; we simply had to eat the stuff.

We chatted with Ronnie about the campaign, but he was vague about everything. He kept saying, 'We own this territory and that territory' but, in fact, when you looked on the map he owned very little territory. However, he was very proud of himself, keen, dead eager and raring to go. That was a good sign. If he'd have been like any of his men, a marijuana-smoking no-hoper, I think I'd have turned around and gone home at that point.

Next morning, a short, plump, bearded white man, wearing shorts, a neat T-shirt and flip-flops, arrived on our doorstep. He spoke excellent English and introduced himself as Orlando, Ronnie's pilot. He turned out to be the son of Surinam's Minister of Sport and Recreation. Orlando worked for a small air charter company called Goni Air and had landed his Cessna somewhere in the jungle when Ronnie's boys hijacked the plane and forced him to fly to Langatabbetje. 'I've been here four weeks and I'm pissed off,' he moaned. 'Thank God you guys have turned up.'

We'd only been chatting a while when Ronnie burst into the room. 'OK boys,' he announced, 'come, come, I want to show you something.' Ronnie had been working while we were having our coffee. On the cookhouse table were three FN-FAL automatic rifles. They were Brazilian-made copies of weapons originally manufactured in Belgium. Six magazines, three of them filled with 7.62mm rounds, were also piled on the table. We cracked them open. They were a bit shitty inside, but basically sound. All they needed was a damned good clean.

'OK boys,' said Ronnie, 'let's go.' We arrived at the airstrip as a small group of JCs were stripping off the palm-leaf camouflage from the Cessna. Orlando started his pre-flight checks – a tap and a bang here and there, checked the flaps, gave the rudder a jerk. Moments later, the engine burst into life. Orlando slowed the engine down to idle as he waved us over. The co-pilot's duel control had been ripped out to make an extra passenger seat. Ronnie sat next to Orlando. I was directly behind Orlando, with John Richards beside me and Keith Kenton next to the open doorway. The doors had been taken off. We banged the loaded mags into our FALs as Orlando gunned the engine. The runway was rapidly running out as the heavily loaded plane lifted wearily over a stand of trees, and banked low to the left above the river. This was our chance to survey the territory we'd soon be fighting in. Below, a necklace of emerald-green islands dotted the silver Marowijne River. To the right, the Surinam side, a carpet of dense jungle spread as far as the eye could see. Nothing else. No sign of any villages. Fifteen minutes later, we started to descend. It was impossible to talk through the wind rush in the doorless cabin, so Ronnie leant round, poked me in the chest and pointed out through the front window. Through my Japanese binoculars I could see another island below, with a small township and an airstrip. It

looked bigger than Langatabbetje and from the air
seemed very civilised. I could make out a building with a
huge red cross painted on the roof. With flaps down
ready for a landing, the Cessna drifted slowly towards
the strip, which to my horror, I saw was covered in
objects. If we land now, I thought, we'll be dead. Still the
plane descended. Fucking hell, what was happening
here? At the last minute Orlando pulled out of the
landing and the plane screamed along ten feet above the
runway. Ronnie turned around, flashed us a manic grin
and gave the thumbs up as if it say, 'What do you think
about that, boys?' Shit. As the aircraft careered towards
the forest, Orlando pulled hard back on the control
column and we lifted right up. He levelled off, brought
the throttle back to three-quarter power and turned in a
big circle to the left. This time as we approached, a
swarm of tiny figures in the distance pushed those
objects off our flight path. As we bumped and bounced
along the grass strip, I could clearly see they'd been
moving forty-five-gallon oil drums. Jungle Commandos
lined the strip, waving their guns. Ronnie looked like
Prince Philip, acknowledging them with that little back-
of-the-hand wave the British royal family uses. Jungle
Commandos swarmed the plane as we pulled out our
gear; Ronnie introduced us to a couple of his boys and
then disappeared. Left to our own devices, we walked
down a track to a modern-looking village. As in
Langatabbetje, at one time the houses here had been
smart homes, built up on stilts. You can imagine the state

they were in now. Welcome to Stoelman's Island, the rebel army's headquarters.

A large concrete building that looked like a hotel sat in the bottom of the village. It had once been a guest house for tourists. Believe it or not, this jungle island had been popular with holidaymakers, who came from Holland to look at the wildlife. A flagpole was still standing beside the entrance arch. Through the archway I could see a large patio by the river. The place must have been beautiful until these guys got hold of it. Now it was crawling with Jungle Commandos who were billeted there. We took a couple of rooms on the first floor. John and I in one, Keith in another.

Stoelman's Island is actually made up of two villages – the one we were in was obviously where the people with money lived. It even had a hospital, where two white doctors worked. Ronnie lived near the hospital with his wife and kids, but there was no sign of him. We passed the day stripping down our FALs, getting them in working order. In the evening, a white man and a white woman came into the guesthouse. They were Alain and Bayer, the doctors from the hospital. When I told them who we were, their eyes opened wide. This was the first time they'd ever seen mercenaries. 'Aren't you afraid to die?' asked Bayer, in her lilting Belgian accent.

'No, no, take it easy,' I said, trying to reassure them. 'We're only going to have a look at the situation here. We're not about to start murdering people. We're quite civilised, we don't go around biting babies' heads off.'

To bring the conversation down to a normal level and put all this Rambo crap out of their heads, I told them about Liverpool, my home life, my friends.

Ronnie finally emerged next morning just as we were finishing off our three-course breakfast – cough, smoke and a coffee. Ronbo took us to meet his Jungle Commandos. As we arrived at the top end of the village, a large group of them were standing in a circle around a wooden post with jars full of what looked like shit hanging from branches nailed to the pole. A circle of beer bottles stood around the bottom of the pole. Keith Kenton's eyes lit up at the sight of the bottles.

Ronnie pointed to a weird-looking pole. 'Tomorrow we fight, today we must get you protection.'

This was another voodoo shrine, although his commandos didn't call it voodoo, referring to it instead as 'culture'. You are not allowed to take your weapons to one of these shrines, so we leaned our FALs against the side of a hut and joined the circle. Now this *was* interesting. I'd seen voodoo ceremonies in West Africa before, but had never actually taken part in one.

As the Jungle Commandos in the circle started chanting and jumping around, an old guy – obviously the chief voodoo man – walked backwards and forwards, poking people in the chest with a stick and speaking to them in Taki Taki. He'd go back and poke at the post and then poke at somebody else. Suddenly he came up to me and shoved his stick into my chest. I must have shown some kind of an expression of mock horror on my face, because

I noticed Ronnie started to grin. Our leader obviously had a sense of humour. The voodoo chief came back and gave me friendly slap on the back of the head, still chanting all the time. He grabbed my hand and started to feel along my left arm. Christ! I thought to myself, this guy's in love! Then he did the same to John and Keith. More blah, blah, blah and the circle began to break up.

I turned to Ronnie. 'Very nice ceremony, Ron, please thank the vicar for me.'

'It's not over yet,' replied Ronbo, 'The man is going to make a charm for you. One charm will protect you from bullets, so if you get shot by a fifty calibre it will bounce off your head... the other one will protect you from disease.' 'Bloody hell,' I thought, 'if these things work I could make a fortune back in Europe. Syphilis, Aids, bullet wounds – I've got the cure here!'

So, with great aplomb and, as Shakespeare said, much ado about nothing, the voodoo man bent a lump of concrete reinforcing rod into a circle and wrapped a twisted piece of dirty old cloth around it. We had to endure another ceremony, which involved drinking a mixture of water, rum, crushed leaves and soil from an old coffee jar. It represents everything from God's earth and you're supposed to swallow it, but while no one was looking I spat mine on the floor. Once the band was placed on our arms we were protected; bulletproof. God help the enemy!

Ronnie spent the next hour showing off his white mercenaries to the whole island. Everybody was happy, there was backslapping all round, and then we climbed back aboard the Cessna. This time I asked Orlando if I could have a go. Ronnie sat in the back with Keith and John. As the plane reached 2,000 feet, Orlando eased out of his seat and I hopped across to take the controls. I admit I was a little nervous at first. It had been many years since I'd flown a plane, but it's like riding a bike – you don't forget. Feet on the rudder pedals. Don't grasp the control column, hold it gently with thumb and two fingers, so you can feel the slightest movement. Nose down a touch, back up, left and right on the pedals to bank the wings slightly, all the time watching the altimeter. I didn't need the compass, because we were following the river. I glanced behind me. Keith looked like he was about to jump out!

A couple of hours after Orlando had landed us safely back at Langatabbetje, Ronnie came into the house. 'It's time to go up to the front line, boys,' he announced

'Just one problem, Ronnie,' I interjected. 'We've only got twenty rounds of ammunition.'

'Don't worry about that,' he replied, 'all the goodies are up at the line.'

Surinam was just 300 yards across the river. Six of us, including Ronnie, Keith, me and John, landed near a road, where a few vehicles were parked up. Ronnie ignored a long-wheelbase Toyota Land Cruiser and leapt into a beaten-up Mazda pick-up truck instead. We declined the front seats and climbed in the back, so we could get out pretty damned quick if anything happened. Ronnie took the driver's seat and with the wheels squealing, screamed off in a blood-red cloud of oxide dust whipped up from the road. One kilometre from the river we came to a badly damaged Bailey bridge. Two thin planks spanned the yawing gap. That didn't matter to Ronnie, he drove across at fifty miles an hour, sending us bouncing up and down in the back. I thought we were going to break our necks, but we braced ourselves as the pick-up see-sawed across.

A black guy called Coffee – his real name was Oki – sat in the back of the truck, hugging a Remington shotgun. He started ranting at us almost immediately: 'Bouterse's men shot my cousin. They are bastards. We work together at the front, we kill plenty soldier.' Then, with no warning at all, Coffee whipped up the pump-action shotgun. Bang... he fired a shot!

The pick-up truck came to a roaring stop; we all leaped out and took cover. Slowly and calmly, Ronnie walked up to Coffee and called him a shithead, in Taki Taki, of course. Coffee had spotted a bird a bit like a vulture in the trees and thought, 'Here's tonight's dinner....' Crack!

A couple of hours later, the pick-up ground to a halt at the bottom of a long rise. In the distance I could see a vehicle parked up near a pile of burnt wood. Through my binoculars, I could make out the remains of a bridge. It appears the Jungle Commandos were able to hold this area because they poured diesel over all the wooden bridges like this one and set fire to them, stopping Bouterse's soldiers getting their armoured cars across. We sat for a moment and drove cautiously towards it. The three of us in the back leaned over the top of the cab, FALs pointing down the road. We'd only got sixty rounds, but anybody trying to pop at us in an ambush was going to get three mags at once. The bridge was so badly damaged that we had to abandon the pick-up and wade knee-deep across the shallowest part of the creek. Another truck had been hidden in the bushes on the other side. The sun was setting as we climbed in the back; it goes pitch-back very quickly in the jungle.

We'd been driving for an hour when we bumped into a small group of Jungle Commandos waiting by a broken-down car. It was pretty cramped in the back as we bounced along the rutted, pot-holed road. We knew the military had three Britten Norman Islander aircraft with machine guns pointing out of the doors. I wasn't happy that we were driving along with headlights on full; then, John spotted a bright light in the sky behind us. It looked like an aircraft with landing lights on. My stomach knotted. We hammered our fists on the cab roof, shouting, 'Stop! Stop! Get out!' The truck screamed to a halt. Ronnie leaped out, looked up at the 'aircraft' and burst out laughing. It was the North Star; down on the Equator, it is extremely bright. Looking sheepish, we climbed back on the truck. Soon we came to another burnt-out bridge over another creek, only this time there was no vehicle hidden on the other side. Carefully, Ronnie eased the truck down the bank and into two feet of water. With the engine screaming, ten guys heaved, pushed and shoved the damn thing up the other bank and back onto the road. We'd gone a few yards when a military plane roared overhead, attracted by our headlights like a moth to flame. One of the blacks hollered, 'Plane! Plane!' and hammered his fists on the cab roof. Ronnie slammed the brakes on and turned the lights out. Everybody started bailing out. I dived straight into the jungle, nearly knocking myself unconscious as my head hit a tree with a juddering crack.

I scrambled into the dense undergrowth. The darkness was absolute. I tracked the engine noise with the FAL. The plane began to circle around, then the engine roar began to fade. It was flying off. Somewhere in the blackness, Ronnie hissed, 'Right come on, up the road. He might come back, let's get away from here.'

So we ran up the road. I hadn't run for a long, long time. The night was steaming hot and sweat poured out of me like a tap. John Richards and the blacks were away like bullets. Keith and I struggled, but we managed to keep right behind them. When we finally stopped we were half a kilometre up the road from the truck. As we strained to listen for the plane, I could hardly get my breath back.

I gasped to Ronnie, 'Look, if the plane's gone what are we doing up here?'

'Sorry about this,' he replied, 'I meant to tell you before but last night some of the boys had vehicles parked here and a plane came down during the day and dropped bombs on them.'

'Oh, charming. And you're still parking the vehicles in the same place,' I said in disbelief.

'Yeah, but we've no choice.'

We waited twenty minutes to make sure the aircraft wasn't coming back. Another hour down the dirt road, we turned on to a jungle track. From nowhere, a Jungle Commando armed with a shotgun popped out and gave us a wave. Dense undergrowth brushed against us on the back of the truck. We stopped in a clearing. The truck's lights revealed a clutch of bashers made from palm leaves and poles. Our first jungle camp was run by a Hindu called Yankie; all the commandants there were bloody Hindus. Yankie led us into a basher. In the flickering light of an oil lamp, I could make out three white men lying in hammocks; a large TV camera and sound equipment lay on the floor. They were journalists and all three of them sat up at once when we entered. What have we got here? Mercenaries. Great.

We didn't want to talk to these guys – two French and a Dutchman – and we certainly didn't want to be photographed. It was imperative that no one find out we were there. The journalists didn't say a word – they simply lay back down, though I could tell they were trying to listen to everything we said. Consequently, we spoke in whispers, and decided we'd deal with them in the morning.

Before we got our heads down for the night, the boys were called to yet another voodoo ceremony. Keith wanted to go because he knew they passed rum around and everyone gets sprayed with beer during these ceremonies. Now that I was bulletproof and disease-proof,

I wanted nothing more to do with this voodoo stuff. But Keith went. The voodoo man splashed all fifty of them who were there, Keith included, with water from a bucket near the shrine.

The next morning Keith went out to look at the shrine and came back with a face like thunder. He'd just seen what was in the bucket – a couple of inches of water and the severed head of an enemy soldier. Nearby, he found a forty-five-gallon drum three-quarters full of water with the hearts, hands, feet and heads of enemy soldiers floating in it. Every time the commandos shot one of Bouterse's men, they butchered parts of his body and threw them in the drum. The voodoo man would then pick out the severed body parts and organs he needed for a particular ceremony. These people believed that you can actually take on the qualities of one of your victims. You want the brains of this man? Then they'd bung his head in the bucket and you'd wash yourself in water with his head floating in it. If you wanted his spirit, you'd throw his heart in. If you want the skill of his hands or the speed of his feet, the voodoo man would put the appropriate dismembered limb in the bucket. When Keith realised he'd been given his victim's brain, he grabbed his FAL, cocked it and walked around camp like a madman, ranting and raving: 'You fucking bastards, I'm going to get disease. You bunch of arseholes, why didn't you tell me there was a frigging head in the bucket?'

I felt the need to have a quiet word with him. 'The price of rum around here is pretty expensive,' I said. 'Get off the booze, behave yourself and you'll know what's going on. Keep away from the voodoo stuff.' Pointing to the FAL, I added, 'This is my voodoo.'

The television crew went to have a little chat with Ronnie, who came over. 'Listen, Karel, can you come and stand with me and have your photograph taken?'

'Now look, Ronnie,' I replied, 'we had a deal. We came out as quietly as possible. Please, no photographs.'

Then Yankie butted in. 'The thing is, nobody knows this war is going on. By showing pictures of you, they'll know what's really happening.'

'Please Karel, please,' Ronnie pleaded. 'You'll be doing me a big favour. What harm can it do for you? Surely it will only do you good?'

'It won't do me any good,' I answered. 'If I get a great deal of publicity back in Europe, people won't really want to employ me, Ronnie. That's the problem, I've got to remain like the invisible man. If I suddenly become a well known face, not many people are really going to want to employ me,' I explained.

All their begging was making me feel cold-hearted, though. It was difficult to refuse Ronnie's big, pleading eyes. And in the end I found myself saying, 'What the hell... yeah, we'll do it.'

John had been sitting there praying for me to say 'yes'. He'd always wanted to be a movie star. Keith didn't give a shit, so we all walked up the track a bit, where we were filmed standing next to Ronnie. The journalists couldn't believe their luck but despite their scoop, they were clearly nervous. You can understand why, stuck in the middle of the jungle with this load of loonies. They asked if they could come with us up to the front line, a couple of hours away at a place called Blackwater. Ronnie would join us later. Before we left camp, I told Ronnie that having twenty rounds each was not going to be good enough, old chap. He disappeared into his basher and came back with 127 rounds in a blue plastic bag. This still was not good, as realistically we needed 300 rounds each.

Blackwater is an abandoned logging camp by a creek that flows into the Surinam River. Huge machines that virtually rip trees out of the ground stood abandoned, like rusting dinosaurs. We arrived caked in red oxide clay and made straight for the disused workers' mess room, where the Jungle Commandos served up cold Parbo beer, the local brew. In the distance we could hear heavy machine-gun fire. It sounded like the boom of a fifty-calibre. The noise was coming from the nearby army garrison of Carolina, across the other side of the river. The bridges had been burnt out and the Jungle Commandos had used one of the logging machines to dig up the road to make an embankment. It would take the enemy a good day to clear it, one of the commandos noted. I reckoned five minutes.

The noise was getting louder. I estimated the shooting was a just a couple of miles away. It didn't sound healthy. As I cracked open the FAL to start cleaning it, I picked up my webbing and put it on a bench nearby, ready to throw on. Another of the commandos tried to reassure me.

'Don't worry, mister. It's okay,' he explained. 'They just come a little bit close to try and frighten us away.'

I'd got a funny feeling we were going to get a real fright shortly, but John and Keith took the guy's word for it and stripped off to have a shower.

Next minute a shout went up: 'ALARM! ALARM!' I pulled on my webbing, grabbed my rifle, ran out across the road in front of the mess hall and made a flying leap behind a pile of logs. I cocked my rifle, stuck a spare mag in the sand and muttered, 'Come on you bastards.' A moment later, John Richards was diving down beside me wearing only his underpants. He had his webbing and FAL in one hand, and his uniform and boots in the other. 'You'd better go and get fucking dressed,' I snapped, 'because the shit's going to hit the fan in a minute and you'd better be ready for it. And while you're at it, get Keith.'

John disappeared and returned a couple of minutes later with Keith and one of Ronnie's commanders, Johan, who asked, 'What do we do now? The army are actually coming for us this time.'

'We're going to go up the road and ambush these fucking bastards,' I replied.

Webbing clanking, John and I jogged up the road towards the firing, now about a mile away. After 400 yards I looked behind me, expecting to see Keith and about forty black guys. Instead I beheld the sight of a French television crew and a Dutch journalist with his cameras and a tape recorder around his neck. He was talking into his microphone, while the French TV man had his camera switched on, pointed at me. Where was Keith? All the Jungle Commandos except two had disappeared. Wonderful.

I'd spotted a nice little gap in the jungle about a kilometre from the camp. I ducked into the opening and got down behind a great big tree. I shouted to the cameraman, 'Get in there!' John and the three journalists disappeared out of sight. I was alone behind this large tree, FAL on auto, finger on the trigger, when the road where we'd been standing moments earlier exploded with the loud 'whoosh!' of a shell. I was wearing my voodoo band, but I didn't feel the least bit invincible. I was as nervous as hell.

With a loud roar, a large, six-wheeled Cascavel armoured reconnaissance car with a 90mm gun on it drove past. A guy wearing a green fibreglass helmet, with a microphone attached, poked out of the turret. 'What a shot,' I thought to myself – 'I can take his fucking head off from here.' I couldn't have been more than six or eight yards from the road. Armchair commandos or weekend Rambos might be wondering why the hell I was so close. The answer is, I couldn't get any deeper because the vegetation was so thick. I felt the trigger. 'Don't fire, Karl, don't fire,' I told myself. 'Let him go, you don't know what's behind him.' I eased my trigger finger. He drove on, letting off another couple of rounds, which exploded down the road.

Seconds later, another one drove by at slightly faster than walking pace. It was a Brazilian-manufactured Urutu armoured personnel carrier, which holds eight men in the back. The fifty-calibre blasted away. Again, a glass-fibre helmet came into my sights. And again, my brain raced: 'Don't shoot. You don't know what's behind.'

I waited. It seemed like an eternity, but it was probably only thirty seconds later that a truck full of young soldiers in green berets, FALs in their hands, ground to a halt right in front of me. It would be an absolute fucking sacrilege to let this lot go. They'd all been sitting down but now they were starting to get up off the benches in the back of the open-backed truck. I took careful aim. My senses on full, I could hear the Cascavel blasting away down the road. The soldiers were up off the bench seats and going forwards, and there was a large group of them leaning over the cab. I glanced down the road to see what the Urutu was up to.

I got onto my knees and peeked around the tree, I had my finger on the trigger, and brought the barrel of the FAL up from behind the tree, pointing it towards the truck. A soldier filled the sights. His right elbow was leaning over the side of the truck, to get a good view down the road. His FAL was in his left hand. As I took aim, the young soldier turned around and looked straight at me. I fired two bursts.

Automatic fire ripped into the group hanging on the side of the truck. Through the muzzle blast, I saw men in green berets bouncing and falling as the FAL's 7.62mm bullets tore into the mass of bodies on the back of the truck. Faces fixed in horror. Change mag. I let off two more bursts straight into them until the FAL went click. Mag empty. I ducked quickly back behind the cover of the giant tree trunk. Somewhere close by, John popped up and gave one burst, full mag twenty rounds, straight into the screaming, terrified enemy. I cocked my rifle. Nothing. I cocked the rifle again. Click. Nothing. You bastard!

BOOM! BOOM! BOOM! Loud rapid-firing was now coming from my right. Experience teaches you the difference between indiscriminate rounds – going here, there, everywhere – and direct fire. And this was direct firing at one target: me.

CHAPTER 3

Bullets from the fifty-cal showered dirt and leaves on top of me. This was getting too close for comfort. The firing stopped. This was my chance to get out. I moved to the side of the tree. Suddenly, a thundering diesel engine revved to screaming point. The Urutu roared backwards and with a sickening crash, smashed into the truck. The wrecked vehicle and its cargo of bleeding, terrified men catapulted back up the track. BANG! BANG! BANG! Bullets half the size of man's thumb, spewing from the fifty-cal on top of the APC, ripped down branches all around me. I dived back behind the tree. Its trunk was so fat that two men would have struggled to circle it with their arms outstretched, but it gave me no comfort. A fifty-cal bullet is designed to take out aircraft and, fired from close range, can blast straight through three feet of pine.

Another shower of foliage crashed on top of me. I hadn't seen the guy on the gun yet, but he'd definitely seen me. Bang! Bang! Another burst of fire ripped shards of bark from the tree like a chain saw. I got down on my stomach behind the tree, as close to the earth as possible. BOOM!

Another loud burst of fire. I rolled to my right, I look up and there he was in the Urutu's turret. He stitched the ground with bullets. I felt one of them touch my trousers. In the millisecond before, I thought, fuck, there goes my leg. Amazingly, the bullet didn't touch my flesh. I leaned over to my left. Bang! Bang! Bang... I could feel the heat from the gun's muzzle. My only chance of survival was to roll backwards and forwards and hope this clown would miss me. I looked up again. He was shouting into his microphone. The Urutu shot forwards then backed up again, smashing back into the truck. I knew he had a hundred rounds of ammunition in an eleven-foot belt and he was going to have me. My only hope was that one of the Jungle Commandos hidden in the bush on the other side of the road would take his head off any second now. I rolled backwards and forwards for what seemed like an eternity. He was still there, high in the turret, firing round after round. It looked very much as though I was fucked.

Then, the firing stopped. 'John! Cover me!' I shouted, 'I'm coming across.' John didn't fire back; I couldn't see the others. The gun had obviously run out of ammo. This was it. I grabbed my chance. Go, go, go. At high speed, I took five long paces and threw myself into a patch of heavy, spiky vegetation and landed right on top of the French cameraman. I scrambled out of the way. Bang! Bang! Bang! We were under fire again. The machine gunner had obviously changed belts and was still blasting away at the tree. I dug myself down into the earth. I still couldn't see John.

The cameraman hadn't moved. My mind raced. Was he dead? Had he been shot? I grabbed his ankle and gave it a tug. His ankle moved; he was alive. I scrambled forward to grab the back of his pants and pull him away from the fifty-calibre raining down on us. I grabbed his leather belt and heaved to lift him towards me; as I did so, his jeans and underpants came down. So there I was, in the middle of a battle, staring at a big white arse. I dragged him back behind the cover of the bushes. He was in a terrible state of shock.

There was only one way to get out alive: wriggling backwards on our stomachs. Some of the firing was so low that you'd get your head blown off if you raised yourself up onto your hands and knees. As I dragged the cameraman back, he moaned, 'Where's my camera? Where's my camera?'

'Fuck your camera.' I hissed back. 'Don't worry about the bloody thing.'

As I continued dragging him backwards, I came across the soundman, who was actually joined to the camera by an umbilical cord that links the two operators together when they're filming. I pulled on the cord but it quickly came to a stop. I tugged the fucking thing again, hard, and it still wouldn't come.

'Come on, leave it. Let's go,' I ordered.

'I can't leave the camera.'

'You bastard,' I shouted as I scrambled forward to discover the camera jammed between two saplings growing out of the ground. I flipped the camera up on its back, dragged it free and struggled back with it. Now I still had a FAL in my right hand and this fucking camera in the other; and it's heavy, very heavy.

We were twenty feet further back in the jungle when the machine-gun operator on the Urutu realised there was no one behind the tree any more. So he started to spray the whole place. Scary, very scary. 'We've got to pull back one kilometre,' I told John and the journalists, 'We don't know what's behind that truck that we've just hit. Maybe there's more vehicles full of troops. They might get out, sweep each side of the jungle and encircle us. We've got to get back.' I was starting to sound like Major Getback. We turned around and with our arses to the enemy started to crawl deeper into the jungle. The journalists were struggling with their bloody camera and sound recorder, so I helped drag them through the incredibly thick vegetation. Twenty yards back, we stumbled across two black guys. It was the pair of Jungle Commandos who had jogged behind me up the road. One was a loud-mouthed son-of-a-bitch called Django, who was wanted by the police on suspicion of being a rapist. The other was Oki. The pair of them hadn't fired a shot.

We scrambled back fifty or sixty yards where, because of the dense vegetation, we were just about safe from the fifty-calibre fire. Every now and then, bullets would whiz past us a few feet high. Deeper into the jungle, we were able to stand up and move quickly. If the army was sweeping the area, we had to get away.

The cameraman kept pleading, 'Please get us out of here. Get us out of here.' I pleaded with him too – to be quiet. Expecting troops to appear on our flank at any moment, every so often I motioned everybody to crouch down, be silent and listen. We could hear rustling. I pulled out a Browning from my holster. The sweat pouring down my arms and my shaking hands made it difficult to cock the damn thing. Would you believe it, Oki and Jango now decide to have a full-scale row, arguing in frantic Taki Taki! I hissed across to them, 'Oki, shut your fucking mouth up or I'll blow your face off.' It did the trick: the two of them quickly went quiet. We moved off again, trying to head parallel to the road, and made about 400 metres. We stopped once more and this time we heard engine noises in the distance. The army was on the move again. Were they moving out or towards our camp for the final kill? I let Oki and Django take over: they were bushmen, this was their territory. We were moving faster now. John was on my right, carrying only his FAL, out for nobody except himself. I had the cameraman with his arms hanging around my neck. I was supporting him and his bloody camera and the umbilical cord kept getting caught in the vegetation.

'Ow! Ow!' Oki started making the call of a Macaque monkey. The same call came back. We were close to camp. Totally exhausted, sweat pouring out of me, I gasped to the journalist, 'Come on, pull yourself together, now you can walk a bit.'

John picked up my webbing up. At last he was showing he could help somebody instead of himself. We staggered on. I was so drenched in sweat, I must have looked as though I'd jumped in the creek. And there was Keith on the side of the road near the camp. He was smiling from ear to ear.

'Keith, what happened to you, man? Everything all right?' I asked.

'I fucking killed the tank commander,' he replied.

Keith and a Jungle Commando called Surinder had taken a pop at the soldier on the top of the Cascavel. Surinder claimed he'd got him with an Uzi from about fifty yards away. That was a bit hard to believe. Keith had done a sniper course in the British Army and was a pretty good shot. He took careful aim at the back of the guy's head and fired one round. The soldier's helmet split wide open and he dropped down into the turret.

Fifty minutes later, Ronnie appeared. He'd been driving to Blackwater when he heard a battle going on and decided in his great wisdom to stay where he was until the firing stopped. He was talking to his boys, trying to collect as much information as possible. They were all chattering away when a little Hindu guy called Bob pointed at me and said, 'You shoot very good, you shoot very good. You fucking crazy man. How many soldiers you killed in the truck?' Ronnie asked what had happened. As I was I telling him how I popped out from behind a tree and fired into a truck full of troops, Bob started doing a mime of men being shot and falling over.

'This is fantastic news,' Ronnie exclaimed, 'Why didn't you tell me before?'

I'd have told him in my own good time after his boys –
who'd run away – had finished telling their war stories,
cheeky bastards! I turned to Bob. 'Where were you when
you saw the guys in the truck being shot?' I asked him.

'I was on the opposite site of the road,' he said, proudly.

'Oh, were you now? Well why the fuck did you not
shoot the guy on the Urutu when he was firing at me with
the fifty-calibre?'

'Karel, I did not shoot him because he had the turret lid
up shielding him at the back. I couldn't shoot him through
the shield.'

I was a bit pissed off now. 'That guy was backing up
twenty yards and going forwards twenty yards. You could
have moved a few yards either way and from an angle you
could have blown his head off!'

'Oh no,' said Bob, 'I only had this double-barrel
shotgun.'

I stared at him accusingly. 'You didn't want to fire the
shot in case he swung around on you.'

Bob looked a bit sheepish and pretended he didn't
understand.

Ronnie stepped in, gave me a big slap on the back, and
said, 'That's great, Karel.'

I rounded on him. 'It's not great, Ronnie. If we'd been
slightly more prepared, if you'd explained before we
arrived in Blackwater how the army were probing each
day, we could have made preparations. Do you know what
we could have done with a few petrol bombs? A Molotov
cocktail lobbed at the Urutu would have shut the bastard

up. It would have made him jump down inside the fucking hatch. And another one lobbed at the truck after we'd fired at it would have made things easier when my FAL jammed.'

Ronnie asked me to describe the soldiers on the truck. I told him they were young, very fit looking, mostly half-castes and wore green berets. 'Green berets!' he exclaimed, when he heard the last bit. 'They're the Echo Commando, the elite special forces.' It transpired later that the elite special forces had found out from spies in Ronnie's camp that we were heading to Blackwater and they were being sent down to wipe out this mercenary menace. 'We'd better clear out of here in case they come back en masse,' Ronnie announced.

'There's no way they are going to come back,' I reassured him. 'They've suffered a lot of casualties. The guy in the armoured car was one of their commanders and they have lost many of their elite commandos who were on the truck. They're going to have to seriously rethink their strategy. They're not coming back just yet.'

While beers and food were being arranged, I wanted to sort out the problem with the FAL. Ronnie offered to look at it. He and John took it away to another table. Two minutes later, John came bounding across the canteen towards me. 'There's fuck all wrong with your FAL!' he shouted.

He stuck in one of Ronnie's mags, cocked it, let the bolt go and bang! Home went the bolt.

'There's fuck all wrong with that, what's the matter with you?'

This pissed me off, and I hit back. 'So I made it all up, did I John? You tell me this, when I shouted across to you to cover me....'

He interrupted. 'When did you do that?'

'I did it during the lull in the firing.' John knew that he hadn't replied to my call for cover. He hadn't fired a fucking bullet to protect my back. I went on, 'If you'd emptied a twenty-round mag just in the general direction of the guy in the Urutu, it might have made him duck down inside the fucking hatch. It would have made life a bit easier for me. That's what friends are for.'

John was tongue-tied. Keith broke the silence. 'Here let's have a look at your FAL.'

He banged one of his mags in, cocked the weapon and, lo and behold, the fucking thing jammed again. We discussed it. Keith thought it was the gas. But it couldn't have been the gas – the gas doesn't come into operation when you cock the damn thing. It was beginning to look like a weak recoil spring. It was jamming with a full mag of twenty rounds, so all we had to do was use eighteen rounds instead. I tested it with eighteen rounds and it went off every time. Problem solved.

We rested up in one of the workers' huts. I was seriously pissed off with John. It wasn't that he didn't cover me while I was firing – he might not have wanted to pop up and have a go in case he got his head shot off, you couldn't blame the guy. It was the fact that he'd tried to make a fool out of me in front of everyone. If there had genuinely been nothing wrong with my FAL, he could have said so discreetly. The three of us were supposed to be in this thing together.

I felt much better after a couple of hours' kip. Arnold Karskens, the Dutch radio journalist I'd last seen running up the road towards the gunfire, had eventually emerged from the jungle. It turned out he'd been twenty yards behind us during the battle and in the canteen he played back the sound of the gunfire. It was pretty ferocious, more ferocious than it had actually sounded at the time.

Ronnie listened. 'Hell you were lucky, you were lucky,' he said, finally. Then he added, 'Boys, tomorrow morning, about two o'clock, I'd like you to go on a recce.'

Our target was the town of Carolina, where the Echo Commando were garrisoned. If you continue four miles up the road from where the ambush was, you come to the Surinam River. Carolina is on the other side of the mile-wide stretch of water. Traffic crosses the river on a large flat-span bridge. The middle section lifts into the air to allow ships through. At night, the garrison raised the bridge to protect the town. We were going to paddle across at dead of night in a canoe 'borrowed' from the Toucayana, the indigenous jungle indians. For obvious reasons, I didn't want the journalists there. I didn't want to have to carry one back. Little Bob, Django, Surinder and a couple of other Jungle Commandos were coming with us to recce the troop strength at Carolina and work out how we could attack the garrison at a later stage.

At two o'clock in the morning, we climbed into the back of two pick-up trucks. The army would have been long gone across the bridge and lifted the section up, so we couldn't come after them. But still we travelled very slowly up the road without headlights on this time. Half a mile before the Surinam River bridge, we turned left off the road into Blackwater village. Soon we were out of the trucks and scrambling down a very steep, fifty-foot high bank into a stinking mangrove swamp. A couple of minutes later we heard the splish-splash of a couple of tiny canoes. As we clambered in, it quickly became obvious they were far too small for all of us; the water almost lapped over the gunwales.

A gunboat from Carolina could have come round the corner at any moment and blown us out of the water, but we were lucky. Eventually, the jungle on other side of the river emerged out of the gloom. Dense mangrove swamp stretched for more than thirty feet out into the river. On a previous trip, the boys had hacked out a channel through the mangrove. It was so narrow that you couldn't paddle – you just pulled yourself along, grabbing stalks and stumps sticking out of the water. We clambered out of the canoes and, knee-deep in mud, groped around in the dark for the river's edge.

We were far too early. It was still two hours before daybreak, when there would be enough light to make our way through the jungle. We sat down, had a smoke and quickly drifted off to sleep. We were woken, about an hour later, by water. The tide had come in. None of the JCs had bothered to tell us this river was tidal. We were sitting in three inches of water with crabs crawling all over our legs. Charming: soaking wet and we hadn't even begun to make a move yet. As we waited for dawn, my voodoo band started to cut off the circulation in my arm, so I chucked the damn thing into the creek.

We tramped a bit further into the jungle and sat down again. As dawn broke we could see traffic moving nearby along a tarmac road leading into Carolina. We picked up our weapons and threaded our way through the jungle, wading through chest-deep creeks. In such an environment, you get everything out of your pockets into the webbing, which you carry on your head. Crocodile attacks are common in Surinam, so one of the team always keeps watch from the bank while the others wade across. Shooting them would have given the game away, so I had my knife between my teeth, like Tarzan! If a crocodile or even a snake had come near me, I'd have stabbed it to death. As we climbed out of one putrid, stinking creek, I stumbled and put my palm against a tree trunk to stop myself falling. My arm felt like it had been wired to an electric socket. Hundreds of large red ants were crawling all over my hand and up my sleeve, each one stinging worse than a bee. Choking back the pain as we silently moved through the jungle, I rubbed my sleeve vigorously to crush the damn things against my arm.

During our jungle jaunt, one of the JCs Surinder started getting pretty nervous. As we sat having a cigarette break, he finally explained what the mission was all about. 'You do know what we're doing on this job, don't you?'

'What's that?' I asked.

'We're going to Carolina to shoot a few soldiers and then run away. It's standard practice.'

Standard practice to pick off a few of their men then leg it back through the jungle with half their special forces after us! Ronnie was taking serious liberties here. If we started shooting, we'd get a great deal more shit back, because something like 300 troops were garrisoned there. And after the mauling they'd taken the day before, the army was certainly not going to let our little group escape unscathed.

I turned to the JCs and told them in no uncertain terms, 'If one of you lot fires a shot, we'll fucking shoot you, OK? We're going to crawl in there, have a recce and get out.'

They weren't happy. I think they were scared – not of us, but of Ronnie. They didn't want to go back and tell their leader that they hadn't had a go. If Ronnie didn't hear gunfire, he'd know they'd ignored his orders. We plodded on, with the commandos muttering away in Taki Taki. As we got near the garrison, I came across a booby trap. A small anti-personnel mine had been stuck on a metal post a foot off the ground to blow the legs off anyone who went past. Luckily, the unusual string trip line had rotted in the steaming jungle heat. It had already taken us three hours to go just a couple of miles. We were now close to Carolina; I could hear the thunder of heavy military vehicles on road nearby. And the JCs were still whinging on about the fact that they should take a pop at the enemy.

Surinder warned us, 'These sons of bitches travel through the jungle like fucking monkeys. They'll fire a few shots then scoot past you at ninety-five miles an hour and leave you with the army on your tail.' Keith said nothing and I don't think John knew what the hell was going on. We were just half a mile from a garrison of over 300 men. It was time to get some order here. So I told the JCs, 'Right, I'm calling this thing off. If you think we're going to get into the same shit as yesterday, you can forget it. If we're going to do something, we're going to plan it and do it properly. We'll be invisible in the jungle. We'll lie there for a few hours and I'll have my binoculars out and I'll mark down in my notebook everything I can see. Then we'll quietly make our way back to our canoes. We'll go back to Blackwater and we'll sit down and come up with a plan.'

They still weren't listening, so in the end I offered them the opportunity to get themselves killed that they so obviously wanted. 'OK, you bastards, you want to shoot a couple of soldiers, do it. Off you go, we'll wait here for you.' Little Bob was off like a shot, determined to salvage some pride after not shooting the machine gunner on the Urutu. Another JC followed him off into the bush.

Surrinder broke the silence. 'Quick, let's start moving back because the shit is about to hit the fan.'

Half an hour later, in the distance, we could hear the pop! pop! pop! of a couple of shotguns going off. All hell let loose. Cascavels opened up followed by the thump of fifty-calibres. We ignored it and made our way back to the river. Surinder was right. Now, we had an hour's head start on these loonies but – incredibly – when we got back to the canoes, Bob and his mate were already there.

Guns thundered all around panic-stricken Carolina as we slipped back on to the river. Bouterse's troops must have thought they were under attack from 20 million Jungle Commandos. We didn't have enough paddles for all of us, so I grabbed a tin plate for baling out the boat and thrashed away. We had to reach the cover of an island in the middle of the river before an army patrol boat spotted us and shot us out of the water.

At last we were out of sight of the bridge and a final quick spurt brought us back to the far side. John and I scrambled back up the high embankment. Flat on my stomach, I peeked over the top towards the deserted village. Darting across to the remains of a blown-up church for cover, we could still hear the army blasting away on the other side. Had they crossed the water? Nope, all clear. Jogging along the road, we dived behind a few tree stumps as the sound of an engine grew louder and louder. It was one of our trucks come to pick us up. Still on action stations, we clambered aboard, the pick-up made a U-turn and sped off towards the main road. As we reached the junction, Ronnie stepped into the road, brandishing his Barnet Commando crossbow. The Dutch radio journalist Arnold Karskens also came running over. Arnold was a nice guy, but a pain in the arse at times. He could see I was covered in mud and swamp shit, but that didn't stop him from shoving a microphone under my nose and asking me, 'Can I ask you where you've been?'

'In a fucking jacuzzi, where do you think I've been? Go away!' My reply was actually translated and broadcast on the radio in Holland a few days later.

'What's happened?' asked Ronnie.

'A couple of your boys have taken a pop at the army and you and me are going to have a good talk when we get back to Blackwater. We've got no time to talk now, the army might come across the bridge at any moment.'

Back behind the barricades at the logging camp I explained the cock-up at Carolina, and then went for broke. 'Look, Ronnie, stop this fucking bullshit. We came here to help but you're gonna get us killed. If you're truthful with us, we'll be honest with you, otherwise it's not going to work. If you continue like this I might as well piss off back to England, 'cos I can't work like this.' Ronnie promised it wouldn't happen again. Then I turned my anger on little Bob, 'You've fucked me up not once now, but twice….'

'I'm so sorry,' he interrupted, head bowed, 'I want to work with you all the time.'

'You must be fucking crazy. I'm not working with a loony like you.'

As he turned round to walk away in disgrace, I noticed he'd painted 'Suicide Commando' on the back of his leather bomber jacket. That just about summed him up. I called after him, 'If you fuck me around much more, you won't need to commit suicide because I'll kill you myself, you little bastard.'

Then I turned my attention to Django. 'Why the hell did you have us crawling through creeks, bitten by every imaginable insect? It's a miracle one of us wasn't eaten by a bloody crocodile. Why did we go through all that shit when there was a perfectly good tarmac road we could have used? We could have jogged along that road and covered two miles in twenty minutes. If a vehicle had come we could have dropped off the road, into the jungle and lay in hiding until the danger had past. Why the fuck did we have to go through that swamp?' That's when I learned that the JCs believe the gods that can protect them live in the jungle; these men only feel safe in the bush.

Ronnie wanted to go back to Langatabbetje to make better plans. I wasn't going to argue, after the last couple of days I'd had enough of Blackwater. The twenty JCs we were leaving behind wanted me to stay. I told them, 'You're brave. Don't be scared of the army. If they can't see you they can't kill you, but that doesn't mean you have to run five miles back in the jungle for cover.'

Just then, I spotted an abandoned American John Deere digging machine nearby. 'I don't think the army's going to cross the bridge for a long time,' I told the JCs, 'but just in case, send some men a kilometre up the road to fire warning shots if the army do come. Get the John Deere out and dig some fucking big holes in the road. Dig one big one, move back half a click, dig another one, move back half a click, dig another one. No armoured vehicles will be able to come through, you'll be all right. It'll give you plenty of time to escape. If they're going to overrun you, they'll send the armoured cars in first. But make sure that your first hole is back more than one kilometre so the shells burst before they even get to you. Make a booby trap as well. Dig a shallow hole and pour in some diesel and vegetation. Put a few petrol bombs in a little hideout on the side of the road. When the armoured car goes down nose first into the diesel, lob a couple of petrol bombs into it. That'll make their eyes water.'

It wasn't much, but at least it would keep them busy and stop them lying around smoking dope. Back in Langatabbetje, we discovered that some of the JCs had been in our room and had done a bit of thieving. There were still some cigarettes left but they'd pinched one of my civilian shoes. Next morning, we went looking for a guy with one leg! John got them all doing press-ups and running around in circles. Don't ask me why, these guys were ten times fitter than us. It was mental education like weapons training they needed, not PE. The JCs loved it, though; they were like school boys. Keith also gave them some useful instruction in field craft.

At one point, Ronnie pulled me to one side. 'Karel, I have another job for you.' The JCs always called me Karel, it was Dutch for Karl.

'Another recce?' I asked.

'No, we have a problem in Cayenne.'

It turned out that staff from the Surinam consulate in French Guiana had been throwing grenades into the houses of Jungle Commando supporters living on French territory.

So far, they'd killed one man and two children. The French authorities were almost powerless to do anything because the culprits had diplomatic immunity. One of them was a Surinam government spy named Koyku.

'We've got the opportunity to catch this bastard,' Ronnie explained.

He told me that a couple of middle-aged businessmen who were JC supporters had set up a meeting with Koyku in the French Guiana township of St Laurent.

'We want to kidnap him. Can you do it, Karel?' asked Ronnie. There he goes with those pleading eyes again. 'You'll have to be careful, you'll be carrying arms and kidnapping on French soil.' Then he added, 'If you can't kidnap him, kill him. But try to do it quietly.'

'Don't worry about that Ronnie,' I assured him, 'I know how to kill somebody quietly. I'll take a look.'

At least it would get me out of the jungle for a while and back to civilisation. I told John and Keith, 'Don't do anything until I get back. I won't be long.' Oki would go with me. He was a dickhead but he was one of the toughest of the lot of them and he knew everyone among the refugees from Surinam who lived in the shanty town beside the river bank at St Laurent. I stripped off my stinking camouflage, washed in the river, and dressed in shorts, T shirt and training shoes. After all, I had to be able to mingle with the local Frogs. I packed the Browning, a pair of handcuffs and a bottle of valium tablets in a small zip-up sports holdall. The bag would act as a silencer and also catch the empty rounds. Fold half a hessian sack into a pad and tape it into the front of a holdall. That's your silencer. Zip up the bag until it's about one-third open, put your hand inside clutching the gun. With the shoulder strap on, move your left hand across to hold the bag. Now push the Browning's muzzle against the hessian sack and fire.

As we arrived in St Laurent, I waited in the canoe while Oki disappeared into the shanty town to make contact. He arrived back with four men and we sneaked through the maze of shacks until we ended up at a hut next to a big old wall. Oki explained this was the old prison where Papillion had been held. I made a note to check it out. As it turned out, I was to see quite a lot of it later. Inside the hut, four locals talked excitedly in Taki Taki about Koyku. Oki spoke English, after a fashion, and said to me, 'Karel, we have a chance for tomorrow. Do you want to take that chance?'

In for a penny, in for a pound. In the morning these four guys would lead Koyku to a nearby café owned by a Surinamese sympathetic to the Jungle Commandos. After days of eating shit, it was time to give my stomach a workout. I had 300 francs, which I gave to one of Oki's pals to get some proper food. He arrived back with chicken and chips and six bottles of Kronenbourg beer. Wonderful. Now, Oki and his pals' idea of heaven was doing drugs and that night, they decided to indulge themselves a bit. They started off on marijuana. I couldn't do anything about that – they live on the stuff. Next thing they were snorting cocaine; then they started burning heroin on pieces of silver foil and inhaling the fumes. By now their eyes were glowing red in the dark; they looked like a bunch of wild men. I retreated to the bedroom with my beer to lie on the floor. I drifted off, but woke with a start as water started lapping around me. Again, they'd forgotten to tell me the place was tidal! Rats nibbled at me a few times in the night. Under normal circumstances it would have been unpleasant, but I'd been bitten so much in the jungle that the rats weren't a problem.

Next morning, keeping our eyes peeled for the French Gendarmes that patrol the area, we threaded our way through the shanty town, along the river to St Laurent proper. The streets were a bit grim; the odd white person drove past. I was armed and had no passport or papers; in short, I could not afford to get caught. We ducked up a side road off the main street and dived into the Café Amsterdam. A group of blokes and a couple of girls hung around in the bar. Music blared from a ghetto blaster.

The owner stepped forward. 'Hello Karl, I'm Bobo. You've come for Mr. Koyku? This is a very bad man, be careful.'

Koyku was due in one hour, maybe two. We had to get organised. I posted two lookouts on a bench across the road and ordered them not to smoke dope. If anybody looking like the law approached, the lookouts would stroll back in and I'd slip out of the back door and onto the river bank. Had anybody else got a gun? Oki had a Browning and one of them had a little Belgian-made pistol. It looked like .25, and it was so rusty that it was almost useless. It would probably do as a frightener, but that's about all. I got my Browning out, cocked it, put the safety back on, and put it on the shelf behind the counter.

In a short while, one of the lookouts wandered in and announced, 'Here he comes! It's Koyku!' He was with two of our boys from Cayenne. They'd parked their car down the road and were strolling to the café. I crouched down behind the counter, pushing the handcuffs into the back of my shorts. In walked a short, stocky bloke in a big expensive white hat with a silk band around it. He wore a white linen suit, white disco dancer's shoes, white socks, and a white shirt. He carried a bulging Le Coq sports holdall. A typical cool motherfucker. As the three of them got through the door, the shutters came down. The café was now closed. I stepped out from behind the counter, the Browning pointing directly at Koyku.

'Do you speak English?' I demanded.

'Yes. What's your problem? Why are you pointing that at me?'

'Listen to me and listen good. Sit down in that chair.'

'Hey, man.'

'I said sit down!'

As he sat down he looked at me shaking his head, a half smile across his face. He tried to make peace again: 'Hey, hey, man.'

'Don't give me any of that shit. Put your left hand on the table.'

He ignored my order, put his hands up in the air and said, 'Hey, what's wrong?'

Bosh. I hit him hard on the nose with the Browning.

'I'm only going to tell you things once and once only. You understand me?'

His hands felt the blood trickling from his nose, 'Oh my God, my God,' he wailed.

Then he put his left hand on the table. Click. The handcuff went on.

'OK, put your hands behind your back – both of them.'

'Yes, yes.' Now he was seeing sense. Both hands went behind his back. Click. The other cuff. 'Hey what's all this about?' he asked.

Bosh. I hit him again with the Browning, this time on the head, knocking his hat flying.

'I told you shut up, just do as I tell you. Come on, move, move get off the chair.'

I dragged him round the back of the counter into a disgusting little hole of a storage room, full of dirt, spiders and empty bottles left lying there for years. I pushed him into a chair. 'Sit and don't fucking move, don't breathe a word, because I will fucking shoot you, do you understand me?'

'Yes, yes.'

His face was covered in blood now, as was much of his white linen suit. The two-inch gash on his head was bleeding quite profusely. I checked him out. He was not going to bleed to death.

'Shut up and be quiet,' I ordered. 'There's two more of you lot to come yet.'

I walked back into the café. All of the black guys were grinning. Would you believe it, on went the ghetto blaster again. I had to shout above the noise, 'Turn that fucking thing down. Be quiet, behave. Have it on by all means so it doesn't sound too silent from outside, making anybody going past suspicious. You can crack the front door open now and open the shutters. Just take it easy boys, relax, and keep off the fucking dope.'

An hour and a half later the four Jungle Commando supporters frog-marched two scruffy-looking men aged about fifty into the café. One towered above all of us, at about six foot six. The other was tiny. Fear was etched on both their faces.

CHAPTER 4

As the Café Amsterdam's iron shutters slammed closed with a clang, I stepped out from behind the bar. Their eyes nearly popped out as they saw the Browning. There was no need for introductions, 'You two, in the back. Now.' They complied swiftly, though they nearly fainted at the sight of Koyku handcuffed and covered in blood.

'Get down in the corner. Kneel. Face the wall,' I ordered. After seeing the treatment their mate Koyku had received, they obeyed smartish. I'd improvised two sets of handcuffs from a couple of coat hangers and I pushed the wire around their wrists.

'Sit down on the floor. Don't speak, don't fucking move.'

Neither of them dared look me in the eye, so they sat staring at the floor. I noticed Koyku had pissed himself with fright. He looked at me. 'Mister please don't hit me, please. I can talk to you. Please let me just ask you something. What have I done?'

I warned him, 'Would you like another belt with this Browning?'

'No, please don't hurt me. Can I just have some drink? I feel sick, I feel bad.'

His mouth was parched. He looked like he was going to crack at any moment. This was the moment for the valium. We had to keep this guy quiet for a long time. The boat to take us out would not arrive until dawn the next day.

'Okay, I'm going to give you a little drink. I don't normally serve drinks to shitheads like you,' I explained to him, 'I'm not taking the handcuffs off, so when I bring your drink, you get it down in one go. I'm not going to stand here being your fucking servant and holding it for you, do you understand me?'

I went out to the bar got a glass from Bobo, half filled it with beer then crushed up twelve small valium tablets into a fine powder and poured them into the drink. When it had cleared, the beer looked clear. Koyku opened his mouth – whoosh, straight down in one go. Ten minutes later he slumped in the chair, chin on his chest.

'You okay?' I asked.

He lifted his head up slowly and gave me a great big smile. 'Yes, everything's OK.' His chin slowly went back down to his chest. The other two still hadn't moved. While Koyku was out for the count, I searched his pockets and the Le Coq bag. He had two passports – one French, the other from Surinam. I also found a notebook full of names, addresses and phone numbers, a return air ticket on Air France to the Caribbean island of Martinique and two thousand quid in French francs.

As night, fell the café reopened. I sat behind the counter, Browning on the shelf, listening to salsa music played endlessly, the same tunes over and over again. I was relieved when finally they played some slow stuff. About two o'clock in the morning the bar closed and I showed Bobo a note from Ronnie that said simply: 'Offer every assistance to this man.' I asked him to arrange a canoe to be brought to the river bank behind the café just before dawn. Bobo would have the boat ready by half-past four. I dragged two tables together to make a bed and conked out.

I woke with a start at five o'clock. No sign of Bobo. I looked in the back room. The three prisoners were wide awake, staring at the walls, not saying a word. I woke Oki and told him to find Bobo and the boat. About an hour later, the door clanked open. In came Bobo and Oki. 'Small problem Karel, small problem. No boat before nine o'clock.'

'Holy shit!' I exploded. 'I've got to get these guys out of here in broad daylight? What's the matter with you?'

'Something wrong with the engine, we've got to find another boat.'

'Oh fuck it. You've had all the time in the world to arrange this and to make sure you got a boat with an engine.' I said. Another cock-up, but I knew that I couldn't afford to panic – we might really have been in trouble if I had.

In the middle of this, Koyku wanted a piss. I made him stand, unlocked one of the cuffs and flicked it onto my wrist. With the Browning shoved in his ribs, I led Koyku out through the back door to what I expected to be the river bank. But the back yard had been blocked off from the river by a high wall of corrugated iron. Bit of a problem there. Bobo revealed that we would have to walk the prisoners fifty metres down the road in broad daylight to reach the canoe. When the initial shock wore off, I realised it wouldn't be too bad. We had enough guys to check up and down the road for danger. However, once we were in the boat we would still not be safe: French marines patrolled the river.

Finally, the boat arrived. I got the prisoners to their feet and they watched as I put my tote bag over my shoulder and put my hand inside the bag, holding the Browning, finger on the trigger.

'See this,' I warned Koyku, 'if you've got any smart ideas about trying to run away or scream in the street, I'll just fire straight through the bag, kill you and then run away. Make no fucking bones about it my friend, pull any stunts and you're a dead man, understand?' I handcuffed him to my left hand. The pair in the coat hangers would walk on ahead. Ronnie's man with the rusty pistol and Oki would be behind them to cover their backs and shield their hands from view. I stepped out of the café door to find a hundred locals standing on the corner. Holy shit! Word had got round like wildfire. Even Jan, whose home we'd stayed at in Cayenne, was there, a big smile on his face. He gave me the thumbs-up sign. I knew he was a bottle-less bastard; if he was grinning and giving me the thumbs up, everything really must be okay. We went off at a brisk pace. No cars in sight. We turned right onto a little track by the side of the house. There was the canoe with two black men in it. Oki clambered aboard; I pushed the prisoners into the boat.

'Let's go!'

Engine in reverse, we roared away from the bank. All I had to do now was keep my eyes open for French patrols. An hour later, safely out of harm's way in the middle of the river, our little prisoner started trying to head-butt his mate. I pointed the pistol at him and shouted, 'Behave yourself there, Rambo'. Suddenly he burst into tears and the big guy handcuffed beside him started crying as well. Koyku, handcuffed to one of the ribs on the canoe, sat there in still shock. Well up the river by now, Oki wanted to stop at a village to give a message to the local JC commander. At least it would let the prisoners stretch their legs. The sun had been blazing, there was no shelter on the canoe, so we all jumped into waist-deep water and waded ashore on a sandy beach where dozens of villagers came out to see Mr. Koyku, the famous spy.

A whole crew of Jungle Commandos bunched outside the local commandant's hut. A couple of them were armed with shotguns; the rest had an evil-looking collection of machetes and knives. The commandant stepped forward, and announced, 'I want to speak with Koyku in my hut.'

'What for?' I asked.

'This Koyku is a big voodoo man. He's put a curse on us.'

'OK,' I said, 'you've got a couple of minutes. Take him in the office.'

A few of them went in, the rest stayed outside. Moments later, slap, thump, ouch! The hut reverberated to the sounds of someone getting a good hiding. I waded into the hut and dragged Koyku outside. A huge group of Jungle Commandos jumped on top of him and the rest laid into the other two poor bastards, kicking them and jumping up and down on their heads. One of the Jungle Commandos levelled a shotgun at me, and another one sidled over with a machete in his hand. Staring the gunman down, I drew the Browning from my bag and walked over to him. I shoved the Browning's nose over the shotgun barrels, literally six inches away from his chin, and snatched the shotgun off him.

'You, fuck off!' I snarled.

I turned around. The rest of these nutcases hadn't even noticed. Bang! bang! I fired two shots into the air. The beating stopped dead and I let them have it – verbally. 'Right, you bunch of arseholes, what's your fucking game? I didn't risk my neck in St Laurent capturing these fucking spies and getting them back here so you lot can all play silly games! You're like a bunch of fucking animals. Get off them!'

Oki came flying over. 'Karel, this is our war.'

'Shut your fucking mouth. I'm not working for you. Ronnie asked me to get these guys – not you or your fucking stupid mates. Go on, just go over and kick 'em… I'll blow your face off.'

Koyku lay in the blood-stained dirt. The other two had been seriously beaten. As they staggered to their feet, the shithead picked up his weapon. I pointed my Browning at him. 'Don't even think about it, sunshine. If I ever see you again, you're in fucking trouble. I won't forget your face. Let's go!'

I got the prisoners back in the canoe; the driver gunned the engine to life. As we backed off the bank, Oki come running along, 'Wait for me!' I still had the Browning in my hand, finger on the trigger. Oki splashed through the water, clambered onto the front and fell into the canoe. We roared in reverse and shot off up the river. Oki came down to my end of the boat, a concerned look on his face. 'Karel, you shouldn't have done that,' he told me. 'You've upset a lot of people.'

'Upset a lot of people? You fucking upset me, you arsehole. You put my life in jeopardy in St Laurent with your heroin and marijuana. I don't know why Ronnie sent you in; you're useless, Oki. I've threatened you once before, I'm going to threaten you now. You ever upset me again, I'll kill you.' I meant it.

'Oh Karel, I'm sorry, I'm sorry.'

Later, as the canoe passed the river checkpoint at walking pace, Frank the local river guard commandant spotted the prisoners in the boat. And like the rest of these sadistic sons of bitches, he wanted to have his little game. He called out, 'Hey, stop! Stop!'

I pointed to my Browning. 'Forget about it arsehole, forget it.'

John and small clutch of JCs were waiting on the bank as we arrived back in Lagatabbetje. Keith had gone on a job to a place called Stolkirtsijver up at the front line. I got the three prisoners out of the boat, gave the big one and the little one to John and took Koyku to the cookhouse myself. There was a secure room above the cookhouse that prisoners were sometimes locked up in. it was one of the few rooms in Langatabbetje that actually had a key to the door. As I took Koyku upstairs to the room and took off his cuff, I said, 'I'll tell you something, you're in big trouble now. You realise that, don't you?'

He burst into tears and sobbed, 'I know nothing, mister. I haven't done anything, I don't know why I'm here.'

'You're lying, Koyku,' I replied. 'I'm going to explain this to you once, so listen and listen good. I will come to you later and we'll have a civilised little chat – or you talk to them. You've had a taste of talking with them back in that village. That was nothing compared to these fuckers. They don't call this Devil's Island for nothing. This Devil's Island has nothing to do with Papillon. Even the bush negroes are afraid to come here.'

Koyku was crying even more now. I locked him in and went to see Little and Large, who were also sobbing their hearts out as Jungle Commandos poked and screamed at them. John stood there, grinning. I pushed my way into the crowd. One Jungle Commando seemed to be doing the most shouting. So I chose him, came up behind him quietly, grabbed him by the shoulder and jerked him back really hard. He stumbled and fell over. I didn't for one moment think he'd fall over, but it did the trick.

I took the two prisoners to the schoolhouse, where there was another room for prisoners. There were already two captured government soldiers in there, living in terrible conditions. They were half-starved and lying on a concrete floor. Prisoners might have been badly treated but at least the JCs took prisoners. To my knowledge, Bouterse's men simply killed rebels rather than capturing them.

I took Little and Large inside and took off the wire handcuffs. Their wrists looked in a pretty sorry state but there didn't seem to be any permanent damage done. With their hands now free, I gave them each a cigarette. I was suspicious about these two. There was something wrong about them. The story I'd heard in St Laurent was that they'd been talking to some of the Jungle Commandos about joining up, but one of the pair had been found to have a small tape recorder running in his pocket. I think some pillock had sent them in just to try and gather information and they probably thought that they were safe in St Laurent. I'd have to sort the problem out directly with Ronnie – not the local commandant, Radjin. I took the key for the room off the guard; if I had keys to both rooms, the prisoners might be safe from harm. Ronnie was out of contact for a couple of days, so I spoke with Radjin. 'You told me you went to university in Holland and you were in the Dutch Army,' I began.

'Yes, that's correct, Karel,' he replied.

'Well, what's the matter with you, then?' I asked. 'You've got half a brain, you're educated, why are you making those government troops you captured suffer like that? Have you seen the state of the poor bastards?'

'Yes, well, we do that, it's part of the process,' he replied. 'We're busy... we've got other things to do.'

'Busy? Every time I see you, you're busy lying on your fucking hammock. Listen, find some mattresses for those poor bastards lying there on the concrete floor and send some food and some water.'

Radjin's response to that was to tell me that he was the commandant and that he didn't have to take orders from me.

'Radjin, when the journalists turn up they're going to see the prisoners in that room and it will get back to Holland.'

'No it won't,' he said, 'we'll keep them away from there.'

I told him straight, 'If any journalists turn up I'm going to take them in the room to show them the conditions that you keep the prisoners in. I'm telling them you're in charge and you're going to end up on telly. See what Mummy and Daddy think about your university education then.'

The prisoners quickly received some smelly mattresses and food. However, I didn't want Koyku eating just yet. I didn't want him to have any distractions. In the middle of the night I unlocked his room. I was carrying my FAL and two spare mags. He was asleep on an old iron bed. I prodded him awake with the FAL. He leapt up. His nightmares were about to become reality.

'Have you thought about what I told you before?'

'I know nothing.'

'For fuck's sake, Koyku, stop playing games.' I looked at
my watch. 'I shall be back in exactly one hour. If you
haven't changed your mind by then, I'm sorry but I will
have to hand you over to the local yokels and they will
extract the information from you.'

'Mister, OK, but I know nothing.'

'Right, smart arse.' Now if you, dear reader, are starting
to feel sorry for Koyku, don't. I took the two passports I'd
found in the disco king's pockets to Radjin's office. I
opened the Surinam one. Inside was a row of Libyan
immigration stamps. As I mentioned earlier, at that time
Libya's Colonel Gaddafi was propping up Bouterse's
regime with $100 million worth of aid. Surinam's dictator
had been to Tripoli several times to see his old mate
Gaddafi Duck. Koyku had obviously been there too.

Radjin's eyes lit up, so I asked what exactly had Koyku
been up to. It turned out he had been implicated in
throwing grenades and assassinating some of Ronnie's
men on French soil in Cayenne. One group of JCs had
disappeared as they drove along a road. It seems this was
Koyku's speciality. He was an assassin and general fucking
scallywag. Now we had proof he'd been on business in
Libya. I opened Koyku's notebook. It was filled with
names and numbers, most of them meaningless to me, but
Radjin spotted the name Gampat and an address. It
appeared Bouterse's agents had thrown grenades at
Gampat's house to try to assassinate a man called Krishna
Mahabir who was staying there. He was lucky: the
grenade missed him.

Now, I'm no Inspector Maigret, but the evidence against our friend Koyku was starting to look a bit strong. Judging by the number of package tours Koyku had been on to Libya, he would be well trained. Getting information from him would be difficult. Even if you battered him with a hammer he wasn't going to talk. He was going to hang on and hang on because as soon as he confessed to what he'd been up to, he'd sign his own death warrant. It wouldn't be a bullet through the back of the head – the Jungle Commandos would most likely end up chopping him into mincemeat. I brought Koyku from the cookhouse to Radjin's office. John stood guard outside to slap any JCs that tried to get in and attack Koyku.

'Your hour is up, have you anything else to say?'

Tears rolled down his face. 'No, mister. I don't know why you people have got me. What have I done? Why are you doing this to me?'

Don't be taken in by the tears, this guy was tough. Radjin started barking at him in Taki Taki. However, as he and Koyku could both speak English, I decided this particular conversation would be in a language I could understand.

'Look Koyku,' I began, 'I'm a busy man. I can't hang around with you lying to me all the fucking time. I've got other things to do; you've had your chance.'

I took him out of the office and locked him in a storage room where they kept bits and pieces for the airstrip – marker flags and stuff like that. 'I've finished with you now,' I told him. 'Bye bye.'

He was crying again as I walked back to the office to arrange part two of the interrogation. I told one of the gofers, 'Go and fetch number one loony. Bring me Oki.'

Oki's eyes were glowing red again when he wandered in, still cocky. 'Karel, we done a good job, hey?'

'Listen, the job's not finished yet,' I told him. 'I want you and a couple of your friends to give Koyku a little hiding. Oki, I'm going to make it clear now: you don't have to hurt him too much. Koyku's already terrified of you.'

'I do good, Karel, I don't kill him.'

'This man is important, so yes, do not under any circumstances kill him. Don't even break a bone, not even one bone. You beat him by all means, but do not fucking kill him. This is a chance to redeem yourself. You do this properly and I won't tell Ronnie what you've been up to in St Laurent and in the village down the river.'

'Okay, you and me good friends, we're gonna work together all the time now.'

He disappeared and came back a couple of minutes later with three more lunatics who had all been on something. One had a FAL, another brandished a machete.

'What are you going to do with that?' I asked him.

'Er, er, I'm not going to cut him, I'm going to cut a branch off a tree, we're going to beat him with a stick.'

He went off and returned with a four-foot long, two-inch thick branch. I told them to only hit the arse and the back of the legs. Then, I threw back the bolt, opened the locker door and ordered Koyku out.

'You won't talk to me so these guys want to talk to you,'
I said, pointing at Oki and his chums. When Koyku saw
the stick, then realised they were stoned out of their
brains, he gasped, 'Oh my God!'

Just then Oki pulled Koyku by the ears; another one
grabbed him by half his cheek. They dragged him around
the island, past the cookhouse, past the clinic, up onto the
airstrip. I wanted them away from the family huts. There
was no way I wanted civilians to see this.

John and I stood a hundred yards away by the airport
building, FALs at the ready. The three talked to Koyku
first and slapped him a few times. Then Oki ran at him,
punched him in the gut and knocked him flat on his back.
Now they were screaming at him. Koyku curled up in a
ball on the floor to protect himself, his hands covering his
face. The guy with the stick got stuck into him – in all the
places I told him not to touch. He stopped. Koyku
screamed his head off as they knelt on top of him,
spreading his arms and legs out. Then, they pointed the
FAL at his body spread-eagled on the ground. John and I
were convinced they were about to bump Koyku off there
and then. We cocked our weapons and took aim in Oki's
general direction.

But before we could fire, bang! bang! bang! Oki opened
up; 7.62mm bullets tore up the earth around Koyku's
head. Bam! bam! bam! Now they were ripping around his
legs. Koyku clawed the ground like a cat. Oki emptied the
full mag. Koyku endured twenty rounds. Any one of them
could have killed him. Then they laid into him again with

the stick. One of them started to take little running jumps onto Koyku, feet first, going for his head.

The whole seedy business lasted no more than four minutes before I decided it was time to end it. I raised the FAL again and fired one shot down the strip. This was part of my plan. John and I went running up, 'Clear off you lot!'

I pointed at Koyku still lying motionless. 'You, up off the fucking ground.' Paralysed with fear, Koyku couldn't move. He'd pissed himself again and was shaking like a leaf, but he didn't dare move a muscle.

'Hey, it's me, the honky,' I told him. 'Off the ground, get up.'

Gingerly, Koyku raised himself up on to his knees. He clung on to my camouflage pants, sobbing, 'Oh my God, oh my God.'

Both his eyes were virtually closed from the beating; his lip was split wide open. His face and body were covered in wields and welts from the stick. It was the camp cook who'd taken a jump at Koyku's head. I give him an absolutely dirty look, before dragging Koyku off to the airport building. He slumped in a chair, I sat on the desk opposite and lit up a cigarette. 'I told you what would happen.'

Despite the beating, he still kept on, 'Mister please, I don't know anything. I know nothing.'

Then I let him have it. 'They're going to execute you. You know what execute means? They're going to fire a bullet through your head at midnight tonight. They're going to have a voodoo ceremony and exactly at midnight they're going to fire one round through the back of your head.'

'Oh Jesus, oh Jesus,' he moaned.

'There's an easy way to stop this: tell me what I want to know.'

'I know nothing, I know nothing.'

I was just thinking, 'You really are a tough fucker', when the door burst open and in flew the cook. Bash, he kicked Koyku straight in the face. I turned around and cracked right into the cook's face with my fist, knocking him back to the door. As he reeled from the blow, I raced in, smacked him a couple more cracks and booted him out of the room.

'Come on, Koyku, let's get you out of here,' I said, helping him to his feet. As we walked down the track back to the village he asked, 'Are they really going to kill me tonight?'

'That,' I replied, 'is for sure. I'm taking you back to that lock-up to save you further torture but other than that I can help you no more. You're going to be executed tonight.'

'Oh Jesus, oh Jesus,' he said. Then he tried a different tack. 'You know the day you captured me in St Laurent? I heard that day that my father had died.'

'Yeah, well I've got news for you: you'll be seeing him tonight.'

'Oh Jesus, Jesus Christ.'

He still couldn't believe it. And what's more, I knew he was lying about his father dying. Who's going to walk into a café going, 'Hey I'm the coolest motherfucker', straight after hearing his dad's just died?

Back in Radjin's office, Koyku claimed he was a tourist who didn't like Bouterse. I held up the passport with the Libyan visa in it. He nearly crapped his pants.

'What's that then?' I asked him

'I went to Libya for culture, a culture thing.'

'What culture thing was that?'

'I'm a culture man, a voodoo man. I showed them how to make voodoo. That passport is not my passport, this is false passport, I have no passport before so I buy passport from another man. I put my photograph in, the other man have the Libyan stamp.'

'That's a nice one. I suppose this notebook belongs to the other guy that you got the passport off?'

He looked at the notebook and nearly crapped himself again.

'Yes, that's my notebook, I have addresses, people to come and see, people who don't like Bouterse, they like Ronnie.'

Radjin couldn't hold back any longer. 'You were seen running away from Gampat's house after the grenades were thrown, right?'

'It wasn't me.'

I'd had enough. 'Back in the lock-up,' I told Koyku. 'I'm too busy to save an arsehole like you.'

'Oh no, please mister, I don't want to die.'

I handed Radjin the lock-up key, gave him instructions to let the boys at Koyku later and went off to relax. It was six o'clock. A couple of hours later, Radjin let Koyku out, but instead of whacking him with a stick, the JCs started prodding him with a bayonet, drawing blood. They also tried to force water down his throat. I arrived to find him lying in a pool of blood, water and vomit. I feigned anger as I chased the Jungle Commandos away. Koyku could hardly stand up. The once-white linen shirt and suit were torn to ribbons and covered in vomit. I dragged him to the office, threw him in a chair and told the gofer to get some coffee. It was his first drink since the valium-spiked beer. I threw him a cigarette. I'd deliberately not given him anything to drink to wear him down. Now I wanted him relaxed. Radjin asked him again about the grenade attack on Gampat's house.

This time, he was willing to admit some involvement in the incident. 'OK, OK, I was at Gampat's house. I just carried the grenades. They asked me to carry them.'

'Who asked to you to do this?'

He named a couple of diplomats at the Surinam Consulate in Cayenne. We asked him about the disappearance of Jungle Commando supporters who had disappeared. What had happened to them? Had they been spirited back to Paramaribo, had they suffered what Koyku was getting now or were they dead?

'I don't know. I'm a very nice guy, really.'

'Oh yeah? Then why did you take the grenades?

'They gave me two hundred dollars every day.'

He obviously thought that because he'd made a confession, he was now safe. He was wrong.

I jumped up. 'You're still lying. Midnight, you're dead. End of story.'

It was already getting on for midnight. I had to speed this thing up. Back to the lock-up. I opened the door, shoved Koyku in and fired a two-second burst from the CS canister. Then I shut the door, stood back and waited for the results, which happened in about fifteen seconds. A loud belching, vomiting noise was followed by screams: 'Please! Please, open the door!' Koyku came flying out at about ninety miles an hour, and collapsed in a heap at my feet. Back in the office, he confessed a little more. By now it was twenty to twelve. Twenty minutes of life left. I shoved him back in the lock-up and shhhhhh, gave him a four-second burst on the gas. This time I left him a little bit longer. The poor bastard must have been crawling the walls. As I opened the door to let him out, the gas hit me. My eyes watered immediately, my face was burning. I couldn't take him straight back into the office because the gas off him was affecting all of us. Finally, he gave us a look of resignation. 'OK you've got me, I'd rather die than have this any more. I'll tell you anything you want to know.'

And could we shut him up after that? Jesus Christ – it was rabbit, rabbit, rabbit! I had to tell the guy to slow down. What was that again? Who said this? Who did that? What car? In the end we had the lot, six pages of details.

When it was all done, he looked up, wearily. 'OK, and now you're going to shoot me,' he said resigned to his fate.

'That was a bluff. Nobody's going to shoot you. Even Ronnie won't shoot you – he doesn't believe in killing prisoners. Have a coffee and a cigarette.'

Koyku looked down at the floor. He was taken away and locked back up in his room at the cook house with strict orders to leave him alone. He'd done his bit. Ronnie was going to be a happy chappy when he got back.

Next morning I checked on Koyku. He still couldn't believe they weren't going to execute him at midnight. I know that they would have killed him if they'd had their way. What do you think the guy brought the machete for? That wasn't just for cutting off a branch, believe me.

CHAPTER

5

A canoe appeared out of the morning mist from the Surinam side of the river. Four Jungle Commandos lay on the bottom boards. They'd been shot in a fire fight with the army up on the front line at a town called Stolkirtsijver, which lay on the main road between the capital Paramaribo and French Guiana. The wounded men had bullet holes through their legs and arms. A bullet had left a deep gouge right across the back of one of them. It had taken so long to get the casualties through the jungle that some of them had stopped bleeding. A swarm of tiny flies that feasted on coagulated blood covered the wounds. I had the only medical kit on the island, an NBC pouch full of antibiotics, bandages and antiseptic creams, which Major Getback had put together. It was very basic, not ideal for treating gunshot wounds that were rapidly going putrid in the heat. I sprayed each wound with fly repellent, then plastered on antiseptic cream. I bandaged and taped up each casualty. Hopefully that would stop the infection until Ronnie got back with the plane and the wounded could be flown to the hospital at Stoelman's Island.

The Commandos were in shock. Some of them asked me whether they were going to die. I gave them a little pep talk. 'Don't worry you're not going to die. You're safe with me, Karl, the number one doctor from Liverpool. I know what I'm talking about because I used to be a brain surgeon, take it easy.' After patching up the still-terrified soldiers, I put them in hammocks in the big classroom at the school. As more stragglers arrived at Langatabbetje, we learned Keith had still been at Stolkirtsijver when the shooting started. He'd travelled out with another guy called Oki – not the number one loony. Little Oki, as we called him, was a bush negro with a lovely nature. Eventually little Oki turned up from the skirmish, but there was no sign of Keith.

Little Oki explained, 'We got separated at Stolkirtsijver, a Cascavel came after us and we got split up. Keith ran one way and we ran the other.'

'What, Keith's gone off on his own?'

'Yeah, he ran off on his own into the jungle.'

We were starting to get a little bit concerned now. Maybe Keith would show up later on in the day. A slow trickle of stragglers came in bringing a few more wounded with them. I patched up all the casualties and there was still no sign of Keith. Next morning, more stragglers arrived, plus a Dutch television crew. I asked them all whether anyone had seen anything of Keith, but no one had.

Now I really was starting to get worried in case the poor bastard was lost – or worse, lying injured in the jungle. Where would we start searching in hundreds of square miles of rainforest? And then, at midday, guess who turned up? Keith, of course.

'Where have you been you, bastard?' I enquired.

'Have you been worried about me, boys?'

'Yeah, I've been worried about you, Keith. What happened?'

'Fucking hell,' he exclaimed, 'a Cascavel came after us, I ran off into the jungle and I got lost overnight. I couldn't move through the jungle in the dark, it's physically impossible.'

It seemed he'd lost his compass but somehow he'd found a bottle of rum. He pulled out one of his water bottles. 'Does anybody want a drink of this?'

'No, it's all right, Keith.'

Remember I told Koyku that Lagatabbetje was known as Devil's Island? I wasn't kidding. Many of the JCs there were the scum of the earth; they were wanted for murder and rape. They'd joined Ronnie's little band to escape the law but these reprobates never went anywhere near the front line. Instead, they hung around Langatabbetje making a nuisance of themselves. Radjin had a discipline problem with some of them – and with two in particular, Mario and Castile. When he'd tackled them they'd shoved a shotgun under his nose and told him to fuck off or they'd blow his brains out. Radjin went white with fear and came looking for me and John. We warned them off. But that night Radjin flew up to our room. 'Karel, they're at it again.'

Enough was enough. This pair were not going to take the piss out of me or anybody else. John and I grabbed

Castile and smacked him right in the face. He put up a struggle, so I brought up the rifle and bashed the butt into the back of his neck. Now he had the barrels of both FALs jammed up against his face. 'Up to the room, you bastard,'. At this point, Castile clearly realised that he'd made a big mistake. Going up the stairs, I rammed the barrel of my FAL up his arse, violently, hurting him. We tied his thumbs with wire and Keith stood guard while John and I hunted for Mario. We found him in a hut that stank of marijuana; the warm glow of an oil lamp revealed a huge smirk on his face. I pointed the FAL at him, and barked, 'Get out now, you fucker.' A rifle butt across the head wiped away the smirk. He went down, and I put in a few kicks, before shouting, 'Get up, get up on your feet.' Violent jabs in his back all the way to the house. Mario really panicked when he saw his pal already there – Castile was the tough guy of the two. For good measure we picked up another troublemaker while we were at it. Wired up, they all sat solemnly in silence.

I crouched down in front of Mario and poked him in the eye, a good one that really hurt. And off I went. 'You think you're a fucking smart arse,' I told him. 'I warned you, and what did you do? You ignored me.' He answered back in Taki Taki, so I slugged him right in the mouth. I started losing my temper a bit then and laid into Castile – slap, crack, whack. 'Get hold of that you cheeky bastard.' All three of them had seen what had happened to Koyku and now they started screaming. They weren't going to get the same treatment, of course, just a few slaps for misbehaving. Other Jungle Commandos in our house or sleeping nearby heard the commotion and started gathering at the bottom of our steps to our house, shouting and bawling. Most of them had guns, so we had to be careful now. They could fire up through the wooden floor below. As well as my FAL, I had a Beretta Model 12 sub-machine gun. I pointed it at our three prisoners, 'One shot comes up here and you get it.'

Mario shouted out in Taki Taki, telling them, 'Go away or this guy will kill us.' The chanting carried on, followed by the sound of feet on the stairs. I swivelled round, the Berretta aimed at the door. In came two of the more responsible JCs, Blakka and a Rastafarian called Boycee. 'What's happening, Karel?' they asked. After I explained, they went out onto the stairs and started arguing with the mob below. Everything went quiet. I walked outside and shouted down, 'Fire one round and I'll empty the clip into the lot of you.'

Boycee spoke up, 'Let these three go, I've just told everybody we're going to get Ronnie to deal with them.'

Not a bad idea that. Eight o'clock in the morning was radio time. Ronnie was back at Stoelman's Island, so I told him on the radio, 'You'd better get these troublemakers sorted out now because if you think we're staying here with this load of jerks you've got another think coming.'

The radio crackled. 'Okay, I'll be there in twenty minutes.'

Ronnie must have jumped straight in the Cessna with Orlando. As he stepped off the plane, it was the first time I'd seen real anger in his face. Next thing, 150 Jungle Commandos were crowded around the cookhouse.

Ronnie signalled to me, 'Karel, come over here, stand by me. Who are they?'

I pointed out Castile, Mario and the third troublemaker.

Ronnie ordered, 'Get down on the floor, on your stomachs.' The cook who likes to score penalty kicks on prisoners dived into the cookhouse and came out with a four-foot length of thick electric cable with a knot in the end of it. Ronnie gave another speech for a couple of minutes to let the three on the floor sweat a bit. As he ranted and raved, the Jungle Commandos all looked a bit sheepish, trying to hide their faces as he pointed out individuals in the crowd. Then the cook got stuck in with the electric cable. He started on Castile first. Swash! swash! Ronnie grabbed the cable off him, 'You're not doing it hard enough, like this!' Crack! crack! Castile screamed his head off. He tried to jump up, but Ronnie slapped him around the head, yelling, 'Get down or you'll get it worse.' Big, tough Castile was in tears as Ronnie laid in to him. The cook took over and thrashed the other two.

To my mind, it wasn't enough. I told Ronnie they should have been shot. He replied, 'I know this, Karel, but if I shoot these three, half of my men will desert. I have a big discipline problem.'

While we were talking, one of the voodoo men suddenly went into a trance. Apparently he was being visited by a ghost. He ranted and raved and then started slapping Ronnie, on the arm, on the back and pounding him on the chest, because the ghost was 'telling him to speak to Ronnie'. I don't know what he told him but the voodoo man suddenly started to go among the crowd. He pointed at one, then another. Ronnie told all of the ones the voodoo man picked out to stand against the cookhouse wall. Then the voodoo man pointed to the three lying on the floor still crying their eyes out and bleeding. Ronnie shook his head, they weren't going against the wall. Ronnie turned to the men who were stood beside the wall and laid into them. 'You are a useless bunch of fuckers, you don't go near the front, you're just a bunch of hangers on, you're nothing. Get your gear and go.'

They started pleading, 'Please, we've nowhere to go. The police are after us in French Guiana and if the army pick us up in Surinam, we're dead men.'

Ronnie refused to give in, 'Get off the island, you motherfuckers. Off!'

Great stuff, but why didn't he get rid of the three stooges on the floor at the same time?

'No, no, no,' Ronnie replied, when I asked him, 'I'm going to make those bastards suffer. They're not going to get away so easily.'

Ronnie had more business to deal with, so I went back to the house for a lie down. As I walked past Castile, Mario and their friend, I said, 'I told you didn't I, naughty boys!' Even John burst out laughing.

I was lying on my bed when I heard deep, heavy-breathing noises coming up the stairs. In came the voodoo man, followed by Radjin, who looked terrified, and Ronnie behind him. The voodoo man pointed at me and started growling.

'What's the matter with this loony?' I demanded, 'I'm trying to get my head down, now piss off.'

Ronnie stifled a grin. 'This is serious, Karel. You must not sleep on that bed any more. The bed is cursed. The man has seen a vision, you're going to be killed. We have got to get rid of the bed.'

'What am I supposed to sleep on, for fuck's sake?'

'You can have the mattress,' said Ronnie, 'But we have to take away the bed.' I'd just about had enough of this voodoo stuff. I slung the mattress on the floor and the voodoo man hauled the bedstead outside. I later found out he'd given it to his best mate, the cheeky bastard!

I turned to Ronnie, 'We need to have a serious talk, me and you alone.'

We went to Radjin's office, I spread out my map of Surinam and looked Ronnie in the eye. 'I've been here a week and a half and what have we done? We've given the enemy a bloody nose at Blackwater and captured a couple of spies, but what's your overall plan? Where are we going with this war?'

'It's sort of hit and miss Karel,' Ronnie admitted, somewhat sheepishly, 'we don't have the weapons.'

'Of course you don't have enough weapons, but there's plenty in Surinam for the taking. We can ambush the army and take their weapons off them, but we must prepare the ambushes properly.'

'But we've got no explosives,' said Ronnie.

'Can you buy gunpowder in large quantities, say fifty kilos?' I asked him.

'It would take a while, but no problem,' said Ronnie, 'But what are we going to use as detonators?'

As we sat there, I took a six-volt battery from Radjin's flashlight and made a detonator from brown parcel tape, filament wire from an old phone and some gunpowder. I placed it all in an ashtray, touched the wires to the battery and... bang!

Ronnie jumped up. This was incredible stuff to him. 'Show me again,' he stammered. I quickly knocked up another one, but this time I put in a bit more powder for greater effect. Off it went again. Ronnie was made up. He had a go at making one, while I explained, 'The army are not going to know it was a home-made mine under the road. They're going to think we've got our hands on supply of landmines.'

Outside the office, Keith and I manufactured a few bottle bombs and exploded them using trip lines and trigger switches made from clothes pegs. The Jungle Commandos had seen nothing like it. You'd think we'd shown them the atomic bomb.

I turned to Ronnie. 'The army have about three thousand men, we can call on two hundred who will have a go, at most. It's no good shooting at an armoured car with FAL or a shotgun. We'll ignore the army and concentrate on bringing down the economy. We'll blow up pylons, bridges and roads.'

This group was seriously lacking many things, especially money. We needed to get our hands on something of great value to help fund us. Unbeknown to me, Ronnie had already robbed a bank truck full of worthless Surinamese money. We threw many ideas about but the problem was that most things of great value in this country were privately owned. Then someone mentioned that Bouterse owned most of the shares in the country's national airline, Surinam Airways. It was a tricky one this because we weren't a terrorist organisation. Let's look at the reality. Surinam Airways owned three 22-seat Twin Otter passenger planes and one DC 8. At that time a Twin Otter was worth around two million US dollars.If we stole one we'd be stealing a plane from a bunch of gangsters. What about the passengers? We needed some ground rules.

Number one – we do not take passengers. We do not point weapons at them or even threaten them. Ronbo thinks otherwise. He wants to bring the passengers briefly to Stoelman's Island for the Press to see them and then release them to the safe custody of the French. He believed it would bring massive publicity for the cause. We argued about it for too long and in the end, just to shut him up, I agreed. We needed to start making a plan. Ronbo reckoned he had a buyer lined up and we also had the radio frequencies Surinam Airways operated on. Lets' suck it and see.

Ronnie was delighted. 'Nice idea Karel, very nice idea. I'll take you back to Stoelman's Island.' By now, he'd noticed Keith was pissed. 'You leave Keith here,' he added. 'You and John come with me.' Keith was happy as a pig in shit. He had bottles of rum stashed all over the house and plenty of fags.

Back at Stoelman's we said hello to Belgian doctors Alain and Bayer. They'd heard about the business at

Blackwater. 'It was on the Dutch news,' said Alain, 'You killed thirty men there.'

Bloody hell. Thirty Echo Commandos dead. Bouterse had tried to keep our activities at Blackwater a secret but staff from the Dutch Embassy in Paramaribo had been outside the military mortuary when thirty bodies were brought out of a fleet of ambulances. A crowd of families had gathered outside to identify the bodies. We knew that during the ambush at Blackwater Keith had got the tank commander, so John and I must have got the rest in the truck. Thirty in total. Not a bad score. As John and I sat discussing the best way to steal a Twin Otter, a half-caste wearing shorts, a blue tracksuit top and a camouflage bush hat wandered over and introduced himself as Henk. It turned out Henk had been the chief of Bouterse's Echo Commando. It was his men we'd killed at Blackwater. Henck had been stationed at Awira Camp on the Marowijne River, which had come under fire from the Jungle Commando. Henck and four of his men were in a high-speed glass fibre boat on the river when the attack happened. Ronnie's boys riddled the boat with bullets, killing the other commandos. The vessel was like a sieve. Henk had no idea how he survived. He arranged a meal for us, potatoes, bread, tea and two cans of fruit for desert. We couldn't believe it. Bayer and Alain joined us on the guest house veranda, drinking beer by candlelight. It was like being on holiday.

Later, Orlando the captured pilot joined us. We grilled him about Surinam Air's internal Twin Otter flights. Orlando had wanted nothing to do with it, but we persuaded him to talk. It emerged that the best place to steal the plane would be at Possu Goomu, forty-five minutes in the Cessna from Stoelman's Island. I asked Henk if he would come with us to act as interpreter. 'Okay,' he agreed, 'if it's just you and John I'll go. I don't want to go with any of these Jungle Commandos.'

We took off in the Cessna – me, Henk, John and little guy called Max. He would not be taking part in the hijack. His job was to make sure Orlando went directly back to Stoelman's with the Cessna and not fly back home to daddy. Fifteen minutes into the flight, Orlando was listening in to the radio. The bloody Twin Otter was early. We'd never get there in time; we had to abort. We turned round and landed again at Stoelman's Island. However, we'd only been monitoring air traffic radio for a short while when we discovered the Twin Otter was flying from Possu Goomu back to the capital Paramaribo, then flying on to Raleigh Falls, a beauty spot in a nature reserve on the Coppename River, to pick up tourists. We had to move now, otherwise we might not get another chance for a week.

Henk knew Raleigh Falls quite well. He drew us a plan of the airstrip, the airport terminal and a couple of other buildings. There was also a policeman's house there and a track leading down a steep embankment to a small holiday village. We made our plans in half an hour flat. The Cessna would leave us there and fly off. The Twin Otter crew would become suspicious if it was parked on the strip. If we fucked up, it would take us a month to walk back. There'd be no cock-ups. First we had to capture the airport building and monitor the radio. We learned from the radio the plane would be arriving with a small group of tourists and twenty would be going back to the capital. In his great wisdom, Ronnie decided he wanted the tourists brought back to Stoelman's Island for a huge publicity coup. There was no way I was bringing civilians back, but I didn't tell him that.

I had to be able to move quickly from the plane when we landed, so I took only the FAL, four spare mags in pouches on my pistol belt, a bottle of water, map and fags. I told Henk we were changing the plan slightly. We would keep the Cessna on the ground for a while while we monitored radio traffic. Only when we were sure the plane was on its way to Raleigh Falls would we let the Cessna go. I wasn't walking through the jungle for a month with just two packets of fags and a bottle of water. No thank you.

Before we left I explained to Ronnie that because we had spies in the camp, Bouterse may already have known about our plan. To avoid the Twin Otter landing with a load of Bouterse's crack Echo Commandos on board, we arranged a landing procedure so the men on the ground could be sure it was us in the stolen plane. I told Ronnie, 'We'll have no radio contact with the ground, so we'll approach from the west with the landing lights on. As we get closer in, we'll flash the lights. Do not remove the oil barrels from the runway. We'll do one fly past very low, flashing the lights so you'll know everything's okay. When we come back round and approach for the second time you can clear the barrels and we'll land.'

Orlando gunned the Cessna's engine. Beside him sat Max, with Henk directly behind the pilot's seat. John sat on the other side of him, safely out of the way and I would sit next to Henk in the open doorway. As Ronnie stood in the wash from the propeller shaking my hand, a big crowd of locals gathered. They didn't know what was going on – they always came to look at the plane when it was started up. A few of the Jungle Commandos who did know all about it stood standing giving me the clenched 'Black Power' salute. As I climbed aboard I told Ronnie, 'This should shake them up in Holland a bit and bring some more publicity to your cause. Who knows, it may even raise a few shillings.'

Orlando was waiting for my signal. I got my FAL ready and did a last check – yes, everything was there. Thumbs up to Orlando. Let's go. I was feeling pretty tense as the Cessna climbed high over the forest cover and turned west. First things first, lean forward, light a fag up, ease the tension bit. Everybody's looking pretty serious and slightly paler than their normal shade. It was time to show them a few big false grins to buck them up. 'We're going to do this boys, don't worry about it.'

An hour passed before Orlando announced, 'Ten minutes to go.' The tension rose; big false smiles again. I strained to get a good look out of the open door as we lost height for our approach from the east. We would make one pass over the trees parallel to the runway. Down we went, skimming the treetops. The runway was clear, I could see a couple of people moseying around at the airport building; they hadn't even looked at us. Orlando looked around at me. I had to shout through the wind rush in the open door: 'Right, do it. Go round, turn left, come back on your track the opposite way, and straight down onto the grass. No fucking about.'

Henk looked at me, wide eyed. I wouldn't say Max was petrified, but he was more alarmed than anybody else. Orlando looked pale. We came around, and there it was right in front of us: the runway. This was it, shit or bust; got my rifle ready. Bang, down we came on the grass, then it was seat belts off. We were still going like the clappers, but we couldn't jump out yet, we were still going much too fast. As we slowed down, you could feel the heat. We were belting along on the grass, shaking and rattling. John was trying to push me through the door and he was shouting, 'Get out now, now!'

'You fucking lunatic, John, take it easy, I'll tell you when,' I shouted back.

If I'd jumped out then when John had said, the tail section of the aircraft would have cut me in half. That would have been a good hijack job, me lying there in two bits on the runway! The buildings were closing in on us. 'Out, do it do it, out!' We ran towards the embankment, up the embankment. John raced off to my right at high speed; the Cessna continued but it was out of my mind now. All I had to do now was get to the door of that airport building. At the top of the embankment, standing outside the airport door, was a little old white lady in a hat and floral dress, carrying a handbag. She looked at me as though I was something that had just landed from outer space. I ran towards her, too quick for her to get out of the way, and flung open the door with a bang. Out of the corner of my eye, I caught a fleeting glimpse of a man darting off to my right along the corridor and screamed, 'Don't move! Everybody stay perfectly still or I will fire. You lot quick! Down in the corner!'

I did a quick squint around at the corridor to see the man disappearing towards a back door. I shouted out, 'HALT!' and he came to a dead stop, hands in the air.' 'Come to me,' I yelled out, 'get down here quick, fast.' He ran down the alley towards me and I pushed him on the pile of airfield staff cowering in the corner. Henk had his pistol. 'Watch them,' I told him, 'I'll be back in a second.'

I shot down the corridor and out of the back door to find John standing there pointing his weapon at two more who had their hands in the air. I screamed at them, 'You two come here quick, down the corridor back into the radio room with the other lot.' It had only taken a matter of seconds and now we were in total control of the airport. There was a knock at a side door. It was the little old lady in the floral dress. 'Excuse me,' she said, ' but are you making a film?'

'Absolutely correct, madam,' I replied, 'I'm very sorry but can you just wait outside one moment, I'll be with you and explain everything.'

There were windows all around for viewing the runway, so I had a good view of all that was going on. I told John to hide in the bushes out back and watch everything. I asked Henk to tell the airport crew to stand up. They were petrified. I spoke to them. 'Do you speak English?'

'Yes, yes,' they mumbled.

'You must understand, we are here to take the Twin Otter when it arrives. The only way we're going to leave here is on the Twin Otter or in a body bag so do exactly as you're told. Any messing around and I swear by God I'll kill you.' Just bluffing, of course. 'If you do what I tell you, you will have not the slightest problem in the world. You've got nothing to fear, but please cooperate with us and everything will be fine.'

I made them sit down on a bench, while Henk spoke to the radio operator in Taki Taki. Henk then picked up the microphone and started talking, again in Taki Taki, to the Twin Otter. Their ETA was three o'clock. We were well in time; there was an hour and a half to wait.

I went outside to see the little old lady and explain to her what was happening. She was with her husband, who was dozing on a bench under a tree. It turns out that he had a heart problem and was in Raleigh Falls for some tranquillity. However, when he found out what we were up to, he wasn't very tranquil; he mouthed off quite a bit at me in Dutch. He was not a well man himself, and well entitled to be pissed off. I apologised and told him, 'This is the way life is at the moment. There's no harm done, just inconvenience.'

The Cessna was still parked up with the engine running, so I gave Orlando and Max the all-clear to take off. Among the airport staff was a tour guide who'd been mouthing off – until I shut him up with a threat to take him on a tour with the Jungle Commandos. He told me more tourists were still in the holiday village at the foot of a waterfall below the airfield. I told John to check it out and keep an eye open for the local policeman. A few minutes later, John swaggered back up the track; he was doing some serious swaggering now, a big smile on his face.

'Did you see the tourists, John?'

'Yeah, they're all down there having a drink in the restaurant. I stuck my head around the corner, they all saw me and I said hello and came back up here.'

'Fuck's sake, John. Wait here I'll go down.'

I raced along the track to find an open-air restaurant surrounded by huts. The restaurant, a long hut with open sides, was full of white people with their brightly coloured luggage lying around. I held my rifle down by my side to avoid sparking alarm. When I said 'Hello', they all looked up. I raised my left hand, flat palm gesture, 'Cool, cool, don't worry, does anybody speak English, please?'

Most of them did, so I carried on. 'You've heard about the war in Surinam, yes? Well it's here now. Please do not panic, just bear with me and I'll explain everything. I'm one of the Jungle Commandos working for Ronnie Brunswijk, whom you've all heard about, I'm sure. I am going to hijack the Twin Otter plane that you're waiting for.'

As soon as I said the word hijack, there were gasps all round. I continued, 'Have a drink, relax, there'll be no violence. Now ladies and gentlemen, please pick up your baggage and drinks make your way up the track back to the airport building.'

The black holiday camp staff stood at the back, their eyes like saucers. I told them, 'What I require from you, please, is a case of soft drinks and a case of beer – cold beer. I will pay you. Would you please take them up to the airport building?'

Note the many 'pleases' and 'thank yous' with which I peppered my speech. These people were in fear; I wanted it to be polite. In the airport building, I told the tourists to help themselves to the drinks I'd bought. John was in his element. There were about five young women among the tourists and there was John in his Foreign Legion beret, flashing his badge at them and wearing an inane grin. In fact, John seemed to be getting worse and worse. Not to worry, things were going well. I told him to cool it with all the posing for the girls and we steeped outside into the raging heat – it was easily 100 degrees – to plan for the plane's arrival away from the tourists. There was a real possibility that our plan had been rumbled and there would be a couple of government agents on board, armed with Berretta Model 12 sub-machine guns. The Twin Otter would land on the strip, taxi towards the terminal, go past it, turn around again on the strip and then taxi to a stop outside the airport building to let the passengers off. John would be hidden on the far side of the runway, not directly opposite but further down, so the tourists would not be in his line of fire. At this stage I wasn't actually in charge of John. We were supposed to be partners but I told him, 'Drink your Coke, get away from the girls and go to your position. Stay cool and start acting a bit serious, because I don't fancy a month tabbing it back through the jungle to Stoelman's Island eating trees and bugs.' In fact, if John fucked this up I'd be eating him on the way back. I looked up in the afternoon sky and noticed the two big halogen landing lights of an aircraft. Fucking hell!

'John, quick, into position.'

By the time John had put down his Coke bottle, the aircraft was touching the grass. It was the Twin Otter, painted in Surinam Airways' orange-and-yellow livery. John darted across the strip into the bushes. Henk took up his position as a civilian airport worker, standing to the right of the waiting passengers. 'Everybody please stand up now,' I told the tourists, 'don't be afraid. There'll be no shooting.' They weren't happy. From the radio room doorway, I watched the Twin Otter land. It taxied past the airport building, turned around, and taxied back down. The twin turbo prop engines shut down. Everything went quiet. The passengers were still moaning. I pleaded with them again: 'Please be calm. There will be no shooting.' Cool as a cucumber, Henk casually walked down the embankment towards the aircraft. The pilot was taking off his headset. The pilot's door opened. A boy and a girl stepped out of the passenger door. The girl carried a tomato crate of coffee and sandwiches. The two pilots climbed out, stood on the grass and watched the rest of the passengers get off. Finally, they were all off. Henk checked the passenger cabin then gave the all-clear signal. He shouted to the pilots to distract them. I pushed a tourist to one side and rushed forward. I was down the embankment in a couple of seconds. The two pilots hadn't seen me. They both turned around, a look of horror on their faces as they saw me standing there.

'Both of you, on the ground, now!' I barked.

I grabbed the one with the most stripes on his epaulettes. 'Do everything I tell you to do. If not, this man here,' I said, pointing to the co-pilot, 'I will kill him.' The co-pilot looked at me from the right. I still remember his face – he was as white as a sheet.

'Okay, stand up,' I ordered them. 'We are going to take your Twin Otter and you two are coming with us. You will fly us to our destination. Don't ask me any questions, just do exactly what you're told and everything will be fine.'

Now I'd got the message through, I stepped back out of their faces and said, 'I'm English by the way, my name's Karl, how do you do?' Let's keep it a bit civilised....

The captain quickly regained his composure, 'Before we go could I please have a drink?' he asked. His mouth had gone dry with fear. Henck gave them a Coke each, while John came darting across the runway. We had locked the airfield crew in a room, so I unlocked the door and let them out. Then I nipped into the radio room, dismantled the microphones on the radio set and threw them onto the roof. The tourists were beginning to realise that the possibility of any shooting had passed. There was a big sigh of relief. We were in a hurry to leave, but I had to make one last apology, 'Ladies and gentlemen, I'm sorry for spoiling your holiday, I didn't like doing it....' Blah, blah.

A middle-aged woman, who seemed to have become the party's spokeswoman, piped up. 'That's okay. You promised you wouldn't hurt us and you didn't. In fact, you're very nice! Can we take some photographs for our holiday albums?' So, bizarre though it may seem now, John and I had our photographs taken. Henk declined the offer.

CHAPTER 6

'OK Mr. Pilot, start the engines up.' I had the Browning pointed at him, 'But before you do, my friend, do not blow them.'

I'd been warned the pilot might try and flood the Twin Otter's engines with fuel so that the turbo props would burst into flames when the ignition was pressed. I looked out of the window for the last time; all the passengers stood outside the terminal building, still looking gobsmacked. The twin engines roared into life. After a couple of minutes' warm-up, we were ready. We charged down the runway; the earth dropped away beneath us. Thank God for that, there was no question now of being caught or compromised. 'OK Mr. Pilot, climb to two thousand feet, then turn to one one seven degrees.'

I took away his headset, I didn't want him talking on the radio to anyone. I put on the co-pilot's headset, flicked the switch and announced over the PA system, 'Good afternoon ladies and gentlemen this is your new co-pilot speaking. Due to a misunderstanding back at Raleigh Falls, there will be no refreshments served on this flight. Also due to a misunderstanding, we are not flying to Paramaribo. We are, in fact, flying somewhere else

entirely. Enjoy your flight with Surinam Airways and I
hope you will fly with us again.' I went into the passenger
cabin. John gave me the thumbs up and a big grin. Henk
looked relieved; the co-pilot, who was sat staring at John's
FAL, didn't look so happy about things, but such is life.

We'd been flying for fifteen minutes. The captain, still
looking pale and nervous, was touching switches and
knobs trying to take his mind off the situation. I put my
feet up on the rudder pedals, and told him, 'Now Mr.
Pilot, release the control.'

'What are you doing?'

'Release the controls and shut your mouth. I'll tell you
what to do.' He released the controls. I banked the plane
to the left and the right and settled back on course again.
I turned to the pilot. 'Did you see what I did just then? I'm
capable of keeping this plane under control, so any
messing about from you, you're a dead man and I will fly
back myself.' There was no question of me being able to
land the plane, of course – I'd have killed the lot of us. But
I thought it best not to mention that at the time.

'No problem, no funny business,' he promised. I put the
Browning back in its holster. A few minutes later, he spoke
again. 'Please, can I just ask you something? When we
arrive at the place we're going to go to, what is going to
happen to us?

'They'll torture you for a couple of days and beat you up
badly, but they won't kill you.' The already-ashen pilot
went white as a sheet.

'Take it easy, I'm only joking,' I reassured him. 'When we arrive I'll buy you a drink.'

We passed my first visual reference – the southern end of a huge expanse of water, known as Brokopondo Lake. Then, as we crossed the 2,400-foot high Lely Mountains, I told the pilot to drop down towards Stoelman's Island. Our final destination was now in sight.

'I want you to do a low pass – and I mean a low pass,' I emphasised. 'I don't want you to carry on like you're still working for Surinam Airways. I want you to flash along that runway at fifty feet.'

I reached for the switches above my head. Click, click, click, I flashed the landing lights. All the barrels were still on the runway and there wasn't a soul in sight. The place was deserted.

Back out now beyond the strip, we turned hard left, then banked out over the river, and circled back around again. On the ground, the boys appeared from nowhere, moving barrels. By the time we lined up to come into our landing the runway was clear, but everyone had disappeared.

Once down on the grass, we taxied to the top of the runway and turned around. As the pilot switched off the engines, I looked out of the windows. The place was deserted. Ordering the pilot to stay still, I swung open my door, ducked under the aircraft, and opened the passenger door. Henck and the co-pilot climbed out. Just as I motioned up to the pilot to get out too, dozens of heads appeared up out of a drainage ditch at the side of the runway.

Armed to the teeth, and with some of them sporting feathers that stuck out of their hair at crazy angles, the JCs looked like a bunch of lunatics. The pilot and the co-pilot went into shock at the sight. Ronnie, his eyes on stalks, forced his way through the boys. He looked at the aircraft; he looked at me. He didn't know what to say, so I took the situation in hand quickly before he made a pillock of himself.

I went straight to him, 'Ronnie come here, come here.' He shook my hand. 'Karel, this is brilliant. Oh man, excellent job! Where's the tourisits?'

I exclaimed to him, 'I don't do tourists, Ronnie.'

'Okay, Karel, okay.'

'Ronnie listen,' I told him, 'stop, before you get too excited. This is the captain. His name's John, he's a very, very nice guy. He has co-operated in every way. This other man here, his name is Juno. He's also been spot on.' I didn't want any antagonism towards the pilots, who were shaking in their shoes, as a large crowd milled around them. We led them to the guesthouse, where they were given drinks to try and calm their nerves.

'I know it's a difficult situation, but try to relax,' I explained to them. 'You'll be released in a couple of days. We're only after the aircraft.' Even so, John was still extremely nervous; he was just not a happy man. He looked like he was going to burst into tears any moment. Then I had an idea. I went to look for the doctors, Alain and Bayer. Eventually, I found them among the crowd still mobbing the Twin Otter. 'Can you do me a favour, please?' I asked them, with as much politeness as I could muster. 'We've just hijacked this thing. The pilots are in the guesthouse and the captain looks upset. Perhaps you can give him a tranquilliser? You're a doctor, maybe talking to you will make him feel a bit more comfortable. Please come down.'

After about an hour talking to Alain and Bayer, the captain produced a set of car keys. 'I have a big, big problem,' he explained, 'my car is parked at Zandarjit airport but my wife is at home and she needs the car. We live outside Paramaribo in a small village but my wife needs the car to go into town to take my little daughter to school. She needs the car to go to work. In fact, she's lost without the car.'

Bloody hell, I thought, he's just been hijacked and all he's worried about is fucking car keys. We sent the keys on to his home so his wife could use the car. All right it took a few days, but sometimes you've just got to do these things....

A large number of new recruits had found their way to Ronnie's hideout at Stoelman's Island. Now we had men, I sat down in the guesthouse with a map of Surinam and worked out a plan to bring the country to its knees. We'd start by crippling roads and power lines, shut down the airport, followed by the ferries into and out of the country. Finally, we'd hit Bouterse's main exports, forcing him to the negotiating table. If he didn't talk, Surinam's economy would be wrecked.

Ronnie also had a plan... to build an assault course to train the recruits. We were in the back of beyond, where it was extremely difficult to find an elastic band, let alone materials to build a full-blown assault course. So they ended up with two pieces of rope between two trees, a step ladder and several oil barrels to jump across. It was unbelievable. The boys ran around all day shouting 'pay! pay!' which means 'bang! bang!' Ronnie was in his element, roaring around the assault course with the boys following. In fact, Ronnie shouted 'pay! pay!' louder than anybody else. It was side-splitting fun. Keith decided to have a go at the assault course. We watched him climb up the ladder into the tree and inch his way precariously across the ropes. Wobbling like crazy, his feet rocked wildly from left to right as he hung onto the top rope for grim death. He slowly made it across. Very comic at the time, but on the whole I was now becoming more and more concerned about Keith.

By the way, Keith hadn't wasted his time while we were away hijacking the plane. He'd spent hours with a cheeky eighteen-year-old kid called Anton who, for some reason, had found favour with Henk. Keith had been teaching Anton to speak English. When we all sat down, Keith called Anton over, and told him, 'Come and talk in English for Karl.'

So Anton came over stood by the table and with great pride slapped himself on the chest and said, 'I am a dickhead.' Apparently, Keith had told him that a dickhead was a type of super commando. Sadly, later on Anton was killed in French Guiana. He'd been arrested but had escaped from the police and ran away still wearing handcuffs. He sprinted about fifty yards up the road. A black French

Guianan out hunting was walking towards him. The two policemen who'd arrested Anton shouted out, 'Hey, stop that guy!' And the man walking down the road pulled out a pump-action shotgun and blasted Anton in the back.

One night, the two doctors invited us and the two pilots for a drink. Keith was invited too, but I didn't tell him. We were all sat on the veranda at the doctors' house exchanging pleasantries when Keith rolled up. He'd been on the rum. 'Where the fuck have you lot been?' he enquired, 'Give us one of them fucking bottles of beer!'

Within half an hour he was up on the table singing, 'Get 'em down you Zulu Warriors'. Off with his T-shirt, down came his shorts. He was standing on the table stark naked with his jungle boots on, his FAL hanging around his neck, and his voodoo bands on his arm. Bayer the Belgian doctor was flabbergasted when Keith asked her for a newspaper. Why would anyone want to read the paper while dancing naked on a tabletop? She came back with a couple of pages from an old newspaper, which Keith screwed up into a stick shape. He shoved it between the cheeks of his arse, clenched his buttocks tight and set fire to the paper. The trick is to dance and jiggle your arse to put the flames out before they burn your backside; all the while you have to keep singing. Good old British Army fun. Henk and the two pilots almost fell over backwards with laughter, tears streaming down their faces. Bayer ran back inside the house, came out carrying a camera and proceeded to take loads of pictures of Keith, the savage Englishman. It was a great little party but all too soon we ran out of drink. With no electric lights, there was nothing to do at night so everyone went to bed. Not Keith, though. He disappeared off to see his mates in the voodoo gang – they'd always got rum. Next morning, he was in his room, still half-pissed, laughing and joking about how he'd walked barefoot on broken glass.

Keith was now becoming a bit of a problem. Let me explain. Keith's a very nice guy – funny and loyal too – but for me, his big downfall has always been the booze: he likes a lot of it. He was at the voodoo every night and during the day he was starting to argue with me about my plan to cripple the country. It was too over the top for him. I couldn't make him see that unless we brought the country to its knees we would get no political or financial support from anybody. We would only ever be regarded as a bunch of amateurs.

Keith didn't want to know, he just wanted to stay on a holiday on Stoelman's Island. I thought to myself, 'Keith, I've got to send you home before we really fall out.' As it turned out, a solution to the problem presented itself very quickly. A boat arrived from Langatabbetje with a message from Major Getback, in the civilised world. Unfortunately, it seemed that he'd somehow misinterpreted the code I'd told him to use, and consequently the message was gibberish: 'Keith's wife's had three kids'! We were none the wiser about our finances. We could be killed any day and we still didn't know if we'd been paid. So I went for a stroll with Keith well out of earshot of everyone else.

'Listen Keith,' I told him 'you're going to have to do me a big favour. I'm busy here, can you go into St Laurent and call the U.K. to find out if there's some money in the bank? I can't send John, he's too daft. Can you do it?' Keith readily agreed; he loved the idea of being our secret agent. 'Before you go off, Keith, get your passport and take your civvie clothes with you, your bergen, everything you've got, just in case. You never know what can happen.'

Bye, bye, Keith. Now I could get on with the real job in hand – taking the war to the enemy. And, of course, Keith took the next flight to Paris and joined the Major back in Manchester.

Surinam's version of the M1 is the N1, a main road that runs from the border with French Guiana to Paramaribo. The N1 starts in Albina, opposite St Laurent and runs for fifty miles to the capital. To have any chance of bringing the country to its knees, we were going to have to close that road. We had no explosives, but I was going to make bombs from fire extinguishers. Load the fire extinguishers up with gunpowder, screw the caps back on and link them to an improvised detonator made from paper, wire filament and gunpowder. The detonator is triggered by a command line via a switch made from a clothes peg. I ordered more gunpowder from Ronnie and went round Stoelman's Island collecting all the fire extinguishers I could find. Most of them had been hadn't been touched for years and were covered in cobwebs. They were old and they were really heavy – ideal for shrapnel. I took one down to the river bank to empty out the powder inside it. As I unscrewed the top, a light breeze wafted the powder flame retardant out of the extinguisher and away. Next thing I knew, there was shouting from up in the guest house. It was Henk, looking like a snowman! Sorry, but Merry Christmas anyway.

We used the Twin Otter to move our newly trained men up towards the front line. Ronnie's commandos scrambled aboard the hijacked plane in cobbled-together uniforms; some had bits of rope instead of webbing, other carried fire extinguishers. They probably thought they were going to fight fires. The Twin Otter had just half an hour's fuel left, so we flew downriver to Langatabbetje, fifteen minutes away. When we landed, Radjin, the commandant, lined the boys up smartly and marched them down to the schoolhouse, where they slung up their hammocks. Then they went to the cookhouse for a plate of rice.

As we stood in the queue, an awful, gagging stench filled the air. Round the back of the cookhouse there was a voodoo shrine and on a little post sticking into the ground was a badly decomposed human head wearing a tin helmet. It stank and was swarming with flies. I lost my rag, ran over, kicked the head off the post to get rid of the flies and picked it up by the chinstrap. This was somebody's son, someone's husband. I shouldn't even have kicked it. He had to be buried. I took the severed head to Radjin. 'What the fuck's this?' I demanded.

'Oh, I can't stop those guys. They do the voodoo all the time.'

'This is for you, Radjin,' I replied giving him the head, 'Don't throw it in the river, bury it somewhere and mark the spot.'

I went back and ripped up the voodoo shrine, which caused some shouting and consternation, but I told the JCs to fuck off, in no uncertain terms. Then I went and had a word with Ronnie about it.

'If your guys want to use the bodies of soldiers they kill,' I said, 'leave them on the side of the road with a note by them warning any troops coming this way, this is what you get. Use psychological warfare, not splitting the chest open, pulling their hearts out and chopping their heads off.' Ronnie had a talk with Thoma, the mad axeman who'd been carving the bodies up. Apparently Thoma was going a bit loopy. You'd never have guessed....

Still, there were soon other things to think about. 'Karel, Karel,' a JC told me, excitedly, 'somebody's come to see you. A white man.'

Who could that be? I climbed the house stairs to be met by a man in a French gendarme's uniform. A strange black guy was with him, along with Radjin and John Richards. 'Karel this man is from the French police he wants to talk with you,' explained Radjin.

Now, the policeman's translator spoke French and Taki Taki, but not English. So the French guy talked to his translator, who talked to Radjin, who then talked to me. If I wanted to ask the French guy a question, I put it to Radjin, who put it through his translator, who put it back to him. Follow that? The conversation went on like that for an hour, with the French cop asking us why we were there, and who was paying us.

Then he asked, 'Have you ever been to St Laurent?'

'Yes we passed through there to come in.'

'Have you been back?'

'No, no, I haven't been back.'

He was quite a friendly guy, but he may have been sent to find out what had happened to Koyku. We were very evasive and gave him duff names. Eventually he left with his translator in a rubber dinghy with an outboard engine.

The village of Moengotapoe lies up a dirt track just off the main N1, ten miles outside Albina. A bullet-riddled cinema, built by Ronnie Brunswijk's family, squats in the middle of town. Moengotapoe was to be our base on the main road. We had to be there before first light. We were already late and thirty miles of pot-holed dirt track lay ahead of us. We said goodbye to Henk and the pilots. To make up lost time, Ronnie hammered the Daihatsu pick-up, headlights full on to avoid the biggest craters. I was just thinking we'd be lucky to get there in one piece when the front of the pick-up truck collapsed with a loud bang. I'm not a mechanic, but it seemed the front axle had snapped. Talk about improvisation, I'll give Ronnie and his men their due, they cut a branch off a tree, got some bits of rope out of the back of the truck and put a splint on it. We were off again, but this time more cautiously. As we clocked up the kilometres, the vehicle began to sag by the minute until it was scraping on the road. Our only hope was to abandon the wrecked car in the bush and hijack the first vehicle that came along.

We'd only been there a couple of minutes when the boys flagged down a pick-up truck with a metal canopy in the back. We piled it up with fire extinguishers and climbed aboard. It was tension time again; the lump in my throat felt as big as a house brick. At any moment we could have run into a passing patrol. We pulled off the side of the road onto the tarmac highway, my rifle pointing out of the cab.

Hero Ronnie followed 500 yards behind us in a little blue Mazda and we raced on down towards Moengotapoe. It was a very tense time. The jungle thinned out with houses on either side. A right-hand turn up a side street took us into Moengotapoe. Only a small clutch of people going to work saw us drive through the back of the village then jump out into the bushes, down a steep jungle track to a clearing by a creek. A couple of our boys were already there, sent on ahead in civvies.

'This,' announced Ronnie, 'is our new home sweet home.' He was convinced it was safe. Well, maybe, but I wasn't going to take his word for it. We were only 200 yards from the main road and banditos could come walking up on us any moment. I spent the next few hours leaving early warning devices and booby traps around the camp.

As dusk fell, John and I went with Ronnie and six of his best-dressed commandos – the ones with reasonable uniforms, proper webbing and decent weapons. We made our way through the back alleys of Moengotapoe to a house on the main road. Ronnie put the JCs on 'wachtee', keeping guard, while we went inside. There were twenty people in the living room, sitting on chairs, boxes, anywhere they could park their backsides, watching *Rambo* on video in honour of Ronbo. Christ, this was surreal but

Ronbo loved it. We shook hands with the big chief, a pleasant, educated guy who asked if we were hungry. Hungry? We'd been permanently hungry since arriving in Surinam. He returned a few minutes later with a cup of tea and a fried egg sandwich on fresh bread. It was unbelievable. 'Would you like another cup of tea?' Ronbo, all is forgiven; for tea and a fried egg sandwich I'll sit here and watch *Rambo* till the cows come home. Everyone in the room started gesturing at the screen when Rambo came on with his M60 machine gun and sweatband. I must agree, it did look a bit like Ronnie – they were both twats.

As the final credits rolled, I told Ronnie it was imperative that we went outside and found our bearings. I made a map on little pieces of paper as we tippy-toed around in the warm tropical evening, checking out escape routes. My face was smeared in cammo cream, and I was wearing Portuguese camouflage kit, bush hat, webbing and carrying my weapon. I was ready for anything. The only thing missing was a sweatband!

Suddenly a pair of headlights appeared out of the gloom. It could have been a Cascavel. When I'm in such a situation, I'm continuously planning escape routes; if I sit in a house or stand by a tree, I know where to go if the shit hits the fan. It's second nature. To the left of the main road as you face towards Albina is a swamp. I made my way there quickly, followed by John and Ronnie. We ducked down behind the cover of trees. Cascavels are fitted with a searchlight. Now Mr. Gorgeous – John – hated wearing cammo cream, making him a liability to be around in situations like this. So I hissed in his lughole, 'John, get away from me. Don't fucking come crouching next to me all the time with your big white face. I've warned you time and time again, I'm sick of it.'

I put my hand in a big clump of swamp mud and said, 'John, close your eyes, close your mouth.' Slap! I daubed him with stinking mud – at least you couldn't see him now. The Cascavel turned out to be a big dump truck and John was now stood there covered in shit.

As well as planning ambushes, I also ran a campaign to get the message to Bouterse that the Jungle Commandos were active and about to strike at the government. I was over the top on that and took a big chance, but thankfully it paid off.

Luxury air-conditioned coaches raced along the N1 day and night, carrying tourists and businessmen between Cayenne and Paramaribo. They crossed the river by ferry between St Laurent and Albina. On a recce along the road, I found the perfect spot to stop these coaches. Near the town of Moengo, halfway between Albina and Paramaribo, the road climbed a hill and through a gorge that sliced through a hill. My plan was to stop a few of these coaches, but I'd be the perfect Englishman – all I needed was a bowler hat and brolly.

The crack of a rifle shot echoed through the gorge. One shot. That was the signal for a vehicle approaching. I scrambled down onto the road. I was nervous – this was a bus travelling from Paramaribo, maybe carrying soldiers back to the garrison at Albina. Watch out, Karl, watch out. I could lose my life in a second even stopping a civilian bus. A smart-looking coach came over the rise. I stood out in the middle of the road, my FN rifle in my right hand with the butt on my hip, so I could snatch it up quickly and grab it with my left hand, which was now raised up in flat-palmed gesture. Stop.

Here came the bus, over the hill; the driver slowed down and I waved again. I pointed my rifle because he wasn't slowing down quickly enough.

He got the message then, slowed down and pulled over to the side of the road, twenty yards in front of me. He couldn't believe his eyes. I jogged towards him; the door opened with a whoosh of compressed air. I climbed inside. A quick glance told me it was full of civilians and children of all colours. The driver shook with fear as I asked if there were any soldiers on board.

'I don't know, boss, I don't think so.'

'Easy, easy, no problem,' I said, loudly enough for some of the passengers to hear.

I looked round. Mums and dads were holding their children to them to protect them from the savage who'd just climbed on the bus. I had to act quickly. I didn't want them to be unnecessarily afraid, so I gave them all a big smile and shouted, 'Hello, excuse me does anybody speak English please?' They weren't too keen on shouting out, but I could hear a few mumble, 'Yes, I speak English.' 'Please don't be afraid,' I continued, 'I'm a Jungle Commando working for Ronnie Brunswijk. I want to know now if there are any soldiers on board. There's no problem for the soldiers, I want them to come off the bus now.'

Any soldiers coming off that bus were going to get fucked – I don't mean killed, just captured. Nobody owned up to being a soldier, so I made my way down the bus, very, very slowly, looking from side to side at the passengers. It was bloody awkward because I couldn't move my FAL around in the narrow aisle on the bus. I hadn't thought of this. So I walked backwards along the bus, checking over my shoulder, and when I got back down by the driver I slung the FN over my shoulder and pulled the Browning out of its holster. The pistol was already cocked, but with the safety on. I went back down the bus again, checking for anybody who looked like a soldier – someone the right age, with a short haircut. I was convinced a pair of them were Surinam soldiers but they showed me French passports. Some passengers offered me money and cigarettes. One lady offered four oranges. I took the fruit and a bar of chocolate from somebody else. I took no money, not one cent. I didn't want people saying afterwards that I'd robbed them, but the oranges were luxury. 'Merci, madame.'

I needed the army to think we were here in force, so I told the wary passengers, 'There are many, many Jungle Commandos in the area and very shortly we will be closing the road. It's entirely up to yourselves if you wish to return to Paramaribo or to continue your journey through to Albina and onto French Guiana. But once you go through, that is it, there's no coming back.'

I was banking on the ferry operators at Albina deciding that if the road to Paramaribo was closed they'd stop the ferries. The French would question their nationals from the buses in some detail to find out what the hell was going on. I was hoping the French passengers would say they were held up by a very nice English gentleman. I genuinely didn't want to frighten people. I had no gripe with them; my problem was with the army of Surinam, not with French or Surinamese civilians. In the end, I stopped about four or five coaches and minibuses, just to make sure the authorities knew we were there.

This was it, time to make the big move I'd been planning. An orange glow from the street lights of Albina filled the horizon as we roused stunned workers from their beds at a logging camp near Moengotapoe. Half-awake, the frightened lumberjacks stared dazedly into the barrels of the shotguns pointing at their beds.

'All of you out of bed, please. Don't fuck about, do exactly what I tell you.' I wanted these men to drive the huge logging machines we needed to lift dozens of tree trunks to form a barricade on the main road.

'On your machines. I want two men per machine. Have you got diesel?' Luckily, the machinery had been filled up the night before. With a unit scouting ahead of us, we set off down the road towards Albina in a convoy of pick-up trucks followed by a large Fiat machine with a big grab to lift logs and a John Deere digger fitted with a spike for smashing concrete.

After a recce along the whole length of the road , I'd chosen to close two bridges twenty-five kilometres apart, one near Albina, the other up near Moeng. At the Albina bridge there was a wonderful pile of trees lying to one side of the road, destined for a sawmill. Well, they wouldn't be going to the lumber mill just yet, because I was going to put them across the road in front of the bridge. The grab on the large Fiat picked up the huge trunks as though they were matchwood and began constructing a barricade. The giant machine trundled backwards and forwards, stacking the logs up across the road. Meanwhile, the long steel finger on the John Deere digger pierced a gaping hole in the tarmac across the road. Then the driver changed the steel spear for a bucket and shovelled earth out of the hole. While this was happening, a small party of JCs worked feverishly, filling rice sacks that would be used for tamping these fire extinguisher mines into position.

The extinguisher bombs were not powerful enough to blow the bridge and I couldn't camouflage them under the tarmac road, so I decided to make them directional, to detonate at Bouterse's troops when they stopped at the roadblock.

I took a fire extinguisher bomb, plus battery pack, command line and a switch made from a clothes peg, and picked a spot beside the road. I laid the mine on the ground in front of two rice sacks filled with earth. I put a sack on each side, and then a sack on the top of the mine, before shovelling sand from the side of the road all over it, forming a hillock about three feet high. I scurried around with a flashlight, pulling plants out by the roots, taking them over to what looked now like a heap of sand and placing each plant in it so it seemed like they were growing there naturally. The sweat just pissed out of me.

I walked back up the road a few metres to check them from different angles – a plant here, maybe one there to make it look natural. I put three mines at that position then went back down to the bridge, where I attached more mines to the side by the handrails and camouflaged them. I also booby-trapped the logs. If the army did manage get over the hole in the road and across the log roadblock without being blown up, I could detonate the bombs on the bridge.

We worked until three o'clock in the morning, constantly worrying that the army in Albina would hear the noise of our engines. Would the spies among us have told them? I had an OP down the road to give us an early warning. We weren't in danger of our lives, the army weren't just going to spring out of nowhere and kill us. But we were in danger of the extreme embarrassment of being chased away. Thirty men manned the roadblock, while I ran out command lines and covered them in sand. I picked precise firing angles, so when the army came and fired, the men would be in cover and quite safe. With all that exertion we were really tired and physically worn out. It had been a long, hot, dodgy night. As the new day dawned, Ronnie became concerned the army might make a show. If Bouterse had any decent commandos they'd have been all over us by now. Ronnie took a group of boys to the Albina roadblock, leaving John and I to watch the other end near Moengo with a young interpreter, whom we christened Michael Jackson because he was a dead ringer for Wacko Jacko. He carried a Winchester 30:30 lever-action rifle, a modern version of the gun John Wayne always carried in westerns.

God was on our side again – beside the road was a deserted concrete building, a shop, in fact. It was lovely cover for us. I worked out a safe escape route into the bush, but I wasn't going to run without pulling the command line. As the first rays of daylight broke, you could hear a vehicle. 'John,' I hissed, 'watch the command line.' It was a pick-up truck. It slowed down and pulled up right beside me, I jumped out, rifle to my shoulder, and pointed it at the driver.

There were three men in the cab and back of the pick-up was full of people. There were a couple of women and one of them, a girl of about fifteen, started screaming her head off when she saw the rifle.

As I put my hand up to calm them down, I thought to myself, 'This is no good Karl you've frightened the life out of everybody.' One of the women in the back put her hands over her ears and ducked her head down as if she was about to be shot. I was going to have think up a better system. This was frightening the life out of people for no reason whatsoever.

'Right, matey, listen... whoa! whoa!' I called out, as the driver started to reverse up the road. I shouted out, 'Stop!' He slammed on the brakes. 'You fucking dickhead, I told you to stop and when I say stop I mean stop.' This was nerves; the set-up wasn't right. Mind you, you can't do a lot with just me, John and Michael Jackson.

'We're from the Jungle Commandos,' I began. 'I'm not going to hurt anybody. You cannot travel on this road. Go back, you go home, that's the end of it.'

'What are we going to do?' asked the driver.

'None of my fucking business what you're going to do, just go back to Moengo. Look on the other side of the road,' I bluffed. 'It's full of Jungle Commandos. If you'd driven this truck away from me, they'd have shot you to fucking bits and all the people in the back. Now turn around and go back. Tell anyone else going this way, forget it.'

He turned around and drove off. I moved about forty metres further back up the road. Three more vehicles came along without incident. At the Albina end of the roadblock, a crazy doctor in a little red car started to protest when Ronnie stopped him going through. He turned the car round, drove 500 metres down the road, turned round and roared back at fifty miles an hour... and straight into the hole! Only the boot of his car stuck out above the ground. Amazingly, the doctor wasn't killed. He'd shot forward, smashed his face on the dashboard and was in a terrible state. Ronnie's boys jumped in the hole and manhandled the wrecked car back up onto the road. They dragged him out, and Ronnie beat out of him what little sense he still had. He was last seen staggering towards Albina – probably looking for a doctor....

CHAPTER

The walkie-talkie hanging in the basher down by the creek below Moengotapoe crackled into life, 'They're coming! The army's coming.'

Here we go, this is what we've been waiting for. The warning was from the boys up on the Albina side of the roadblock. John, me and about ten others climbed into the back of a couple of pick-up trucks with no doors and roared flat-out towards our killing zones. Feeling very apprehensive, we leaned out of the doors, rifles pointed down the road, straining to see as far ahead as we possibly could. We dumped the vehicles up a track off the road, about one hundred yards from the roadblock, and jogged towards the trees piled across the road. We were in the open and could be shot. Boom! boom! Shots, a long way off. It was the army all right. Just like at Blackwater. They were warning us, trying to scare us away. Cheeky bastards, they weren't going to intimidate us. Time to get going.

It was the middle of the afternoon, so it was hot again. We ran on the right-hand side of the road; the left-hand side was fairly open, but dense jungle came up to the road on the right – vital cover if we needed it. A couple of the boys stood up waving; you could see the relief on their faces. John and I both had eighty rounds; we were the most heavily armed of the whole lot of them.

The noise of engines and the crack of fifty-calibre rounds grew louder as the army advanced on the other side of the hill. Seconds later, all the boys were in cover as heavy fifty-cal fire from an armoured car raked trees at the side of the road. Branches crashed down around us. The biggest danger at that moment was a branch landing on your head. But many of the young boys who'd come up to fill out the numbers had never experienced anything like this. Some of them were ashen faced. I give them the clenched fist, a sign that said, 'Be strong'. Bang! Bang! Bang! Round after round hit the ground, showering dirt everywhere. By now, the boys were beginning to panic. 'Keep your fucking heads,' I shouted. 'Down, everybody!'

Boom! The Cascavel had started. We were still getting bang, bang, bang from the MAGs (machine guns) and loads of shit from the fifty-calibre still spraying each side of the road. We were still not in any danger, but how do you tell that to a bunch of untrained men? They were flapping. I ordered the group of twenty recruits close by me to 'Fucking stay there!' Then, I scrabbled out of my position and made my way along the line, ordering the JCs to remain calm.

The Cascavel now turned its attention to our position, firing fragmentation shells into the tree above us. With an ear-splitting bang, leaves and branches came down around us. The smell of the cordite lingered long after each round went off. Bang! bang! bang! you could see the panic in some of these poor boys. The Cascavel fired one round then moved fifty yards and let fly with another round. It was pretty grim for a few minutes. They turned their attention to the roadblock, blasting the pile of trees in front of the bridge with 90mm. We waited to see if anyone would get out of the armoured vehicles to take a closer look. Instead, they pulled out, reversing back up the road. I was shaking like a leaf. While I was growling at everybody to try and keep them in position, I hadn't realised I was trembling. I turned my back so the boys couldn't see my hands shake as I lit a cigarette. I took a couple of drags before turning round, a broad grin on my face, and giving them the thumbs-up sign. 'Well done, boys – see, it's easy, isn't it?' The army had not driven into the trap.

JCs crawled out from the bushes and trees where they'd been hiding. Some of them had been shot. We had one dead, the side of his head smashed in, which caused consternation with some of the new boys, who had pale, unhappy faces. I got the dead and wounded on the road back to camp, then started slapping the most shocked ones on the back – 'Well done, good lad, you'll be an excellent commando.' I went round using a bit of psychology on them. What would happen if the army returned in half an hour? Maybe they'd just run out of ammunition, because so many thousands of rounds had gone off. I handed out fags to calm the boys down and told them, 'If another attack comes, don't worry, more men are coming up to relieve you.'

There was no such relief force, of course. I sent a recce party down towards Albina to give us early warning of the army's return. Then, I hung around waiting for it to get dark. The chances of the army coming after us at night were very remote. I went round talking to the boys. 'What's Bouterse going to do to us? Next time he'll come even closer, right into the trap.'

I kicked ideas around in my mind. What were they shooting at? Were they trying to dislodge the mines? Did they know from the spies that the trap was there? We just had to stand firm and not lose our nerve. Stay low and keep out of the way of the bullets.

By nightfall, Ronnie had sent up food and marijuana for the boys, who were soon on cloud nine, swapping war stories. I returned to the camp by the creek at Moengotapoe to check on the wounded. I had the only medical kit and I was down to four band aids, a couple of aspirins and fly spray. Ronnie was in one of the bashers. He'd got one poor boy doing press-ups to check if he had any broken bones. Blood was squirting out of ferocious wound on his back. The boy was in shock. I got him into a hammock, where he lay face down, his arms and legs dangling over the side. He moaned weakly, 'Karel I think I die.'

'You ain't gonna die,' I told him, 'certainly not today, nor tomorrow, because I need you back up on the front.' That caused a few grins.

He'd been struck just below the base of his neck. The bullet made a rivulet under the flesh on the left hand side of his back. As it came out near the kidneys, the bullet had ripped a large piece of flesh, which flapped around. The wound was covered in flies – but mind you, don't forget, I'd still got my fly spray! I needed to straighten out this piece of meat. As he lay face down on his hammock, I squashed the wound with the flat of my hand. The boy moaned in pain. It started to bleed heavily. I took out a relatively clean towel from my bergen – it was probably the cleanest thing there – and padded the wound. He was weeping with agony. I cracked a few jokes to try and ease his discomfort, but he desperately needed to get to Langatabbetje and then down to the hospital at Stoelman's Island. Eventually, the bleeding stopped and we were able to send him on a convoy of trucks to Langatabbetje.

Later, I sat down with Ronnie and warned him not to be too jubilant. 'We've got to get a little more serious,' I told him, 'the next attack that comes may be two or three times as strong as the first one.'

'What are we going to do, Karel?' he asked.

'You remember that night when we crossed the river at Carolina? The army were totally paranoid. They've only got to hear a dog bark and they'll expend thousands of rounds of ammunition. Let's make them think they're being attacked. I want ten pairs of men with shotguns, I want them to go to the outskirts of Albina and start shooting towards the town. Let's keep that going day and night; we won't let them sleep.'

I paired off some the men, gave them loads of shotgun cartridges, plenty of fags and food and explained my plan using a map drawn in the sand. 'Don't put yourselves in any danger,' I told them. 'If you see soldiers run back, don't try and defend. When you shoot, move away from that position in case there's any accurate retaliatory fire. Keep moving about, enjoy yourselves.'

Things were looking good so far. We'd repelled an attack – well, we'd sat there while the attack went on and never budged. The army hadn't come back and I could hear the boys in the distance – bang, bang, bang, from their shotguns followed by machine-gun fire back from the Albina garrison. Yep, I felt wonderful.

I sat with Ronnie beside a crackling fire next to the creek and discussed my next idea. Some of the boys had hunting rifles, which had been badly mistreated. One had a beautiful Remington 7mm Magnum with telescopic sights. You were supposed to be able to see for miles through it, but you'd be lucky to see three yards with this one because there was about half a pint of water splashing around inside the 'scope.

'Can you buy some new high-powered hunting rifles and telescopic sights?' I asked Ronnie.

I explained how I planned to pick the best shots and put a team of snipers all around Albina, twenty-four hours a day, taking pot shots at anything that moved to keep the pressure off the roadblock.

Ronnie suddenly livened up. And if he liked that idea, he was going to love the next one. A company called SurAlco, a Surinamese subsidiary of the giant United States aluminium conglomerate Alcoa, ran one of the world's biggest bauxite mines at the nearby town of Moengo. Bauxite is the main raw material used in the manufacture of aluminium. To get the brown bauxite out of the ground, SurAlco used tons of explosives. My plan was to get my hands on those explosives. SurAlco had always been part of the master plan that I'd devised back at the schoolhouse in Langatabbetje.

Desi Bouterse decided in his great wisdom that at night SurAlco workers must lock away their explosives in the army camp at Moengo. Trucks carrying the explosives were supposed to have a military police escort. But we learned that on one particular day there'd be no escort. The two men in the three-ton, open-back truck had been told to drive like fury on the short journey between the barracks and the mine. Unfortunately for them, some of our boys, dressed in civvies, flagged them down with a ruse that they'd broken down. Our vehicle was stopped across the road on a right-hand bend. The driver and the guy riding shotgun in the explosives truck had no choice but to stop. The driver slammed the truck into reverse – only to find we'd closed the trap. The guard, who carried a Beretta sub-machine gun, went as white as a sheet, panicked and ran off down the road. I shouted for him to stop. He kept on running. The driver jumped out, pissed himself, threw his weapon down and burst into tears. He was convinced he'd be shot. The boys quickly dragged him off the road and took him prisoner. Back at camp we inspected the load. It was beyond my wildest dreams. I'd expected a few hundred kilos of explosives, but the truck was piled high with boxes of Dupont plastic explosive and dynamite. Two thousand kilos in all, plus box upon box of detonators, safety detonators and safety fuse. I couldn't believe it.

'What do you think, Karel?' asked Ronnie.

'I think, Ronnie, we've won the war!' I exclaimed. To us it was like pinching the atom bomb. Now we really were going to shut this place down. I was going to start getting nasty, do some real damage. From now on, no bridge or power line in Surinam would be safe.

The relief was immense. I was so pleased I must have walked round the truck nearly 400 times looking at it all and pulling boxes off. Many of the boxes were filled with pink-and-black Dupont det cord. We stashed the explosives in two caches in the jungle in case we were compromised. Afterwards, I showed Ronnie what det cord could do. I wrapped some around a tree trunk and blew the tree in half. Needless to say, Ronnie loved it.

My confidence was contagious and spread like wildfire among the boys. Over the next couple of days, I replaced gunpowder in the fire extinguisher mines with proper explosive as well as training the boys in how to light fuses.

Bush negroes have no sense of time or distance. If you ask, 'How far is it to that town?' you'll get a reply like, 'It's a long way.'

'But how many kilometres?'

'Plenty.'

I taped sticks of dynamite into packs of five and cut seven-second safety fuses. I'd put a piece of fuse into a safety detonator, crimp it with my teeth and push it into the middle stick of dynamite, then ignite it with a sparkler. You could light it with a match, but that would take half an hour, so it was best to light it with a sparkler. Every pack of dynamite had a sparkler taped to the side of it. The boys loved it. They were like a bunch of kids as the dynamite exploded. In one of the demonstrations, I detonated an old truck and the whole cab blew off, spiralling forty feet into the air. The boys danced around in circles when the cab hit the road with an almighty crash. I taught them that you could put the shits up the army with five sticks of dynamite. I also gave them a serious warning.

'We are not the IRA, there will be no acts of terrorism,' I insisted, 'There will be no throwing dynamite into people's houses. This is for the army only.'

I'd asked John Richards to help me put together packs of dynamite to hand to the boys, but he'd replied, 'No mate, fuck that, I don't know fuck all about explosives.' And with those words, he went back to his pit.

Next time the army showed up, I was really going to fuck them. There was a culvert under the road near the Albina roadblock. When the army passed over it, I'd detonate explosive packed in the culvert under the road, leaving a hole so big that they wouldn't be able to reverse their vehicles. All they'd be able to do was sit there and shoot until they ran out of ammunition. Then we'll be on them like a pack of hyenas, with petrol bombs and shotguns.

I calculated that two boxes of dynamite inside the culvert would do the trick. I would run two lengths of det cord out of the pipe into the safety of the jungle, where we couldn't be seen for love nor money. Six bush negroes watched the road while I examined the culvert. It was the pipe from hell. The whole of the floor inside the four-foot high tube was covered in stagnant sludge. It stank to high heaven because the culvert was also home to several thousand bats, hanging upside down and shitting everywhere.

I unloaded the explosives from our truck along with a pile of rice sacks. That's when John announced, 'I told you before, Karl, I know fuck all about explosives and I don't want to go in the fucking pipe.'

'I thought you were a Legionnaire, John,' I replied, testily. I put him in charge of filling the rice sacks with sand to block up both ends of the culvert. This was it, shit or bust. I passed my FN to one of the JCs and told him to keep his eyes peeled.

Crouched at the entrance to the pipe, I was already ankle-deep in shit and thinking of horrible snakes that could be lurking in the slime to feast off the bats. Browning out, I fired a shot down the pipe. Bang! A huge cloud of bats shot out of the pipe, did a quick circle and flew straight back in again. Bastards. Right, bats, you've asked for it now.

I fired three more shots. Out they went again, and straight back in. OK, nose to the grindstone, Karl. I lifted the first box of dynamite. It must have weighed about sixty pounds. My job was made even harder by the fact that the water was eight inches deep. You couldn't see into it because of the shit, so I placed my feet out on each side of the circular pipe to keep them out of the slime. It was hot in there, and the smell was ferocious. Holding the box of the dynamite and walking on the side of the pipe really killed my feet. I tell you what killed me even more, though: I was covered in panicking bats. They were all over me, in my hair; on my shirt. John Richards was looking down the pipe at me, shouting, 'Fucking hell, Karl, get out of there.'

Get out? How could I get out? The dynamite wasn't going to lay itself. I made my way forward. It was slow going. I was doing six-inch steps until I got to what I presumed was the middle of the pipe. I prised open the lid with a Yankie pilot's knife. All the while, I was flicking bats off me. They were on my arms, bashing into my face. Get the box open, peel back the lid, push it down, that's open. Right, next box. I worked my way back through the pipe. By now, I was covered in shit. I'd frightened the bats and they were shitting themselves, all over me. I gave John a hard stare. He stood there with his Foreign Legion beret and a stupid smirk on his face. I'll deal with you later, I vowed. The next box was positioned this side of the halfway line.

Detonators were in my pockets, all prepared. Get to the first box, stick of dynamite, ease the det in nice and steady. I picked up a handful of dynamite sticks placed them in the centre of the box. That was my booster to get it going. I went to the next box and did the same again. They both had individual det cords. If one failed to go off, the other box would detonate it. I reeled out pink-and-black det cord as I inched my way towards the end of the pipe, which came out in a swamp. I had to feed the cord through the swamp and up into the firing position in the jungle. I stepped out of the pipe and ended up chest-deep in stinking water. I kept tripping over broken, rotted trees lying in the water. Halfway through the swamp, I spotted a big snake in the water, slowly moving past.

'Oh my God, I've just seen a fucking big snake. Stand by there on the bank with a shotgun. When I tell you, fire. Don't shoot me.'

My nerves were going a bit now. I knew the snake wasn't going to attack and I was really pissed off at myself for panicking. I had to reel the det cord out and put loose branches over it to sink it. Eventually, with drenching wet boots and uniform, I climbed out and supervised bagging off both ends of the pipe.

I went off into the jungle to find a firing position. I picked what I thought was an excellent place, somewhere from which you could see the road clearly, but not be seen by anyone on it. I attached a twenty-second safety fuse to the det cord. The JCs liked long safety fuses, but I didn't. I wanted the explosives to go off as soon as army vehicles had driven past. With the whole jungle to disappear into, Ronnie's men were not going to be caught. I wrapped the det cord around a tree and tied a knot so it couldn't be dislodged. The safety fuses hung down. I stuffed half a dozen sparklers, for lighting the fuses, into the bark of a tree. Then, I pulled out two cheap plastic cigarette lighters, which I taped to the sparklers. I told the four commandos who'd be manning the post, 'If any one of you pinches the lighters, I'll shoot you myself. Those lighters are for fuses only. When the next people take over, you tell them the same thing, do not fuck off with the lighters.' I also told them to build a little basher because this position would now be manned twenty-four hours a day.

I went down to the roadblock to let everyone know about the explosives under the culvert. I was soaking wet, with bat shit in my hair, down my shirt, and in my eyes and ears. I smelled vile but I felt chuffed.

Now it was time to have a word with John Richards. I asked him to come with me to the pick-up. I didn't say a word until we reached the truck, then suddenly I turned on him. 'I thought we were in this together. I've been very patient, I've listened to your rootin', tootin' stories of the Foreign Legion. How come when you were in the Foreign Legion you were so tasty and yet when you're here with me you're so fucking useless? In the Foreign Legion you saw no action whatsoever, in fact you didn't even leave Corsica. Now you've seen a bit of action, why don't you pull your finger out? You don't want to get your beret wet, you don't want to get your feet wet, you don't like wearing cammo cream because it makes your face dirty. John, I'm really fucking sick of you now. Listen to me, matey, if this goes on much longer, me and you are going to part company. I know which way you're going to go and I know which way I'm going, believe me.'

He tried to remonstrate with me, 'I told you about the explosives....'

I hit back, 'Don't come out with your feeble excuses, this is a serious situation we're in. Look John, I know it's difficult, stick with me, just give me a helping hand, that's all I require. Do you seriously want me to bin you? I can pick up a black oppo who can stay by me twenty-four hours a day if I need to. But I feel safe with you around, John, watching my back – or, at least, I used to.'

We drove back to Moengotapoe, John sulking like a schoolboy. He got out of the pick-up truck and walked straight away from me. No apologies, no 'I'll try to do better' or any of that. Still moping, he went back to his pit.

I spent the next couple of days going up and down to the roadblock like a blue-arsed fly, hoping the army would turn up. Of course, they didn't. Every now and again, a Defender plane came over to have a look. With the equivalent of the M1 shut, you can imagine all the jumping up and down that was going on in Paramaribo.

It was becoming obvious that the boys I'd sent down to Albina to fire shotguns in the air were having an effect. Every night you could hear loads of shooting. The army were so paranoid, they sent out their Dutch-built S-class boats out onto the river to defend Albina. These huge patrol boats were fitted with big searchlights, 40mm Bofors guns, fifty-calibres and MAGs. They would pull away from the jetty at high speed, turn both Bofors guns onto a given position and let rip. And they did – I could hear it through the night. Things were falling into place; very satisfying.

One thing that wasn't satisfying was our food. Living off nothing but boiled rice and a corn-like substance called Kwak, I rapidly lost weight. You take kwak with a mug of river water and it swells up in your stomach and eases the hunger pains for a short while. Mentally I was as sharp as a Stanley knife but unfortunately, physically, I was getting weaker and weaker. The JCs were dug in around the roadblock and were much more confident. I was desperate for food and sleep. I also needed to find out if Keith had sent news about our money. Ronbo was going back to Langatabbetje, so John and I went with him. To put spies off the scent, we told the boys we were going down to a jungle camp ten miles away at Patamaka. As we were driving back to Langatabbetje, Ronnie revealed he'd had a highly unofficial approach from the French military intelligence service offering help to the Jungle Commandos. A French Colonel flew to Apatou by Puma helicopter to meet Ronnie, who had known about the meet for two days but decided to do nothing – at the time the meeting was due to take place, Ronnie had still been with us on the front line. When Ronnie finally turned up there, the Colonel had gone. For his efforts, the Colonel was demoted and sent to the sweltering hell-hole outpost of Chad on the fringes of the Sahara desert.

I wrote out a list of food I wanted brought back from St. Laurent. There was a knock at the door, and into the schoolhouse at Langatabbetje walked a white guy, covered in cameras. He was French but spoke very good English, with a very faint American accent. His name was Patrick Chauvel, we didn't know him from Adam but it turned out that he was a famous combat photographer. The son of a French war hero, Patrick was one of the last men out of the French Embassy in Phnom Penh when the Cambodian capital fell to the Khmer Rouge. Patrick is top-of-the-range, brave, switched-on, humorous and likeable; we were in real company. We chatted, drank coffee and swapped jokes, before he announced that he was here with two doctors from the French AMI medical organisation. They had brought huge aluminium trunks full of medical equipment. Doctors Michel Bonnot and Didier Pouly were great guys who planned to set up a field surgery on the front line. Having them there would certainly boost the boys' morale. Perhaps unsurprisingly, as I was explaining the grim realities of life at the front to them, John Richards whipped his top off and posed for us in his Foreign Legion beret, flashing his tattoos. The man was seriously getting on my tits.

Keen to get back to the pressing matters in hand, I turned to Patrick. 'We're really short of food at the front,' I told him.

'Don't worry boys, I've got food supplies to last us for about six years,' he said, opening his bag to reveal four tins of pâté, two bottles of brown sauce, some other bits and pieces, a couple of jars of coffee and tea bags.

'You'll do. You can come to the front line with me any time.'

Michel Bonnot brought out a bottle of Scotch and we sat there with a tape recorder playing music; in fact, the four of us had quite a little party in the doctors' house. It did me the world of good. I would have gone back to the front line with a heavy heart knowing I had to face starvation and worry, but taking these guys along it was going to be party time. I couldn't wait to get back. Unlike most journalists I'd met, Patrick didn't jump up straight away and start taking photographs. At first he played it a bit cool. Then, when we'd got the measure of each other, he got into top gear, the flash on the camera was going off every thirty seconds. He's a funny man with a very dry wit. It helps to have good company like that in a life-or-death situation, no question.

There had been no messages from Keith Kenton, but we did get more men and a load of new pump-action shotguns. It was time to go back and have a look at the culvert pipe and my little pet bats. After a long drive from Langatabbetje, we set up home in a hut in Moengotapoe village, because it was closer to the Albina roadblock than the camp down by the creek. The hut John and I shared with Patrick, Michel and Didier had one double bed, a wardrobe and a vile smell. Michel tracked the source of the stench to a wardrobe. When he moved it, he discovered a dead, maggot-ridden rat. He put on surgical rubber gloves, held his nose with one hand and picked the rat up with the other. Walking like a pantomime dame he carried it away. This guy had a sense of humour.

While I'd been away, more Jungle Commandos had arrived at Moengotapoe. One of them was a voodoo man called Baku Gadu, a name that apparently meant 'behind God'. He wore a 'Davy Crockett' hat made out of green palm leaves and, to be honest, he was a complete nuisance. He'd take the boys off on suicide missions, totally against my orders, and I had to get Ronnie to bring him back in line.

The doctors set up their equipment in a wooden hut and within hours people started turning up from miles away. Pregnant women, old folk needing treatment and even a man who'd been bitten by an alligator. When he arrived, his body covered in teeth marks, I couldn't help bursting out laughing. A couple of days later we were really grateful for those doctors.

Gunfire erupted in Albina. Two of our boys took cover in an abandoned house as the army shot at them from a Dutch-built DAF YP armoured car. One Jungle Commando was killed outright by a burst of fire from a MAG. The other took a bullet in his temple, which exited through his mouth. He must have tried to scream and the bullet must have ripped out the top of his mouth. His teeth hung down with the gum. He'd also been hit in the elbow, which came up like a football. He crawled out, leaving his mate dead in the porch. Somehow he came across Baku Gadu, who'd promoted himself from voodoo chief to ambulance driver and carted the injured boy in a wheelbarrow. It was nearly dark when Baku wheeled his casualty into the field hospital. By rights the boy should have been dead. How he had survived a bullet through the temple, I'll never know. He was in shock, though, and didn't know what day it was. There was no electricity, so Michel and Didier operated by the light from the headlights of a truck that shone through the doorway.

It was a grim business; the makeshift hospital was like a butcher's shop. Sweat poured off the two men as they set about their task; watching them, though, it was obvious they knew exactly what they were doing. I stood in awe, only becoming involved once, when they asked me to pour cleansing fluid onto a piece of toilet roll, which Didier pulled in and out of the gaping hole in the boy's head to clean out the wound. By now, the large dose of morphine they'd administered was taking effect. Michel Bonnot wanted to put the kid in traction, but first he needed to insert a pin through the smashed elbow joint. The pin had a thread but Michel had nothing in his kit to screw the pin in with.

'Do you have a hammer? he asked. I didn't carry one around with me. 'Lend me your pistol.' I told him to get lost, but I did remember seeing a tool box in a disused shop nearby, so I sent John to look for it. He soon returned with a hammer and Michel smashed the pin through the elbow; the wounded man couldn't feel a thing. I lit a cigarette and put it in the injured JC's mouth. He couldn't raise his arms, so I held the fag to his mouth and he inhaled the smoke. I tell you now… there was smoke coming out of the hole in his temple. Next morning, the wounded man was sitting by a camp fire with his arm in a metal frame, a bolt sticking through his arm and a gaping hole in his head. Subdued but alive, he was having a cup of coffee. I told you these guys were tough little bastards.

There was no doubt we were hurting Bouterse. A recce in Albina told us the townsfolk were getting short of food. We'd stopped all the country's exports by land that went through French Guiana. But we still had to keep the pressure on the army. We couldn't just sit up on the road like a bunch of numb nuts. We had Albina shut down tight, so my next target was the town of Moengo, which lay halfway between Albina and Paramaribo. Moengo was split in half by the Cottica River, which was spanned by an old concrete bridge that had seen better days. When the structure became dangerous, the government had simply slung a metal Bailey bridge on top of the concrete span. My next plan was to blow it up and cut off Moengo. To drop the concrete bridge would have taken a huge amount of dynamite and a large number of men to carry all that explosive. Instead, I was going to damage the Bailey bridge beyond repair. I'd only need eight kilos of plastic explosive to do the job.

It was three o'clock in the morning as we tabbed along SurAlco's private railway line towards the heart of Moengo. Suddenly, I froze. Just 400 yards away stood a man. Had he seen us? Eighty per cent convinced that he hadn't caught a glimpse of us, we dropped down an embankment. We were deep behind enemy lines and the last thing we wanted to do was kill a civilian. If he came too close we would be left with no alternative but to shoot him. Slowly, he walked towards us. I slipped the safety off my Browning. A hundred yards more.... I raised the pistol and took aim. Just then, he turned sharp left and wandered off into the town. We sat there for ten more minutes. If that guy was onto us, the baddies would arrive pretty quick. No one came. Paranoia must have overtaken us; it was about time we concentrated on the job in hand.

We were now within 200 yards of the bridge and very close to the army camp. I ordered two JCs to go down to the bridge and take a look. It was like watching the Keystone Cops. They disappeared just twenty yards into the darkness and then reappeared – 'Everything's cool.'

'Cool? It's not fucking cool. You arseholes you haven't even been to look.'

Ordering everyone to stay put, I crept to within ten yards of the bridge. I got my thoughts together as I watched. If we blew up the bridge, we couldn't come back along this road. Our only escape would be down the river in a boat. I sent the two cowards down to some nearby houses where I could see a load of canoes. We watched them steal the best one, paddle it fifty yards across the river and hide under an overhanging tree. The rest of us tip-toed across the steel floor of the bridge like bloody ballerinas, carrying explosives and a roll of det cord. I warned Patrick not to let off his flash while I put the charges in place, but as I was concentrating on them, bugger me if a flash didn't go off. I nearly died of fright. It was Patrick snatching pictures with his camera. I didn't have time to argue. I quickly placed four kilos of explosive under one of the main girders. On the SurAlco truck we'd found what looked like pink hosepipe in three-inch lengths. It was, in fact, rubber impregnated with explosive, impregnated with explosive small boosters in fact. You run det/cord through the hole in them. I ran four boosters to four charges, I then said to John 'Foot on this' (det/cord) then ran down to the other main girder, sliding the remaining four boosters along the cord and repeated the same. All nicely tucked in, made a knot to lock it in place and ran to the other end of the bridge as I ran I pulled out the safety fuse and taped it to the det/cord. Sparkler out – whoosh, let's go! It was all done in under a minute.

The bridge would blow in thirty seconds. We were down the embankment when the metal structure exploded. A flash of flame, an almighty bang, the Bailey bridge shook and shards of metal flew in all directions. Job done.

CHAPTER 8

An armoured car opened up just as our canoe rounded a bend. Bullets from the fifty-calibre whizzed harmlessly way over our heads. The two guys in the canoe more than made up for their cock-up on the bridge recce by paddling like fury. Bouterse's men could shoot shit out of the river bank for as long as they wanted. We were gone, round a bend in the river and safely out of harm's way for now.

We turned off the main river into a creek filled with crocodiles. You could just make out their eyes. I'd never seen so many crocs in my life. In Surinam they call these crocs caymans. We drifted along the creek that ran down to the SurAlco bauxite mine. Careful now, the army might just be sitting waiting for us. I certainly didn't fancy having to jump out and end up in the water with a load of teeth marks on my arse.

Safely inside SurAlco's territory, we abandoned the canoe and tabbed to the spot where the Jungle Commando commandant in charge of the Moengo end of the roadblock had arranged to pick us up. This fifty-franc commandant was a real Jack the Lad; I called them that because they bought red berets for fifty francs and strutted around like they were God's Gift. The bastard didn't turn up. I'm ashamed to say we snatched a local man from a house at gunpoint and sent him down to the Moengo roadblock on his motorbike in fear of his life. I threatened to shoot his family if he didn't go. We never even saw his family and didn't even know whether he had any relatives in the house, but it was a good guess. When we finally got down there, I screamed at the commandant, 'Where were you, you fucking bastard?'

It wasn't just that they'd failed to send a vehicle to pick us up. They were also supposed to be back up if we were pursued by the army. We could have been shot to pieces while they were all lying in their hammocks, stoned out their brains on marijuana. Eventually we returned to Moengotapoe, where I woke Ronnie to tell him the job was done.

'Yes Karel, I heard the explosion. I hear it, very good.'

Every time the boys went to Albina they had to cross a track where a bridge had been burnt out. Without fail, a YP armoured car would turn up and spray the area with a hundred rounds of fifty-cal before reversing back down the track, surrounded by high elephant grass. It happened so often I was sure that whenever our boys did some shooting in Albina, the officers in the military police barracks ordered their men to take a drive down to this particular burnt-out bridge and let rip. I had a little surprise lined up for these guys, though. I buried a fire extinguisher bomb in the sandy track – next time the armoured car stopped there, the crew would be killed.

I took a dependable guy called Blakka, Radjin, a couple of gofers to carry the mine and three boys from the camp who would detonate it. They had to know the firing position and where the det cord and battery were. Working under cover of darkness, and not knowing if the army were laying in wait, was a hairy business. There was no mistaking the spot where the YP stopped. A maze of tyre marks and fifty-calibre shells, scattered where the gun had thrown them out, gave away exactly where the armoured car stopped. I studied the spot hard because I had to leave it looking exactly as I'd found it, scooping sand out with my hands. I put the bomb together in stages. I didn't want the entire kit with me in case the army turned up and whole lot went up.

I buried the extinguisher and bit by bit assembled the trap. Check it. Looks good. Bury the det cord, sweep over it. Run the det cord back into the grass. OK, now the firing position. I'd spotted a couple of trees over to our left. The chances of the armoured car getting in a good shot at those trees were remote. We wouldn't have to spend twenty-four hours a day here. All we had to do was fire off a few shots and the armoured car would come roaring down the track as usual and be blown up. After this explosion, the army would move their armoured cars around with caution.

That was the plan, anyway. To this day, I don't know what happened. The armoured car appeared up the track

Top left: Making 1 kilo plastic explosive charges at Moengotapoe.

Top right: John Richards looking youthful in his Foreign Legion REP badge.

Bottom: Ronnie Brunswijk handing out packs of dynamite to the boys.
I'm keeping my eyes on the road.

Top: Me and 'Michael Jackson'.

Middle: Me, Radjin and John Richards looking at a sand map of the front line.

Right: At Om Leo's camp on the Marowigne river near Appatou.

Top: Ronnie admiring his prize, the hijacked Surinam Airways Twin Otter.

Middle: Me and John at the doctor's house at Langatabbitje.

Left: George Baker at the JC camp in Langatabbetje.

Top: Me with a Cetma 5.56mm assault rifle.

Middle: In the Café Amsterdam in St. Laurent after crossing the river from Surinam.

Right: Ronnie Brunswijk at the wheel with John in the back on the way to the Albina roadblock on the N1.

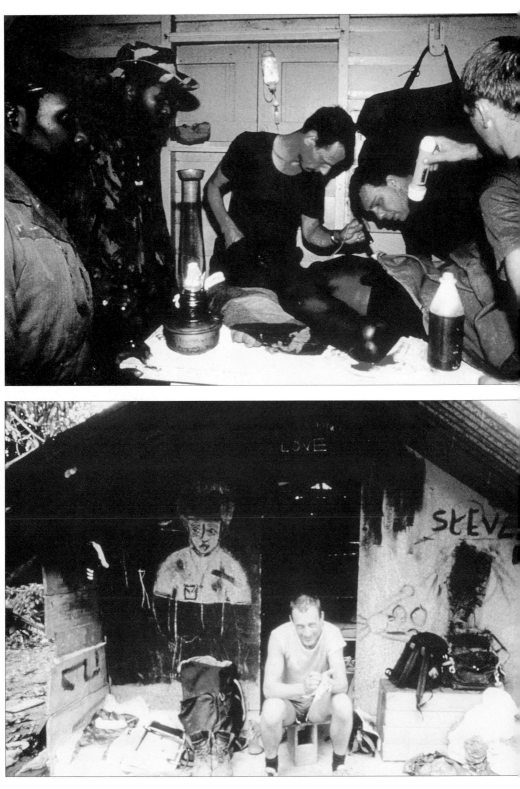

Top: Wounded JC being treated by doctor Michel Bonnot.

Bottom: Our beautiful house in Moengotapoe!

Top: Dropping the bridge at Moengo roadblock.

Bottom: Bouterses's army are just beyond the bend in the road.

Top: John with his cowboy hat in front of Papillon's jail in St. Laurent.

Middle: Me and two Jungle Commandos at Albina roadblock, carrying a fire extinguisher mine and a battery pack.

Left: Me, Ronnie, George Baker and Psycho on our second trip back to Surinam. On the far right is Paco's bodyguard, now deceased.

Top: In a refugee village in French Guiana. To George Baker's left are the two head men who were murdered.

Bottom: Om Leo and one of the murdered head men inside the Café Amsterdam and the excellent Blakka, smiling in the background.

during the firing… and it wasn't blown up. I heard 20,000 excuses why it wasn't detonated. The truth, is no one would fire the battery off. Don't ask me why.

Despite that failure, we were having successes every day. The army was on high-alert everywhere. Even the Defender aircraft weren't flying so low any more, the pilots preferring instead to stay at 2,000 feet and use binoculars to suss out what we were up to. They could look all they liked, because every time we heard them coming we simply disappeared into the jungle. We had teams out all over the place blowing up power lines. Every time the pylons were repaired we went back and blew them up again. Bob the suicide commando and a team shut down half the electricity in the capital by blowing up the main power lines from Brokopondo Lake to Paramaribo. The main road was closed and Surinam's main airport just outside Paramaribo was also forced to shut up. And, of course, there were no exports going through Albina to French Guiana. We had many small fire fights around Albina, but our lack of weapons made them all very one-sided – in favour of the army. My best option was cut the town off by land and make the airfield at Albina unsafe to use. The only way to resupply the garrison would be by sea, and I'd deal with that problem later. All the time, I was learning as much as possible about Bouterse and his mates in Surinam and abroad.

Now it was SurAlco's turn. The company was the world's fourth-largest producer of bauxite, and Moengo was their biggest mine. We shut the place simply by walking into the plant armed to the teeth and politely telling the workers to piss off. Step by step we were tightening our stranglehold on the country. Bouterse called a national emergency and every night a grim-faced news reader told how mercenaries and terrorists were destroying the country. What we didn't realise was that we'd become big news back in Europe too. There was nothing in the U.K., of course, but in Holland, France and Germany we were making headlines. What the news didn't reveal was that we were almost starving and it would have been very difficult for us to repel an all-out attack by the army. If Bouterse's men had summoned up the nerve to get out of the vehicles and flank us, there wouldn't have been a lot we could have done to hold them back. We had no real ammunition except shotgun cartridges and a few hundred 7.62mm bullets.

Michel Bonnot, whom I'd christened Doctor Mengele after his exploits with the hammer, was becoming worried about my physical appearance. Washing in the creek one day, I caught sight of my reflection and didn't recognise myself. I was like a ghost, with huge black rings under my eyes. My body resembled a stick insect. I was so weak that at times I found it difficult to carry my rifle. Michel reckoned I'd got a parasite, but I knew it was really down to malnutrition and stress. I was quickly getting to the stage where I'd become of no use to these people or myself. I needed to get out of the place, have a rest, have something to eat, take half a hundredweight of multivitamins and build my strength up to come back with renewed vigour.

Ronnie didn't want me to go at first; then he suggested I went back to Langabbetje, but the people there were all living off rice as well. It would have taken me years to recuperate if I'd gone there. 'No, Ronnie,' I told him, 'I'm heading for civilisation. I'm going to hide up in French Guiana until I'm better.'

Ronnie was alarmed and pleaded with me to stay. 'Please don't do this, Karel. I need you here.'

I told him, 'I need to get myself sorted out. I ain't going anywhere, I won't be long. Give me a few days to rest up and eat.'

In the end I agreed to be away for five days. Ronnie gave me a list of weapons and ammunition he needed. I had to give it to a man called Robbie Cassie, who had a safe house in Cayenne. Ronnie gave me a letter telling Robbie to pay for everything I needed. I would travel with Blakka and Thoma, the mad axeman. Blakka was a highly trusted man. Thoma – though you may find this hard to believe after his previous behaviour – was also utterly trustworthy and wouldn't let me down. Radjin wanted a break, as did John Richards, who was looking haggard, so they came too. Patrick Chauvel was travelling with us because he wanted to send reports back to whoever from Cayenne.

If the spies in our midst – and I was under no illusions as to the fact that there *were* spies – realised the two Brit mercenaries had gone, maybe the army would attack. So, we told everybody we were just going into Albina for a recce. Our civvie clothes and passports were at Steolman's Island. With no fuel for the Cessna it would take two days to get there by road and river. Instead, we were going to make our way along a loggers' track through the jungle to Pappatam, a small village half an hour's walk upstream from Albina, where we would cross the river into French Guiana in a stolen canoe. There was one slight problem with Pappatam – it had an army garrison manned by Echo Commandos. That stretch of the river also just happened to be patrolled by S-Boats.

'Karel, it will be a dangerous journey for you,' Ronnie warned me.

Now when Ronnie said something was easy, you knew it was dangerous, so when he said it was dangerous, you could guarantee it was almost suicidal. Ronnie was obviously very upset – he threw his arms around me, gave me a kiss on the cheek and said, 'Be careful. God will travel with you.' Wishing Doctor Mengele and Didier 'bon chance', we set off in daylight. From the Albina roadblock we walked in single file, first along the road and then down the loggers' trail. No one had brought an FN. We couldn't use them in French Guiana and the weapons were badly needed on the front line. I'd got my Browning, but invisibility was our best weapon. Thoma acted as point man and Patrick, lugging a huge holdall with all his gear, brought up the rear. It was dark by the time we reached the point where the loggers' trail petered out.

As well as my FN, I'd also left my cammo trousers, bush hat and boots back at camp. I tried to look like a civvie, wearing a T-shirt, shorts and stinking, rotten training shoes. My cammo top was in my tote bag. As we plodded along in the dark, we were up to our ankles in water, and – naturally – succeeded in disturbing the mosquitoes; they chewed my bare legs to pieces. Nerves propelled me along, making me feel strong. Patrick, struggling with his holdall, asked us to slow down. I offered to carry the bag but at this, John took me to one side and said, 'Let him carry his own bag.'

'Be quiet, just keep going, keep your mouth shut,' I told him. Then I helped Patrick.

Fifty feet ahead, Thoma had his hand cupped over a flashlight, like a fire fly darting backwards and forwards as he tried to find his way. At last he stopped. He could hear a motor. I could hear nothing; neither could Blakka nor Patrick. We carried on down a slight incline and suddenly we broke out into open space. Below us the river glinted in the glow from the red light on top of a mast. Now we could all hear the noise of a diesel generator thumping away. The mast was the army camp radio antenna. We made our way down through elephant grass, our eyes peeled for army patrols or booby traps. It was only ten o'clock at night. The whole garrison would still be awake. The village was over to our left along with our old enemy, dogs – four- legged burglar alarms. Blakka and I went forward to pop our heads out of the elephant grass. Pappatam is quite a modern village, not a mud-hut job.

The houses are fairly new and stand on stilts. There was a modern-looking army camp with the bottom half of the fence blanked out so you couldn't see inside. In the moonlight, I could see French Guiana on the other side. Safety. There was no going back, we had to get our hands on a canoe and go for it. I could see a line of canoes over to our left across the main road in front of us. The boats were pulled up on a strip of light sand, which lit up like a white background when the moon broke out from behind clouds. Blakka went to bring the boys forward. I waited alone. I had the Browning in my hand – not that it would do me much good against banditos. It was just very comforting to have. I heard the others coming through the grass. Don't get me wrong, they weren't making much noise, but my ears were like amplifiers. I was like a sprinter on the blocks; when the moon went behind a cloud, I darted across the sand and straight into a palm bush. I could hear people laughing and talking in the houses; music blared, dogs barked. I was nervous, sweat ran down my back. The canoes were now just fifteen feet away. If anybody looked at me I was going to freeze and turn myself into a sofa, like they do on those Ninja films.

I dashed across to a big cargo canoe pulled up on the bank. I fought the urge to panic; my chest felt full of razor blades. 'Calm down, Karl,' I told myself, 'don't take your eyes off that village; it's no good hiding with your head down.' Heart thumping, I looked for a smaller boat. I found a sound one, painted blue and white on the bow. As I made my way around it, I spotted a hole in the bow with a chain through it. The other end of the chain was padlocked to a palm tree. It was then I realised all the boats were chained up. Damn! I hadn't anticipated this. I wondered if the boys would have a piece of wire to pick the lock. Crawling between the canoes, I searched for one that I could get the chain off. Any minute now a dog was going to start barking and give the game away. The army would open up at me with God knows what. I'd only be able to empty my magazine in their general direction, run back to the boys and tab it all the way back at high speed with banditos on our tail. Cool it. Find a canoe. Nobody knows you're here. Stay calm.

I went back to the cargo canoe. It was about forty feet long and must have weighed a ton. But it was old and the two inches of wood above the hole on the left – port side for naval chaps reading this, of course – where the chain went through was rotten. I gouged at it with the Browning. Bits of tar and shit fell off and eventually the wood crumbled away, leaving a hole for me to lift the chain off nice and careful. At last I had my canoe. There were no paddles in the cargo boat, nor in any of them. It dawned on me that they must have taken the paddles home with them in case some bastard like me pinched them. We had to make do with a couple of planks of wood and a metal plate that they normally use for bailing out water.

Waiting until the moon disappeared behind clouds, I darted back to the boys. I took Blakka's shotgun, darted back across the sandy road and ducked down behind a canoe. There was a cartridge already up the spout, so I didn't have to cock it and make a noise. I covered each one as they dashed over.

'This is it, our luxury cruise boat across the river,' I whispered.

On our knees, we slowly pushed the huge canoe back down to the water. With our hearts in our mouths, we let the boat drift silently away from the village. Thoma and Blakka grabbed the planks of wood and Radjin had the plate. I held the shotgun. 'Let's go, quietly, easy.'

Slowly at first, we paddled out 100 yards... 150 yards... then, with a bit more speed. They were strong guys, urgency etched on their faces. I pointed the shotgun back towards the village, receding out of view. We were now about 200 yards out. Hang on, what was that? Jesus Christ, coming up around the bend about a mile away – a searchlight... an S-Boat.

'Let's go – start paddling like fuck,' I hissed.

The boys went into overdrive, Radjin's tin plate flashed as he scooped the water with fury. The searchlight was still a way off but it was getting closer with every minute. Isle Portal, which was the lepers' isolation island in the days of Papillon, loomed out of the dark. The island sits right in the middle of the river and is French territory. That's where we were heading. We kept paddling as the S-Boat got closer and closer. The searchlight swept in a huge, 400-yard arc. Another beam on the boat's stern swept the jungle on the river bank. Patrick Chauvel looked at me with alarm on his face. I don't know what sort of look I flashed back, but I'm not sure how reassuring it was. I was trying to paddle with the butt of my shotgun; it wasn't helping in the least, but it made me feel a little less useless. I must give Blakka and Thoma their due here – they wouldn't give up their planks, they just kept on paddling like fury.

Portal Island was close by but the S-boat had only reached Pappatam. We were safe, we knew it; the patrol boat wasn't going to reach us. However, now we had another problem: we were up to our shins in water. The old canoe was sinking. At least now we weren't going to be shot – we'd drown instead. Isle Portal is surrounded by a dense mangrove swamp. Our only hope was to make for the mangrove and clamber onto the island. We bailed for our lives when the noise of sloshing water was drowned out by the chug of an outboard motor coming from the French side.

Frantically I hissed, 'Let's go! Paddle, paddle, let's go!' But Thoma stood up in the boat and shouted at the top of his voice in Taki Taki. Out of the blackness came a boat with something piled high under a blue tarpaulin. It was another cargo boat and this one was carrying about five tons of bananas. There was family on board, a mother, father and a gang of children. Their faces shone in the light from an oil lamp down inside the canoe, which you couldn't see from a distance because it was behind the cargo. Thoma had shouted out, 'I'm with my family in a boat and we are sinking, help us please!'

They got the shock of their lives when they came over and saw three white men and three black guys. It turned

out the boat family were Surinamese. We abandoned our
boat wallowing among the mangroves. The relief of
climbing on that boat was immense. I patted the man on
the back, telling him, 'I know you don't understand what
I'm saying, but thank you, thank you.' Patrick gave them
big smiles. We sat down. What a night. Through Thoma,
the man offered us coffee. He got a little primus stove
going inside the family tarpaulin shelter. It was wonderful
coffee. We had no cigarettes to offer, but we did have
tobacco, which we all shared. The old man was from a
place called Maripasoula, right down near the Brazilian
border at the southern end of French Guiana. He was
taking his cargo of bananas to Chinoisville, Chinatown,
in St Laurent. I didn't want to put him to any
inconvenience, but we couldn't risk getting out of the
boat in Chinatown. No problem, he would drop us a few
hundred yards further down river in the shanty town
alongside Papillon's jail. We had contacts there and a
couple of safe huts we could use. Don't forget, John and
I had no passports. Getting stopped by the French police
would be a major problem.

An hour later, St Laurent loomed up. We didn't want to
bring our problems on this man and his family. We ducked
under the tarpaulin as the old death camp at Saint-Jean
passed by on our right; the camp was now a French army
garrison. Peeking from under the tarpaulin, Chinatown
looked bustling. Dozens of cargo canoes jostled for
position against the quayside. People milled around, loud
salsa music blared from a bar. No one took any notice of

us. Further on in the sprawling shanty town, the boatman turned right and touched the canoe's bow onto the bank.

We said our goodbyes to the old man and his family. I pumped his hand and offered him twenty quid in francs just to say thanks. He refused to take it. I pointed to the kids, but he still declined. What a guy; I gave him a thumbs-up sign and a big smile.

Then it was time to get wet. Sorry Patrick, there's no gang plank off this cruise liner. We climbed down into the mud and shit. It was over waist high at the back of the boat. We waded our way to the bank. Blakka, Thoma and Radjin were going to go to the bar where I'd kidnapped Koyku so we could get organised. Patrick was going off somewhere else but we were going to wait for him in the Café Amsterdam.

We crouched down under the shadow of Papillion's jail wall while Blakka disappeared. He reappeared a minute later without the shotgun – he'd stashed it somewhere. Thoma went on ahead as point, with Blakka twenty yards behind him and John, Radjin and I bringing up the rear. The Café Amsterdam was heaving, full of Surinamese. The door shut behind us, no more customers were allowed inside. At last we could relax and have a beer. Bobo pumped my hand as Radjin, Blakka and Thoma chatted away in Taki Taki telling him what had happened. Bobo put men outside to keep watch for the French police.

'Don't worry, Karel, everything's okay, you can relax,' Bobo assured me.

We'd got through a couple of bottles of beer each when Patrick arrived with news that we didn't need to stay in the safe huts, as he'd fixed up some nice accommodation.

He explained, 'A friend of mine has a restaurant up the road. He's French and knows the situation. You can come up, have a wash and meal and a sleep in pleasant surroundings.'

I wasn't going to refuse an offer like that. Blakka, Thoma and Radjin escorted us to the restaurant and then disappeared. We'd meet up back at Bobo's place in the morning. We were met by a stocky, tough-looking man and his beautiful wife. Marie Claire was about forty and very chic. The decor almost knocked me out after weeks in the jungle. It was like walking into a smart restaurant in Paris. And there we were, standing like tramps, still stinking of the jungle. They lead us to a table covered with plates of ham, cheese, bread, bottles of wine, glasses, napkins, a white tablecloth. I was in heaven. Marie Claire said something to me in French that I didn't understand. Patrick explained she was apologising for the fact that she couldn't provide a hot a meal because the restaurant was closed and they had no cooked food left. I looked at her as though she was an alien for making such an apology, with that little spread before us. 'Tell her not to worry about it,' I said to Patrick, 'I'll complain to the management another time.'

Unfortunately, after one small sandwich I found I was full and couldn't eat any more. With Patrick translating, Henri asked us lots of questions. He'd heard about us from news reports and having two mercenaries in his bar seemed to fascinate him. Patrick told me Henri was a former French policeman who'd been part of a special shock troop.

A pleasant weariness enveloped me as I sat there drinking French wine and chatting, with soft music in the background. Marie Claire apologised again, this time for not able to give us a room. We'd have to make do with mattresses on the restaurant floor. She brought down a couple of folded, starched white sheets each and pillows with white pillow cases. I couldn't believe it. I woke with a start to see someone walking towards me in the gloom, I whipped out my Browning and pointed it at the shadow. Still half asleep, I called out, 'Who's that?' It was a woman, and – understandably – she recoiled in shock. Then I realised where I was and that I was in my underpants, kneeling on one knee, pointing the Browning at Marie Claire. Cool as you like, Henri walked over with a big smile on his face and said, 'Hey my friend, it's okay no problem, no problem.' and gently patted me on the shoulder. I pointed the gun down at the floor. I looked at his wife and thought oh my God, what have I done?

'I'm so sorry,' I mumbled.

'No, no. It's all right,' With the Browning back under the pillow, I lay back down and went sleep. Apparently, one of us had been moaning in our sleep and the couple had come to see if we were OK. The next thing I knew, Patrick and Henri were waking me up for a breakfast of coffee, bread rolls, marmalade and jam – wonderful. It was after six o'clock and any minute now one of the boys would be here to pick us up. During breakfast Patrick revealed he planned to hire a car to go to Cayenne. He was planning to send his reports from there and stay over for a few days in the capital until we were ready. Then he'd cross back over the border with us and continue reporting on the war. We could go to Cayenne with him in the hire car.

An hour later, there was a knock on the door and the three of them were there: Radjin, Blakka and Thoma. Radjin would come with us in the hire car, while Thoma and Blakka were staying on in St Laurent. I gave Blakka and Thoma hugs, shook their hands and thanked them for their efforts on the river. 'When this war's over, 'I told them, 'if Surinam ever need a rowing team for the Olympics, I'm going to put your two names down.' I told Thoma he was so good I'd let him chop my head off any time he liked!

We arranged to meet at Bobo's bar in five days' time. The morning wore on and at about nine o'clock Patrick arrived with a white Peugeot. As we were leaving, I asked Henri to look after the Browning and the spare mag. Our biggest problem was no longer banditos but the French authorities, which is why I left the gun. With Patrick driving, me in the front seat and John and Radjin in the back, we motored along the main road hacked out of the jungle.

Up ahead, on the right-hand side, was a new-looking wooden building, in front of it was a roadblock. Four policemen in blue uniforms and carrying guns stood on the veranda alongside a handful of soldiers. Another policeman was in the road flagging us down.

I turned to Patrick. 'What's this?'

He looked perplexed. 'I don't know. It wasn't here before when I came across.'

Shit, shit. Stay calm. Big smiles. Try and act natural. Don't look nervous. We stopped. The policeman leaned down and said something in French to Patrick. He peered inside the car, looked at me and clocked the other two in the back. He spoke to me. 'Pardon monsieur,' I said pointing at myself, 'tourist, non parley français.'

'He wants your passport,' Patrick whispered.

'Tell him my passport is in the hotel. We're just going to Cayenne for a couple of hours and we're coming back.' I watched the colour drain from Patrick's face.

Another policeman came over.

'Would you get out of the car please, boys,' said Patrick translating for the cop. An officer in civilian clothes, a big bastard with glasses, wandered out of the cabin and looked in the boot. They found a compass in my bag. Then they pulled out a French Foreign Legion beret. The big guy with the glasses looked at it and pointed at me and John as if to say, which of you owns this? John Richards said, 'Oui'. That did it. Everybody inside.

The police were looking a little bit excited but we tried to remain calm and cool. I said to Patrick, 'Just tell them we're just on holiday and we'll get our passports. We've done nothing wrong.' In the past the only passport check had been at the ferry terminal in St Laurent, but when I'd closed the main road to Paramaribo the ferries stopped running and people started using other crossing points. So the French set up a new passport check on the main road to Cayenne. Therefore, in effect, this was all my fault. Never mind, we were still trying to look cool. With Patrick still translating, I said, 'It's just a mistake, we're tourists, staying at the Hotel Toucan in St Laurent.'

The big guy with the glasses said, 'No you're not, I've seen you two on television: Surinam, mercenaire.'

We weren't so cool when they herded us into a large wooden cage. John, Radjin and I sat in a line on a bench. They couldn't hold Patrick. Peering through the hardwood bars, he told us, 'This guy is telephoning his superiors. Apparently, they've been told to watch out for you. I'm really sorry about this, we've driven right into it.'

Maybe we could salvage something out of this. We knew the French hated Bouterse and his regime, maybe they would let us go. Radjin looked a bit grim. I was feeling pretty weak; I'd also got a hangover. John sat there, fag hanging out of the corner of his mouth, one foot up on the bench, grinning from ear to ear. He announced, 'We'll be all right. I know these French, they're all wankers. They'll let us go.'

'John, shut up. We could still end up in Paramaribo.'

The cops were staring at us as though they'd captured some prize specimen. Don't get me wrong – they were very friendly. One of them even passed three bottles of Kronenbourg beer in to us. The telephone rang. Patrick tried to earwig as the plain-clothes man chatted away. He put the phone down. It turned out that we were now under arrest.

Patrick translated: 'You will be taken to Cayenne for questioning. Then you are to be expelled.'

'Is there any way around this? Can we talk to anyone?' Patrick pleaded on our behalf. 'Can you just forget about it? We'll cross back over immediately.'

'Absolutely impossible.'

The cops handcuffed us and bundled us into a car. Patrick was going to follow. He was still apologetic.

'No problem,' I told him. 'Just one thing. The big fella is talking about expulsion. Can you ask him if there's any possibility of extradition to Surinam?' When Patrick asked him, the plain-clothes man burst out laughing. 'No Surinam.'

Pointing at me he smiled and said, 'You, Paris.'

Patrick was reassuring. 'They'll never send you to Surinam. The rules say you have to be expelled to your own country; both of you will end up in London. Radjin's headed for Amsterdam.' Phew! Thank God for that.

My mind was in turmoil on the drive to Cayenne. What was going to happen with Ronnie? Would the army attack the roadblock when they discovered we had been seized? On the outskirts of the capital we turned right to the airport. The cops had tipped off the press. Television crews and a battery of press cameramen were waiting. Ducking down in the back of the car, we approached the gate. Inside, we were taken to the back of the main terminal building, marched into the police office and put in a cell. The handcuffs came off and I noticed the police didn't lock the door. Half an hour later, in comes Monsieur Chauvel, carrying a case of beer, two pairs of brand new jeans, cans of peanuts and chocolate bars. The police let him in the cell. 'How are you boys? Some guys from the intelligence services are coming to have a chat with you then they'll put you on the next flight back to Paris.'

They opened the cell door and we all sat round a table in the locker room drinking beer and eating peanuts. It was no good fighting it. We were going to London whether we liked it or not. We were interrupted when six policemen burst through the door and ordered, 'Quick back in the cell. Patrick you have to go now.'

One of these policemen spoke English and he explained the Consul from Surinam was outside with his entourage shouting and screaming for our extradition to Paramaribo as terrorists. The press were outside as well.

Alarm bells went off in my head. 'Nobody's going to change their mind are they?' I asked the cop. 'We're not going to be handed over to this man?' Reassuringly, the cop implied that the man outside was an idiot who was going to be in trouble with the police if he didn't behave himself.

I didn't want to appear a smart arse, so I matter-of-factly asked the cop, 'What's his name, this Consul?' His name was Naylam. Mr. Naylam probably didn't realise it, but I knew a lot more about him than I was letting on. Naylam was Koyku's boss and chief of the rat's nest that masqueraded as the Surinam Consulate. I even had

Naylam's phone number. I wondered what Koyku would have thought of the sight of his old boss standing outside with his cronies shouting for my extradition. After twenty minutes, the cops in the locker room started to relax. The big guy with the glasses arrived with his boss. Sitting drinking beer with the three of us, it was blatantly obvious they were sympathetic.

The intelligence people arrived. They took me to an office upstairs and said, 'We've been watching everything. You've done an excellent job.' They told me that after I'd blocked the N1, 7,000 people crossed the Marowijne River to escape the war. Two hundred and fifty Surinamese soldiers had given themselves up in French Guiana. Due to our campaign, the economy of Surinam had collapsed to only a sixth of its previous value. We were doing OK so far! That was when the enormity of the effects of my battle plan began to dawn on me. Seven thousand refugees. Christ Almighty!

The two intelligence men wanted to know how I'd mined the main road, what our set up was, what Ronnie was thinking. I cooperated fully. At the end of our interview, one of them said, 'Karl, if you're going to return here, it's got to be done quietly.'

I couldn't return to Cayenne because I was now top of the official scallywag list for the French Guiana frontier police, the PAF. Unofficially, they explained in great detail the route I must take. They went on, 'Make up a cover story and come back that way.'

'That way' would be via Brazil.

CHAPTER 9

Consul Naylam and his cronies watched from the terminal building balcony as we walked in handcuffs across the tarmac to the waiting Air France BAC 111. Someone shouted, 'Karl! Karl!' I looked round. It was Patrick Chauvel, taking pictures through a huge telephoto lens. I held my hand to my ear in the shape of a telephone and shouted, 'I'll phone you.' As we climbed the rear steps to the plane, I saw him give me the thumbs up. Three seats had been reserved for us on the back row on the left-hand side. All the other passengers were already on board. They stared at us, probably thinking we were criminals.

This plane didn't go direct to Paris. We were flying instead to the island of Martinique in the Lesser Antilles, on the eastern edge of the Caribbean. The police were waiting as the plane taxied to a halt in the capital, Fort de France. They marched us to the airport building and for three hours we sat under guard in an office. The Boeing 747 jumbo jet for Paris was waiting on the tarmac as we were ushered aboard in handcuffs. When the cuffs came off, we were introduced to the captain. I told him we weren't criminals, but soldiers. He seemed to relax a bit after that.

We had a seven-hour flight ahead of us. While Radjin dozed, I had a long talk with John Richards. By now, I was thinking seriously of getting rid of him. He'd been nothing but a weight around my neck. I reminded him of how foolish he'd been, of his continual posing and swaggering around. He sat there nervously as I spelled out that I didn't want him working with me any more. Shame-faced, he pleaded with me to give him one more chance. Now, the airline food was luxury after rice and kwak. The wine even more so. When I was feeling much more relaxed about things, like a fool I said, 'Okay John, we'll give it another go.'

That sorted, I had time to ponder another problem. When we were held at Cayenne airport, we'd been allowed one phone call, so I called Major Getback. The satellite link echoed but I could hear panic in his voice as he told me, 'There's been a lot of trouble, get your arses out of there as quick as possible.'

'What's going on?' I enquired, 'What have you been doing?'

'I can't explain on the phone, just get out of there!'

What could have gone wrong? With Major Getback it could have been anything.

The flight was over. All eyes were on us as a stewardess led us forward to the front door where the captain was stood, stern-faced, holding our expulsion papers. The door opened and two plain-clothes officials were waiting for us. The older, stocky one was a dead-ringer for the actor Ed Asner. He stepped inside the plane, shook our hands and said 'Welcome gentlemen.' He whisked the envelope from the captain, who looked surprised. Over coffee in the cafeteria at Charles de Gaulle airport, he said, 'I was watching you on the television, you're doing a great job out there. Which one of you does the explosives?' He went on to explain that he'd been an explosives man in the French army. He told us about his days in Algeria and the little tricks they used against the Arabs there, how he put some chemical in an Arab's car radiator and it blew him to hell when it heated up. He was laughing about it. Excellent bloke. Then he told us, 'I've a nice surprise for you. You are on the next flight to London. I couldn't get you tickets in economy class, so I've booked you boys in business class.' He put two British Airways club-class tickets on the table. I couldn't believe it.

Radjin was on a later flight to Amsterdam. It was November and freezing cold. I was so skinny and only wearing my T- shirt, the jeans Patrick had bought and stinking trainers. I reached into my holdall and took out my smelly cammo top to try and keep out the cold.

On the plane, John sat by the window and I had the middle seat. A businessman to my right pulled out his *Daily Telegraph* and began to sniff the air, trying to identify the bizarre smell filling his nostrils. It was probably the bat shit on my cammo top. Why should I care? I was in business class, one of the big shots, not with those dirty buggers down in the economy. We arrived at Heathrow with no passports and about fifty quid each in French francs. After holding us for fifteen minutes, Immigration sent us on our way. I was brown, skinny and shaking with the cold. But I didn't care any more. I decided not to call the Major from Euston – I'd find out the real story first.

It was great to be back home. The wages had been paid – I was pleased about that, naturally – but I wasn't so chuffed to learn from George Baker that a lot of money had gone missing. It seemed a bunch of expatriate Surinamese politicians had given Major Getback £20,000 to buy weapons and supply more men. No guns had appeared and the money had apparently vanished. George planned to tell me the whole story when we met up in Amsterdam. I didn't want to speak to the Major until I'd heard everything from George.

It took me a few days to get my hands on a one-year passport, then I flew with John to Schiphol airport, Amsterdam. When we walked into his bar, George threw his arms around us. 'Boys, well done!' You could see the pride in his face. 'You've done an unbelievable job. You've been on the news here every night.' Then he went all confidential. 'Come to my place tonight, there's someone coming to see you. We're going to do an arms deal and I want you to meet this man.' George slipped me a Walther P38 pistol. 'You'd better keep that,' he added, ominously, 'because things are going on.'

Jan, whom I'd last seen standing outside the bar in St Laurent when I kidnapped Koyku, was arriving in Holland from French Guiana. Basically, Jan was a gofer for Ronnie but he thought of himself as a bit of a James Bond. Many of the Jungle Commandos regarded him, rightly or wrongly, as a double agent. When Jan arrived his eyes were glowing red – a sure sign that he'd been indulging in some illegal substances. He soon started arguing with George in Taki Taki, then he turned to me and said, 'You have to be very, very careful here in Amsterdam. Bouterse's men will be looking for you and they'll try to kill you. They've killed before.'

I had a funny feeling I'd have to be careful with Jan. I opened my jacket and showed him the gun – in other words, don't try anything with me. I told him, 'If anyone comes near me, my friend, I'll blow their fucking face off. I'll kill them on the spot.' Jan's face dropped when I gave him that warning.

We were waiting for a man called Dino to arrive. George seemed to think that the guy was okay, but Jan reckoned Dino worked for Bouterse. That was a bit rich! Dino was going to do business for us with a Belgian arms dealer. George wanted me to sort it out. Soon, a short black bloke arrived and introduced himself as Dino. Despite an attempt to appear friendly, he was clearly nervous as hell. He took off his raincoat and went to place it on the pool table. In his nervousness, he put it down a bit too quick. The coat went clunk. There was something heavy in the pocket.

He spoke good English and asked if he could talk in Taki Taki. I let them get into the conversation for a couple of minutes and then I announced I had to go to the toilet. As I stood up from the table, I leaned over and picked up Dino's mac.

'Shall I hang this up for you?' I could feel the handgun in the pocket. Dino looked embarrassed and said, 'No problem, leave it there.' I let it drop with a good clunk, so no one was in any doubt that our friend was armed. When I came back and I was told Dino wanted to take us to see a man in Belgium to arrange for weapons. George was going to pay for everything – literally lock, stock and barrel. The weapons, the shipment, the lot.

When Dino and Jan left, I was able to talk to George privately about Major Getback. While I'd slowly been bringing Surinam to its knees, Ronnie had been praying for the cavalry to arrive. Once we'd started getting Bouterse by the throat, the Hindu community from the west of Surinam, known as the Nickerie side, decided we were worth backing and contacted George Baker. While we were out in the jungle, Robbie Cassie, the guy who ran the safe house in Cayenne, had flown to London with a political heavyweight called Paul, a man called Peeri and his bodyguard. They'd met Major Getback at Heathrow and asked him to buy more weapons and find more men. This was their contribution to the war effort – they were backing Ronnie Brunswijk to fuck up the Bouterse regime with £20,000 cash, which they handed over to the Major in a plastic carrier bag. There was also five grand extra from George Baker for me and John Richards.

At the time, Paul had asked, 'Excuse me Major, but what guarantee can you give me over this money?'

'Don't be silly,' replied the Major, 'You have my best friend, Karl, out there. I know if this money disappeared the Jungle Commandos would kill him.' No wonder he was desperate for us to get our arses out of Surinam!

When Paul the politician tried to get back in contact, the Major's phone was dead. I decided to tell George the truth, that the major was only an NCO. I explained how I'd promoted him only because George had insisted on dealing with an officer. George was dumbfounded. The Major's act had utterly foxed him. It must have been the Sandhurst tie.

After the cock-up at Heathrow, it became more urgent than ever that we got more weapons to send out to Surinam. The next day, Dino arrived in a huge, luxurious Cadillac. John climbed in the back and I sat next to Dino on the drive down to a small town on the Belgian border. Dino was very nervous, to say the least. He was doing his best to act naturally, but he was overly chatty and friendly, trying to hide his nervousness. He must have looked in his rear-view mirror hundreds times just going out of Amsterdam. We were on the A2 motorway when Dino slammed on the brakes, swerved the car to the right, came to a halt and announced we'd been driving the wrong way. He reversed at speed up the hard shoulder to an intersection then drove off down country lanes before rejoining the motorway a bit later. Oh yeah, lost your way, Dino? I played it dumb but thought to myself, I'm watching you, matey. Five minutes over the Belgian border we pulled into a secluded country club. A white man in sports jacket and slacks was waiting in the restaurant. He didn't speak English, so Dino translated. We cut to the chase – he wanted $90,000 up front. I asked what we'd get for our money.

'Anything you want,' he replied, 'it will be delivered to a ship in Antwerp, you can inspect everything. I know the captain of the ship, he will take it to Surinam for you, drop it off the coast or any place you require. That will all be arranged at no extra cost.'

Of course, the arms deal would cost a lot more than $90,000, but this man wanted that much now, in cash, a.s.a.p. 'My friend, why do you require ninety thousand dollars now?' I asked. 'We need to see the weapons and the ship first. Then maybe we can talk some serious business.'

'I don't think you know very much about the arms game, about export licences and end-user certificates,' he replied. I let him waffle on a bit longer. He thought he was a clever bastard, but this was a basic rip-off.

When I'd had enough, I turned on him. 'Listen friend, export licences, on average, cost ten dollars. A bent end-user certificate, which is what I presume we were going to use, is normally ten per cent of the total deal. If you don't know how much we're going to spend, how did you come up with a figure of ninety thousand dollars?'

He went red. Using a translator is always a good way to hide your lies. You can always say that there's been some kind of misunderstanding also it gives you time to think.

He tried that line on me, but I was pissed off and decided that I'd had enough. 'This is a complete and utter waste of time,' I said. 'You brought me all the way down here from Amsterdam. This man,' I indicated Dino, 'is not a very good driver. He gets lost and makes crazy manoeuvres. We'll go back and I'll think about it but don't hold your breath, my friend.' We didn't shake hands. On the way back, I picked up Dino's car phone and called George. Looking straight at Dino, I said loudly, 'Dino has got himself mixed up with a thief. Maybe Dino doesn't know what's happening, but the man's a crook.' I found out later that George would have been quite prepared to lay out ninety grand. I also discovered Dino was on a fifty-fifty share of the money. Wheels within wheels.

The next day we met Paul at his office above a video shop in Rotterdam. Paul is a very intelligent, pleasant man. He's an ex-politician from Surinam, living in exile in Holland because Bouterse wanted him dead. A hit team sent by the dictator to wipe him out ending up shooting Paul's brother by mistake. He answered the door of his home in Rotterdam to be find a man he'd never seen before.

'Paul?' asked the caller.

'Yes,' replied Paul's brother, who was then shot five times in the abdomen. The gunman also put a bullet in his head to finish him off, but remarkably, he survived. Luckily, the gunman had used a .22 weapon.

Paul told us that after the incident with Major Getback, he was very nervous about laying any more money on the line. Well done, Major. However, Paul did want to be associated with us because we'd done so well. He gave John and me 1,000 guilders, about 300 quid each, to keep in touch with him and let him know when we'd be returning to Surinam.

Back in Amsterdam, George took me to a plush Japanese hotel to meet Peeri, the other man who'd met Major Getback at Heathrow. He was waiting in the hotel lobby with Roy, his bodyguard. Ever heard of a Hindu called Roy? It wasn't his real name, and neither was Peeri, for that matter. It seems Peeri was the real aggrieved party in all this: it was his twenty grand that had vanished. And he wanted his money back. During my phone call from Cayenne, the Major had given me a new telephone number to contact him on.

'I can't give you the number because I haven't heard the Major's side of the story yet,' I told Peeri. 'What I will do is call him from a phone booth in the hotel and you can come with me. I'm going to pretend I'm alone. If you butt in on the conversation, I will immediately cut off the call, do you understand?'

I made the call with Peeri standing next to me, ear-wigging. I said, 'Colin I'm in Amsterdam and I met some people yesterday who are very angry with you because apparently they gave you twenty grand. What's more, George gave you five thousand for me and John. The money's disappeared, so do you want to explain yourself?'

'You want to watch yourself, Karl, they're a bunch of bastards,' said the Major. 'Yeah, they did give me that money but I gave it back to them.'

'So you don't have the money and if you don't have it you can't give it back, can you?'

'I haven't got it, I gave it back to the bastards.'

How did I get involved in this? I didn't need it. This is the sort of shit you dragged into with the likes of the bogus Major.

'All right, Colin, I'll be in touch soon.'

I put the phone down and straight away Peeri accused John and I of being in cahoots with the Major.

Now that pissed me right off. I told him, 'You and your bodyguard can fuck off. Find your money yourself. If you need me for anything you can contact me through Paul.'

Back at George's bar, the phone was ringing every five minutes. George picked up the phone for the umpteenth time, then passed the handset to me.

'It's an Englishman, he wants a job,' he explained.

It was John L., an ex-squaddie from Staffordshire who'd been in a tank regiment. He sounded dead game and explained that he'd seen the Ansus Foundation advert and had rung George thirty times but had been given the run around each time.

'I've got no experience as a mercenary or anything like that,' he confessed, 'but I want to get out of this country and do something. If there's no job for me, put me out of my misery now. It's costing me a fortune ringing Amsterdam all the time.'

I promised to let him know. The next day we returned home. Stupidly, I'd agreed that George could give my home number to anyone else who called the bar looking for mercenary work. Jesus, every lunatic on this planet must have rung me. The phone went at two o'clock in the morning on one occasion. It was a Scottish maniac who claimed to be on the run for murder.

Another time, I picked up the phone to hear a Cockney voice. 'I've got a team of men down in New Cross, ruthless we are. We can cut people's throats.'

I cut him off in his prime, 'I'll let you know. Don't ring me back again. I'll call you.' I pretended to take his number.

'All right, mate. Listen, if you're ever down in London way, we've got a field we go to at weekends for training. You're welcome any time.'

Another one rang to recruit *me* for Surinam. I told you George's English was not up to much and maybe something had been lost in the translation.

The caller blundered on, 'I'm thinking about taking you to Surinam. George has told me to ring you.'

'Whoa, hold your horses.' I told him, 'If you ring George back and ask him properly you'll understand what he said.'

A Frenchman rang, who presumed I spoke fluent French. He kept going on about 'mercenaires' this and 'mercenaires' that. I put the phone down on him too. I had guys ringing me up from the United States, Germany, Italy, Scandinavia. It was a nightmare.

One phone call I was glad to get came from Patrick Chauvel. Michel Bonnot had caught severe malaria and was returning to Paris. Patrick had arranged with Michel to pick up our bergens, including our passports, from

Stoelman's Island. He also told me what had been happening in Surinam. The army hadn't launched a major assault on the roadblock. There'd been a minor attack, but Ronnie's boys repulsed it by detonating a couple of the mines at the roadblocks. It had frightened the daylights out of the army.

I called John to tell him we were going to Paris to pick up our passports. It was then John revealed he'd spoken to *Raids* magazine. I'd never heard of it at the time. It was like a French version of *Soldier of Fortune* magazine. The owner, Eric Micheletti, wanted to pay for our story. 'You're going to fuck things up for us getting back,' I warned John. 'I don't think you understand what French Intelligence told us. We've got to sneak back in. You mustn't tell the whole world what's going on.'

'Oh, I haven't told him we're going back. I haven't done that,' he insisted. 'I've only told him what we've done so far and he's going to publish that anyway.'

It was decided that we'd see *Raids* magazine when we went to Paris to pick up the passports. We opted to go by sea and rail, only to discover French train drivers were on strike. Eventually, we ended up in Eric Micheletti's small office. Tall and wiry, Eric is an ex-para from the French Beret Rouge. He's a nice bloke. After some small talk, he asked when we were going back. I said fairly soon, but added that if he printed that fact, we'd be compromised. We agreed he'd stay quiet about our return and we'd give him another story. Eric paid us six hundred quid and picked up our hotel bill. He got a bargain, because he had to reprint that edition of the magazine three times, such was the demand.

We found Michel Bonnot in a flat in an old-fashioned block around a beautiful courtyard in the Montmartre district of Paris. A monkey was chained to the balcony outside the apartment. Michel looked very ill. When he spoke, it sounded as though he had a severe dose of the flu. We weren't going to spend too long with him, but he had grave news. After Ronnie repulsed the army attack on the roadblock, Bouterse's men had taken brutal revenge. They massacred more than forty civilians in the village of Mooiwana, between Moengotapoe and Albina. Two helicopters had flown repeatedly between the Albina garrison and Mooiwana, off-loading troops who massacred virtually everyone living there. There was no military objective to be gained by that, it was just an act of sheer nastiness. Michel videoed the aftermath in the hope that the culprits would be brought to justice. To this day no one has ever been charged with the massacre at Mooiwana.

Because of the rail strike, the train from Paris to Amsterdam was like a cattle truck. John sat on the luggage rack to the Belgian border, where the train wheezed to a halt. A gang of French railwaymen were sat on the track protesting in the freezing weather. John exploded with rage at the sight of them, and spent the next ten minutes hunting for buckets of water to throw over the protesters. Now, that was the funny side of John, the side I used to really like. Trouble was, as time went on, I was seeing less and less of it.

George had arranged another arms deal, this time at the Victoria Hotel in Amsterdam, with two Englishmen who lived in Germany. They were both ex-British army officer types. The one who did all the talking was an arrogant bugger in a black trenchcoat. He deliberately ignored me and started talking to George, showing him photostat copies of Kalashnikov rifles and Browning pistols. He spoke far too fast for George, who eventually told him to talk to me. Reluctantly, he turned towards me and, in his clipped Sandhurst accent, said, 'What I have to do to get this deal through is speak personally to the leader of the rebel group.'

'What you have to do,' I replied, 'is realise that you should have talked to me in the first place. If you'd showed a bit of manners and stopped being so arrogant, we might have been able to do some business. Forget it, George, we're wasting our time.' I've got a sixth sense about these things and it felt to me that we were being set up here for another rip-off.

'I beg your pardon?' spluttered the Englishman.

'I beg your fucking pardon, are you deaf? We're leaving. Let's go, George.' We walked out of the hotel as the two arms dealers grabbed their briefcases and ran out into the street after us. As we strode away, I could hear them shouting, 'What about our expenses? What about our train fare?' Now tell me, have you ever heard of international arms dealers worrying about train fares?

There was another arms dealer waiting for us in George's bar. He was nothing like the last two. He looked like a drug addict. Out of a green American webbing pouch he pulled a night sight – just what we needed in Surinam. At that time, night sights were difficult to get hold of. This one looked in mint condition, but there were no batteries in it. He wanted the equivalent of £500 for it. This particular model, a Varo Starlight scope, was worth $4,500. I gave George a sly wink and said, 'I dunno George, we don't really need this stuff. We've got plenty of night sights over there. With no ni-cad batteries it's worthless. We don't even know if it'll work.' In the end I got him down to two hundred and fifty quid. What the guy didn't seem to know was that there is a way you can wire these sights up even if you don't have the correct battery.

George wasn't ready to go back to Surinam for a couple of weeks, so we returned home. I'm sure I had a mild heart attack in the lounge at Schiphol airport. I felt extremely ill on the flight to Manchester. Since I'd arrived back from Surinam, I hadn't been able to stop coughing. The antibiotics my doctor gave me didn't work. He also put me on valium, because he reckoned I'd got bad nerves. I told him I was in the Merchant Navy; he couldn't understand why my nervous system was shot to pieces.

There were also more phone calls to deal with from loonies far and wide, all looking for a job. I had no intention of taking a lot of men back with me, because you get more trouble off so-called mercenaries, than from the enemy! I'd already got enough problems on my plate.

However, I did phone up John L. – he seemed dead straight. I didn't need guys telling me how to do the job; I needed men who would do what I told them and get the job done. He was astounded I'd actually called him back and offered him a place.

John Richards also told me about a mate of his, an ex-member of the Rhodesian army, with whom he'd worked on a bodyguard job. When I spoke on the phone to the guy, whose name was Charlie Moseley, I realised he had no great love for John. I liked the sound of Charlie on the phone, though, so I give him a job as well.

We all met at Victoria station and as we travelled to Holland, I worked on my plan to get us back to Surinam. We'd travel as civilians, fly first to Brazil and then go into Surinam by the back door. George had been approached by a Dutch TV company who wanted to make a documentary on the war in Surinam. It was the perfect cover, so George agreed to allow a cameraman to travel with us. With him alongside us, we could even carry the night sight without awkward questions being asked.

While we were waiting in Amsterdam for our flight to Rio, George brought an American round to the flat where we were staying. He wore a drab olive combat jacket, jeans, and a pair of U.S. combat boots. He introduced himself as Rex and promptly showed us a brand-new tattoo of the Rhodesian Selous Scouts insignia. He claimed he'd been a member of the Selous Scouts. He then pulled out a huge Rambo knife. 'You be careful with that thing,' I told him.

'Yeah, I know man,' replied Rex.

'If you drop it on your foot, you'll break your toes,' I went on.

George wanted Rex to join the team. I wasn't so sure. Then I had a bright idea. Rambo could carry the night sight.

I told him, 'We don't require visas for Brazil with a U.K. passport. What about you? You've got a U.S. passport.'

He replied, 'Hell, I guess with one of these passports you can get in any goddamn place.'

'Enough of that shit, Rex, at least phone the Brazilian Embassy and ask them about your visa requirements.' Rex returned the following day to assure us everything was sorted out, and that he didn't require a visa either. Anton, the cameraman, was next to arrive at the flat. George turned up with the tickets – we were flying to Rio de Janeiro with Moroccan Airlines, via Casablanca.

Half an hour into the flight the intercom burst into life, 'Bing! bong! Will Mr. George Baker please come forward.' I looked at George. He looked at me. 'Bing! bong! Mr. George Baker please come forward.'

'What's happened, George?'

'I don't know, I'll take a look.' He didn't seem overly concerned. A steward was waiting for him in the middle of the aisle. As the pair of them walked back down past me, I asked George what was going on. 'It's okay,' he said, 'An old friend of mine is on board, he saw me coming onto the plane and I'm just going to have a talk with him.' George disappeared down the back for about half an hour.

What the hell was going on? Why didn't this guy just stroll up the aisle looking for George?

It was pissing down in Casablanca, but at least we were staying in a five-star hotel. Safely ensconced in my double room, I began to wonder about this trip. Who was George's friend? It all seemed very strange. John L. and Charlie were already beginning to get fed up with John Richards's behaviour. I have to say, when John L. and Charlie arrived it was like a breath of fresh air. They were both trained by the British Army, had things to say, opinions to make, and were more intelligent than John. Before long, I realised John was starting to become jealous of the two newcomers. He didn't even like me sitting at the same table as them.

It was a long flight across the Atlantic to Rio, and I was nervy at the airport. Who had George spoken to? Did Bouterse know our travel plans? We went through passport control with no problems. I noticed the customs channel had red and green lights, like traffic lights. They were mostly green, but if you hit a red light you had to have your baggage checked. With my luck, I figured I'd get a red light no problem, but I walked straight through. We all assembled on the other side, except for Rex. This wasn't looking good – they'd probably found the night sight. We took two taxis into the Flamenco district of Rio, where we booked into a hotel. I wasn't bothered about Rex and his new Selous Scouts tattoo, but I was concerned about the night sight.

Anton the documentary guy wasn't on any wanted list, so I asked him to telephone the American Embassy and tell them he'd been on a flight with a young American guy whom he'd lost track of. I told him to say that they had arranged to meet up at a hotel, but had become separated at the airport, and ask if the Embassy could make some enquiries. The answer came back quickly. They were holding an American who had tried to go through immigration without a visa. Guess you did need one after all, Rex.

Anton told the Embassy official, 'He has part of my camera equipment, a lens I use for photographing wildlife at night time. Can I go and collect it?' The answer was affirmative, and Anton travelled back to the airport to pick up the night sight. Bye, bye, Rambo. I'm sure the Rio authorities were pleased when they found his knife. And I hope nobody dropped it on their foot!

CHAPTER 10

The queue at the Varig Airways booking desk seemed to stretch for miles. We'd have been waiting for days to buy a ticket for an internal flight to the northern town of Belem. Instead, we decided to hire a minibus so George and John Richards went off to a car hire depot. Apparently, minibuses are like gold dust in Brazil, so they came back with a car the size of a Ford Escort. Our luggage wouldn't even fit in it. I told John to get rid of it. He eventually returned with a big black American saloon. Our luggage went straight into the boot. Getting six blokes inside was another matter. In the end, we put a plank of wood between the two front seats, so that three people could sit in the front, giving those in the back more room. We drove north out Rio de Janeiro towards Belem, which perches on an inlet just below the mouth of the Amazon river. We drove for thirty hours along a dusty, dirt road. Then, just five miles from our destination, the car lurched violently from side to side at eighty miles an hour. A tyre had blown out. How we weren't killed, I'll never know. The car's paintwork looked like it had been shot-blasted – the front end had been smashed during the blow-out. And John Richards had snapped the indicator switch clean off in a tantrum!

Anton wandered into the reception area of our shack of a hotel, looking agitated. 'Karl, I have to tell you something,' he announced. 'You know when we were on the plane from Amsterdam to Casablanca and a strange man wanted to speak to George? Well, that man was a journalist.' Anton had phoned back to his TV station in Holland to be told that a reporter had gone on the radio telling of how he'd travelled to Casablanca with a gang of British mercenaries who were flying on to Brazil. This was a nightmare. Desi Bouterse had contacts in Brazil, this was where he bought most of his arms and equipment. The Cascavels and Urutus were made there and some of his troops even came to Brazil for training. Crossing the border into French Guiana could now be difficult. There was a good chance the authorities had been alerted and somebody would be waiting to give us a nasty shock.

George had gone on one of his walkabouts, but later I tackled him about it. 'Anton's found you out.'

'No, no, that wasn't the man from the plane. He was an old friend.' George then threw a tantrum. Fuck's sake, man!

Anton sat there with a face like the Archangel Gabriel, as if to say, this is nothing to do with me and George is fucking everything up. George then began to tell me he had problems with Anton who was carrying a lot of money and had so far paid nothing towards the trip. Even better, Charlie and John L. now started to express their doubts about the sanity of this whole expedition.

'On this type of job all roads lead to hell, with nothing but grief all the way,' I told them. 'It's not like in the movies, there'll always be problems. Part of the job is to surmount them. We'll get out of this mess.'

It transpired Bouterse owned chunks of property in Belem and had lots of supporters in the town, so we got out quick. Next morning, George booked tickets for us all to travel by ferry, 400 miles up the Amazon to the town of Santarem to meet a local arms dealer, who'd buy weapons for us and ship them to Surinam. In the hotel, we'd seen posters of a modern, air-conditioned catamaran that sailed up and down the river, and thought we'd give it a go. When we got to the docks, the place was full of old wooden boats. Crowds of people carrying chickens, goats and pigs milled around. There was no sign of a catamaran. George spoke to a docker who led us to a one hundred-foot-long wooden boat. It was a double-decker, with hammocks strewn everywhere, and looked like something Vietnamese boat people escaped on. We couldn't risk going back to town, so we walked up the gang plank. George ripped open a brown paper parcel. Inside were rolls of coloured cotton material and bits of rope; they were our hammocks. There were no cabins, just open decks. At least we were on the upper deck, which was like being in first class.

We made our way to the back of the boat because that was the only place left where there was any room. It was hot and noisy, but at least we were getting out of Belem and all its problems. Santarem was three days away. Chugging along the Amazon was very pleasant, dozing on hammocks during the heat of the day and getting together in the evening for beers. We crossed the distinct dark line that seems to split the river at the point where fresh water from the Amazon rainforest meets sea water. However, despite the pleasures of the trip, I was still feeling nervous when we docked at the colourful town of Santarem.

George's contact was out of town. He turned up after a couple of days, but only to talk crap. There were no weapons; he couldn't even buy a camouflage T-shirt. You may have seen the film *A Bridge Too Far* – well, to me this was *A Trip Too Far*. A desperate feeling that we were all going to end up wearing handcuffs in some mosquito-ridden hell hole overwhelmed me. I'd reached my limit with George. Either I took control, or I went home. Leaving the others at the hotel, I took Anton with me to the local airport.

I went inside the first aircraft company office I came to and explained that I wanted to hire a plane to fly to French Guiana.

'Si señor, no problem.'

'Get your chart out I'll show you where we want to go. It's a French island called Langatabbetje.'

While the guy was working out the distance, 500 miles as the crow flies, he started asking me about the landing strip, only to stop in mid-sentence. 'Oh-oh, problem.'

'What problem?'

'Langatabbetje is marked as belonging to Surinam and there is a war on.'

I tried to bluff him by claiming we'd been told by our TV company that the island was French. I threw in a lot of chaff to try and confuse him, but he wasn't having it. He decided to check with the aviation authorities and get back to us in a couple of hours.

'In the meantime, do you want to look at the aircraft?' he asked.

Feigning calmness, I agreed and he took us outside to a twin-engine Baron beach craft. I pretended I was interested in the plane, but alarm bells were going off in my head. Checking us out with the aviation authorities was the last thing we wanted. All I wanted to do now was get out of there.

'Señor,' I told the guy, 'let me phone back to Europe and clear up this problem; maybe we'll have to fly to Cayenne. Forget about Langatabbetje, just work out a price for Cayenne. We'll be back later.' Bad move that Karl, bad move.

We needed to get on a ferry fast and travel back downriver to Macapá, which lies on the north side of the Amazon delta about a hundred miles up the coast from Belem. That was where we were headed, only to be diverted by George's foolishness. This boat was forty feet smaller than the last one and looked unstable. It was packed with people, but at least we were leaving Santarem. It's a beautiful place, I would have loved to have spent more time there, but not under those circumstances.

A MERCENARY'S TALE

The ferry took a pounding in a raging storm. The boat
pitched and rolled like crazy, people screamed with fear.
The crew slung a plastic sheet over the passengers to try
and keep us dry. Apparently there had been quite a
number of tragedies with overcrowded boats turning
turtle. We arrived in Macapá soaking wet, freezing cold
and severely pissed off. In yet another shanty-town hotel,
I got my map out and decided we had to cross the border
into French Guiana 250 miles away, at the remote outpost
of Oiapoque. The hotel owner put me in touch with a
local air taxi company. The company boss offered to come
down to the hotel and sort out a deal but I went to the
airport instead to make sure the plane wasn't held together
with Sellotape. As it turned out, the Piper Cherokee on
offer was perfect for our needs. Anton paid with a credit
card. It was his way of ending all the arguments with
George over the money.

The Piper Cherokee had been flying above the clouds
for fifteen minutes when I decided I couldn't resist the
temptation to have a little go. The pilot didn't speak a
word of English, only Portuguese, so I pointed at myself
and said, 'Señor, me little pilot.' He gave me the thumbs
up. We were happily flying along at 2,000 feet and the
next thing I knew, the pilot was snoring his head off. He
was asleep and there's me flying along like Captain Kirk! I
flew the plane for one hour while he dozed. He woke with
a start fifteen minutes before landing. Luckily, he quickly
came to his senses. I point at the digital timer, the course
and altitude. He looked quite relieved and took over with

a bit of a razzmatazz to show that he wasn't totally useless. He flew us very low over the village of Oiapoque, did a few tight turns and landed safely. We sat in a minibus at the airport in the pouring rain debating whether to go straight across the border. Before we could cross the river into French territory, we had to have our passports stamped by the local police. The bus driver took us to the concrete cop shop where the one policeman on duty was asleep in a back room. He came out to the front desk, and put his hat and tie on to look official. We all put our passports on the desk, and with great aplomb, he gave us all an exit stamp. Thank God for that. St Georges, the first town in French Guiana, isn't opposite Oiapoque, it's about three miles upriver. We haggled with a group of ten canoe owners for the best price for getting us there. In the end I grabbed one of them by the arm and asked, 'How much?'

'Fifty dollars'

'That'll do, let's go now.' As we travelled up the Oiapoque River, I was still sure that, at best, the French authorities or at worst, the enemy, would be waiting for us. A couple of houses appeared out of the jungle, then we spotted the jetty, with an eighty-foot long cargo boat moored to it. A group of people milled around, watching the boat being unloaded. I scanned the crowd for a uniform. No police there. We weren't out of the woods yet though, so to speak. Climbing onto the jetty, we were hustled by men who were trying make a few quid by taking us to a hotel.

'Monsieur, come with me.' Monsieur, not señor – at last we were on French territory.

'Monsieur, come with me. I take you to the police for a stamp on your passport.'

We needed time to think and to get our story straight, so we booked into a shack hotel, where the rooms were divided by sheets of canvas. It would do until we got our act together. After a couple of hours, I took Anton with me to see the local gendarme. He explained he was from Bordeaux in south-west France and hadn't seen any white people for a long time. I told him we'd been filming in the Amazon but that our gear had been sent to Cayenne. He was very understanding. He took our passports and – bang – we had entry stamps. He added, 'Tell your friends to come up and I'll stamp their passports as well.'

I couldn't believe it was so easy. After all the hassle we'd been through, we were back in French Guiana, and the wonderful thing was, nobody knew. Even now I can't believe that we were so lucky. Nobody picked up on the radio story and alerted Brazilian intelligence that a group of mercenaries were arriving in their country to go back to Surinam. Maybe they did and ignored us. Or, maybe they were watching us. If they were watching us, they would have had a good laugh, I'm sure of that.

There were only two ways out of St Georges, via a once-a-week ferry, or on an air taxi service to Kourou, which lay just off the main road between Cayenne and St Laurent. Next morning, out of the rain came two blue-and-white Cessnas; their pilots wore full uniform, as though they were flying a jumbo jet. As we approached Kourou, the pilot pointed out the Arianne rocket base, but I was looking to see if there were any police cars waiting. Not a soul about; the airport was shut. We'd arrived on a Sunday.

We took a cab to St Laurent after the taxi driver assured us that the checkpoint where we'd been nicked only stopped cars coming out of the town, not going in. Passing the roadblock, I squinted over to my left to see six Legionnaires hanging around outside the police building. One of them actually waved as we went past. Driving through the outskirts, the driver asked, 'What hotel, monsieur?' But I wasn't going to stop outside any hotel. I didn't want anyone clocking two taxis with six of us getting out with their baggage. Instead, we stopped in a side street and made our way separately towards The Star Hotel, where some of Ronnie's men hung out. I'd only been in the lobby thirty seconds when a white woman came over and asked, 'Did you bring any rockets with you?' I looked at her as though she was a lunatic, patted my pockets and said, 'No, I don't have any rockets on me. I don't know what you mean.'

She introduced herself as a Dutch journalist and added, 'I know who you are.'

'Look do us a favour, get lost.' Very rude, especially to a woman, but after what we'd been through, maybe you can understand my response. I recovered my composure and told her I'd try and speak later and tell her what was going on. Just then, Jan appeared out of the people milling around. He told us The Star was being watched by police and he whisked us out to the Toucan Hotel. We were so close now, it was crucial not to make a mistake. I told the rest of the boys to lie low, while I went with John to pick up my Browning from Henri. I knocked on the restaurant door. Henri's wife opened it, looked at me and said, 'Fermé.'

'Don't you remember me?' I asked

Marie Claire didn't understand, so she gestured for me to come inside. Henri was at the table eating with his family as I walked over to him. He looked at me blankly. I pointed at myself, 'Mercenaire Angleterre.' He jumped up from his seat, threw his arms around me, shook my hand and patted me hard, making gestures that said, 'You look so different.' I had looked fucked the last time I saw him, but back in England, on proper grub, I'd piled on the pounds; my hair was longer too. Now I didn't look too bad, though I should have done after that trip with George and John, or 'Psycho' as I was now starting to call him.

'Sit down. Eat with us,' gestured Henri.

I explained to Henri we had a group at the Hotel Toucan and he gestured for me to go and get them. The table was re-laid, and Marie Claire ran around getting food while Henri disappeared upstairs. He came back down with the Browning wrapped up in a piece of cloth, he'd cleaned and oiled it. Thank you Henri. I banged a magazine in and shoved the gun in the back of my pants. Noticing John didn't have a weapon, Henri put his hand inside his shirt and pulled out an old Walther P38 for him.

Our canoe slowed down as we went past the Isle Portal leper colony, which prompted thoughts again of Papillon and his escape. Charlie and John L. were fascinated by it. It was fascinating for me, too. I have this thing about places of human suffering – dungeons, concentration camps and death camps. Maybe I'm a bit weird.

Safely past the place, we headed out towards the middle of the river, the engine going flat out. I was a bit worried about coming under attack from a Surinam patrol boat – we only had my Browning, Psycho's P38 and a shotgun the boatman carried. He seemed confident enough standing up in the canoe, holding the tiller. Near Apatou he throttled back and cruised towards a fifteen-feet-high wooden ladder. As we drifted closer, I could see some of Ronnie's boys armed with machetes and shotguns. Looking for any faces I knew, I spotted Om Leo. He called out in his distinctive croaky voice, 'Karel, my friend, I knew you come back.' He threw his arms around me, shook my hand and asked, 'What you bring for me?' Nothing changes, does it? I dragged a short-sleeve khaki civvie shirt out of my bag. The greedy bastard's face dropped. I think he was expecting a Rolex.

'Where's your radio set?' I asked. He took me to a little basher with a radio inside and an antenna thrown up a tree. He switched it to the Stoelman's Island frequency and I grabbed the microphone. 'Message to Romeo Bravo, Kilo Papa has arrived.'

'Hey, Kilo Papa!' shouted a voice at the other end. Whoever answered was obviously well pleased to hear we were back. As we sailed off for Stoelman's Island, I could see Om Leo looking sadly at his shirt. It was never going to fit him – he was twice my width.

A big crowd was waiting at the landing stage on Langatabbetje. The news of our return had spread like wildfire. The new commandant was a black man in his mid-forties who must have weighed twenty-five stone. He stuck his hand out and announced 'Hello my friend, I'm Paco.' He spoke excellent English and you could see straight away he was intelligent. This made a change!

'Come to the office, Karel.' The office? Things were looking up. The office was, in fact, the jail in the old school. There was a desk with a Surinam flag, and posters hung on the walls. A little white guy with round, gold-rimmed glasses worked away on a typewriter. A brand-new American-made M16 assault rifle leant against his desk. There were even proper seats for guests. Paco explained that since we'd blocked the main road a lot of organisations in Holland had decided to give Ronnie some serious support. I'd been looking forward to meeting Henk but he'd gone off to buy weapons. The Twin Otter pilots were no longer there, either. They'd been freed. We left for Stoelman's Island promising Paco more fireworks to come.

Ronnie Brunswijk grinned like a schoolboy when he saw us and ran the last fifty yards to throw his arms around me. He kissed me and rubbed my head. 'Karel I knew you'd come back,' he said, beaming. 'When I heard you say Kilo Papa on the radio, I was so happy. I'm so pleased you come back.'

I introduced George Baker, then the two new soldiers. We told Ronnie all about our arrest, though I left out the story of our journey through Brazil. I'd made arrangements for George to have a private conversation with Ronnie to discuss finances for the group and Baker's political position in any future government. As we got up to Ronnie's house, a big, bearded, nasty-looking character swaggered down the steps followed by two bodyguards. He shot me a dirty look and stomped off. Ronnie told me that this dead-ringer for UNITA's rebel leader, Jonas Savimbi, was in fact an ex-lieutenant in the Dutch army.

'He doesn't want you here,' Ronnie explained. 'He thinks white mercenaries are no good, and that we can do the job alone. I told him no.' This lieutenant subsequently threatened to leave if we stayed, so Ronnie told him to sling his hook. Apparently he'd gone away to think about it. Cheeky bastard. We do all the work, secure the country, and then he wants to revel in it all. Ronnie also told me the man had come up with a marvellous military plan to overthrow the Bouterse regime. He was going to march up the road to Moengo with several hundred homeless bush negroes singing freedom songs in the hope that Bouterse would be so heartbroken and ashamed of himself that he'd step down. Bloody brilliant plan. I went for a stroll while George had his meeting with Ronnie.

George didn't look happy when he emerged. 'Karel, that man is crazy. I'm giving no more money to this organisation. I have to have a serious talk with you later.'

Now it was my turn for a private chat with Ronnie. I hadn't wasted my time while we'd been travelling through Brazil. I'd come up with an idea to attack Bouterse's armoured vehicles. Urutus and Cascavels weren't actually armoured plated. They were soft-skinned vehicles that were basically bulletproof, up to a certain calibre. A fifty-cal round would puncture them. But we didn't have any. We had to come up with something that would detonate on impact with an armoured vehicle. I decided to make my own rockets plus some 300-pound bombs that could be dropped from a Cessna. These bombs and rockets would explode on impact. It was simple. You'd just need a firing pin, cartridge, detonators, det cord and explosive. Planning all this out, I'd been like a mad scientist, working for more than fifty hours with a pad, pencil and ruler making drawings.

'The Surinam army are not going to sit there forever,' I told Ronnie, 'sooner or later they'll make a move. We can't keep throwing sticks of dynamite at the armoured vehicles. Let's try and use rockets.'

Ronnie thought it was a great idea, 'But how are you going to do it?' he asked.

We'd be like many other rebel armies and make our own weapons. I planned to go back across to French Guiana to find a man with a workshop who could make the rockets from my drawings.

The two Johns and Charlie would stay at Stoleman's and train the rebels, while I returned to St Laurent with George. Ronnie sent his number-one bodyguard, Gary, with us to sort out payment for the rockets and to make arrangements to keep me out of the clutches of the police.

As Gary slept in the boat under a tarpaulin, George decided to have a chat. It turned out George had told Ronnie he wanted to be president of Surinam when the war was won. In return, he would continue to back Ronnie financially. Apparently, as soon as George mentioned finances Ronnie said, 'Sure, you're the new president, don't worry about it.'

Now, George wasn't convinced Ronnie would honour the deal and, as a result, was very unhappy about the prospect of backing him. 'All Ronnie's interested in is money,' he complained to me, 'he wants money off me as quickly as possible. I can't back this organisation. I want to pay you guys for another month, then I'm stopping. I'm going to give you the ticket money to get back home – that's no problem, I'll pay all your expenses – but I can't go on with Brunswijk.' I was very disappointed George was pulling out, but not to worry. now Ronnie had political backing, he could pay our wages. It wasn't a massive blow.

As we approached St Laurent, I could the see searchlight of an S-Boat, sweeping backwards and forwards on its patrol downriver from Albina. I thought to myself, 'One day I'm going to get rid of that boat with a bloody great bomb.' Gary recruited a man in the shanty town to scout ahead and make sure the route to the Hotel Toucan was clear. The hotel owner, Robert, was waiting by a side door with a set of keys. We nipped up a back staircase and Robert opened up two very basic rooms.

They did have at least have air conditioning, which blasted out cold air.

Later, George knocked on my door, a look of alarm on his face.

'Karel, I have to go. The police are looking for us.'

Straight away I thought of Jan who was back in St. Laurent. 'How do you know this, George?' I asked.

'I saw one of the boys in the street. He told me, "Be careful, the police, they are looking for you, they know you are here." I don't want to go to jail, I'm leaving now.'

I told him to calm down. There was one man who would know the truth. I nipped round to Henri's restaurant. Through an English speaker in the restaurant, I was able to make Henri understand what I wanted to know. When the restaurant closed, he went off on a scouting mission. He came back about half an hour later and told me that everything was OK. He'd been to the gendarmerie barracks, where he had brought the subject up about the Jungle Commandos and mercenaries.

'There was nothing said, so I think everything's cool at the moment,' he assured me. 'But you must keep out of sight, that's for sure.'

I went straight back to the hotel and knocked on George's door. There was no answer. The door was unlocked and the room was in disarray. He must have packed his stuff in thirty seconds flat. He'd even left one of his shoes and his hat. George had gone without even a goodbye. Oh well, there goes the end of an era. I must admit, I felt quite sad at the thought of it. Farewell George.

CHAPTER
11

I had been looking for Jan in the lobby of the Star Hotel, when I'd spotted the French Intelligence man who had interviewed me before I'd been expelled. Then he saw me. A look of alarm crossed my face, I shrugged my shoulders and gave him a sigh of resignation that said, okay caught again! He smiled, 'How are you? We've been waiting for you to come back. There's no problem, though I need to talk to you.'

I followed the man, Francois, to his room upstairs where he told me all about Paco, the Dutch Lieutenant and the French stance on the war in their back yard. I told Francois exactly why I was in French Guiana and my plans for making rockets. He told me French Intelligence wanted to find a safe house for me to operate from. A great idea in my opinion. Francois gave me another number to phone in an emergency. From now on, I'd refer to French Intelligence as Room Sixteen, the number of the hotel room he was renting.

I wandered back down to the lobby to find Jan. As I approached, he nodded his head as if to say don't come near me. I walked straight past, sat down at the bar and ordered a beer. The place was almost deserted but Jan was panicking. I finished my beer, gave Gary a nod and made my way back to the Toucan.

Later at the Toucan, Jan was livid with me. 'Why are you dealing with the French, Karl? You work for the Jungle Commandos.'

'Of course I do Jan, just like you,' I replied.

'We don't trust the French. I don't like the French police.'

Of course he didn't like the French police. Intelligence had just told me a few home truths about our friend Jan. They'd tapped his phone and listened in to him calling Paramaribo. The French knew a damn sight more about what was going on in Surinam than Ronnie. Indeed, they were to be my way out of all this, so I had to work with them, but at the same time, I couldn't afford to alienate Ronnie.

Jan was flatly against me staying in a French safe house. He wanted me to stay on a farm belonging to Robert, who owned the Toucan. I told Jan, 'Don't forget, your job is not just to hide me away but to find me a man with a workshop.'

The only such man he knew was in Cayenne. When he told me, I exploded. 'If you think I'm travelling to Cayenne through that roadblock, forget it. There's got to be somebody in St Laurent with a workshop.' Later, Robert told me they'd found a man to do the work and he eventually came to see me at the farm. I managed to phone Room Sixteen and tell them the arrangements. I discovered the only way to the farm safe house was actually through the roadblock. It was only after Room Sixteen assured me I wouldn't be arrested that I agreed to go.

Next morning, I travelled with Robert in a windowless van. As we approached the police roadblock on the road to Cayenne, I climbed in the back; inside my bag I had a Beretta sub-machine gun. My heart was in my mouth, but the Legionnaire on duty knew Robert and waved him through. A couple of hundred yards up the road, we turned left onto a jungle road. After half an hour, we were in the middle of nowhere at a farm hacked out of the hot, steaming jungle. Cattle and a horse grazed in the one field; there was a barn, and a bungalow with a bulldozer and other bits of machinery lying about. A black man wearing wellies, filthy trousers, a T-shirt and a dirty cotton baseball cap wandered over. Robert introduced me to him, but the introduction was more of a humiliation: he pointed at the guy like he was a loony and said, 'Haiti.' The man from Haiti spoke no English.

The kitchen in the bungalow stank; it had a bottled gas cooker, a filthy sink and one tap. Robert pulled out a set of keys and opened the door to a living room straight from a Hammer horror movie. The whole place was covered in huge cobwebs, which Robert immediately set about ripping down. There was a sofa and in the corner a bed. Photographs of naval ships hung on the walls, and there was a sepia picture of a couple taken in the 1920s. Robert explained that the couple were his parents. From the few French words I knew, I gathered his father had been in the navy. Robert pointed at the phone and gave me the number for the Toucan Hotel. Then he pointed at three o'clock on his watch, and said 'Jungle Commando ici.' He shook my hand, climbed in his van and disappeared. The Haitian stared at me from the kitchen. I put my bag down and he still stood there, staring. The guy really was mad. I felt quite sorry for myself. The Toucan was no luxury paradise, but this place – fucking hell.

In the afternoon, Jan, Bonanza and Max arrived in a minibus loaded with supplies: cases of beer, cigarettes, food, a ghetto blaster and about half a dozen cassette tapes. They told me a Belgian guy who owned a workshop would arrive in the morning. They also gave me a warning: 'Look Karl, be very, very careful. Bouterse's men think you're in St Laurent. You're alone now, so be on your guard.' I realised this was not just a cautionary tale. I knew it was true because Room Sixteen had warned me as well.

When they left, I set about cleaning the room out. The process of ripping the rest of the cobwebs away revealed a family of tarantulas, great big hairy bastards with blue tips on their front legs. The place was also swarming with cockroaches and mosquitoes. Mind you, it wasn't as bad as some of the places I've stayed at in Kings Cross! I had to be alert for banditos. There wasn't another house or building for miles, I could hear any vehicles coming along the road from a great distance. The place was so remote a car would go past every few hours. The main entrance to the house was at the back, out of view of the main road. I sat on the veranda with the Beretta Model 12 for protection. I covered it up with an old piece of tarpaulin to avoid alarming the Haitian farm hand. I tucked the Browning in the waistband of my jeans. I'd stacked wooden boxes at the end of the veranda to cut off any of the view of me from the road. I could sit behind the boxes and see straight up the road. The jungle was just fifty yards away. If the shit hit the fan, I could be into the woods before anyone realised.

I telephoned Room Sixteen to let Francois know I was at the Jungle Commando safe house and settled down for a long night. At least now I had some music. Most of the cassettes were crazy Surinamese songs. There was only one I recognised – 'Smooth Operator', by Sade. I must have played it about thirty times; I'll never play it again. I fiddled with the radio and tuned into a station in Cayenne, where the disc jockey spoke French with a Manchester accent!

I waited half the next day before Robert arrived with a white bloke. He was Belgian and spoke English. Jacques was stocky, about fifty years old, tough and a bit of a colonial type. He'd lived in Zaire (now the Democratic Republic of Congo) He was now married to a Surinamese woman and ran a workshop from his home in St Laurent. We sat down and I showed him my drawings of the rockets I wanted him to make. I agreed a price of four thousand quid for forty rockets and two launching tubes. He'd make the launching tubes and the warhead of the rockets. I would arm them and make the motor to propel the rockets. Jacques would return in a couple of days and tell me how he was getting on.

Back at the ranch, I found a saddle in the barn and spent time riding the horse around like John Wayne, chasing the cows up and down the field, just to give me something to do. A couple of days later, Jacques arrived and told me he was progressing well. 'How can you stand to be stuck out in this place with bad guys looking for you?' he asked.

'It's not pleasant, but it's part of the job,' I replied.

'Do you want to come to St Laurent?'

Now, whereas doing a John Wayne impression was fun for a while, most of the time I spent on the farm was sheer bloody boredom. Nights were a bit tricky, because I didn't like going to sleep in case Bouterse's henchmen turned up. I was convinced they knew where I was. Don't forget my fears about Jan. So all in all, I felt as though I could do with a change of scene.

'Okay, let's go,' I told him. I put my little tote bag together and we drove back down towards St Laurent. A couple of miles from town, I climbed into the boot to avoid being seen. Ten minutes later the car stopped, the boot popped open and there was Jacques's smiling face. He parked right outside the house so one of his neighbours, who was a gendarme, wouldn't see me. Inside, Jacques's home was very European, with a proper working fridge and electric lights. There was music on and a TV blared in the living room. A pretty woman, much younger than Jacques, said hello. Her name was Helen and she was from Surinam's Javanese community. She had a little boy in tow. Didier was the cutest kid I'd ever seen. 'Say hello to Jean-Francois,' Helen told him. (I used a false name to prevent the boy telling the neighbours my real name.) I must confess, Didier was such a bundle of fun that he took my mind off matters in hand, if only for a few minutes.

Jacques took me to his workshop in a lean-to next to the house. He pulled back a tarpaulin under the workbench to reveal six rockets and the two launching tubes. The rockets looked a bit on the heavy side, but we didn't expect to have to fire them far. From a hundred yards we could hit armoured cars on the road. One problem was that Jacques hadn't been able to find the correct diameter pipe to fit inside the tube. There was no stockholder in St Laurent, so he'd had to make do with what he had. He'd used the same size tube as the launchers, then cut it down and welded it back together to fit inside the launching tube. It was a very difficult job, and he'd done it well. Things were looking up. After giving me the chance to survey his excellent work, Jacques took me back to the farm.

One night, I was sat at the farm, bored out of my skull, when the phone rang. I was cagey when I picked it up and said, 'Allo'. It was only Aitchen, a Chinese guy who ran a supermarket in Saint Lauren. He supplied ninety-nine per cent of the food supplies for Ronnie's war effort.

'Karl,' he told me, 'the French police are coming to see you. Don't worry, it's not a problem.'

I put on a little act. 'How did they know I'm here? Who told them?'

'Karl, please don't worry, everything is OK. They're only coming to talk with you, there's no problem whatsoever.'

I continued with the pretence. 'Who the hell told them? This is fucking ludicrous.'

Aitchen rang off. Maybe it wasn't the police. Perhaps it was a trap. I kept the Beretta by my side. It was pitch-black outside. Simple Simon the Haitian was in his room – I could hear music playing on his radio. I went out onto the balcony to listen for a vehicle. An hour later I heard the sound of a car in the distance. A car pulled up fifty yards short of the farm gate; the lights went out, the engine died. Well used to seeing in the dark, I watched a man in a light-coloured shirt hop over the fence. Here we go. I looked again. It was Francois. Why didn't he just come through the gate? He'd made a big mistake because, from the road, the land he'd jumped on to looked quite grassy, but it was in fact rough terrain. He tripped over. As he dusted himself off, I put the sub-machine gun out of the way and slipped the Browning back in the waistband. I decided to give Francois a fright. As he came round the side of the bungalow, I sneaked up behind him and shouted 'Boo!'

Francois nearly jumped out of his pants. 'Oh my God! Karl! Karl, how are you, my friend?'

'What's going on, Francois?'

'No problem. Come with us, we have a little surprise for you.'

Before we left, I took the Beretta from under the mattress and stashed it inside a tractor tyre lying on its side in the barn. I put a sack over it and covered the whole lot in cobwebs. Francois opened the back door and I jumped in. The driver turned around; it was another spook. He didn't speak much English, but he shook my hand warmly. They took me to the driver's house for a slap-up meal. Unfortunately, I'd already eaten a huge duck-egg omelette that night, and I couldn't face anything to eat. However, the French are finicky over food and I didn't wish to be rude, so I told them I had an iffy stomach. We spent all evening drinking red wine and talking business. Then they took me back to the farm.

By the end of the second week, Jacques had made thirty rockets, but he needed more money to continue the job. I arranged for Aitchen, the store owner, to pay. When Jacques left, I spoke to Room Sixteen, who wanted me to go back to the Toucan so they could talk to me.

'Bouterse's men are still in town looking for you,' Francois warned me. 'Stay out of the way in the Toucan, you only have a couple of days left.' With one of the boys translating, Robert took me to my room. He pulled back the bed to reveal a service trapdoor leading to an air-conditioning duct. The duct ran for twenty feet and emerged at the side of the hotel, fifteen feet from the ground. I hoped I didn't have to use this escape hatch, because the duct was full of cobwebs and spiders. A couple of gofers turned up at the hotel. Aitchen wouldn't part with the money for Jacques. When it fell dark I zigzagged through the back streets to the supermarket. Aitchen ushered me into a stock room. He had the money, he was just worried the gofers would vanish with it. He handed me a brown envelope with 20,000 French francs inside. 'Thank you, I shall be back for the balance in a couple of days.' He also gave me 400 Marlboro and 1,000 francs.

In Jacques's workshop, I took another look at the rockets. They were exactly as I'd drawn, them only heavier. His son Didier sat on my knee as I explained to Jacques that I'd only managed to get two grand. His eyes lit up, he'd only expected a couple of hundred quid to buy materials to finish the job. He explained he'd be finished the next day and I'd be able to go 'upstairs' – the JC codeword for going upriver to Stoelman's Island.

As we shared a bottle of Ricard to celebrate, Jacques said, 'Moment Monsieur, I have something to show you.' He disappeared into the living room and returned with a copy of *Raids* magazine. In the middle there were photographs of John Richards and I, all kitted up. Jacques wanted me to autograph the magazine!

Squinting through the metal louvre shutters in my room at the Toucan, I watched a black limousine pulled up on the other side of the street, full of coloured guys. Another car appeared. I couldn't see the number plates properly, but they seemed slightly unusual. Something clicked in my head then: they were diplomatic plates. Bouterse's boys were here. A knock at the door. Shit. It was Robert. 'Karl,' he called, 'Karl, open the door.' He came and pointed down towards the street: 'Bouterse men, Bouterse!' I dragged the wardrobe up against the door, pulled the bed to the wardrobe and opened the trap door. Back to the balcony to watch and wait. I looked through the louvres again, convinced this was Naylam's gang from Cayenne. They weren't going to shoot me in broad daylight. They were trying to point the finger at me, follow me round screaming for the police to have me arrested. It would have the same result as a shoot-out, I'd end up on a plane to Paris. My tote bag was packed, I was ready to go down the escape hole. I watched as two black men in suits and sunglasses walked towards the two parked limos and climbed in the rear doors, one in each car. They sat there. They'd probably been to the hotel to talk to Robert. Not a very covert operation. Three or four minutes later, they drove off.

At last the rockets were ready. Jacques left them hidden at a filling station for the boys to collect. I had another meeting with Room Sixteen. On the way back to Stoelman's Island, I pondered over that meeting. Room Sixteen were fed up of Mr. Naylam. They'd had him under heavy surveillance and discovered that he was prone to picking up rent boys. They also knew he carried a gun, which even though he was a diplomat, was illegal. They set him up with a rent boy who caused a massive argument in the street. The cops swooped and – surprise, surprise – they found the gun. Naylem was kicked out of the country.

With me in the boat was an out-of-work French pilot called Jean. I arranged with Ronnie to hire him for £250 a week to fly the Cessna. I wanted him to become Jean Le

Bomb and drop explosives from the plane. When we arrived at Stoelly, Ronnie's eyes were like saucers as he examined Jacques's rockets and the launching tubes. I'd only been away three weeks and John L. and Charlie were already talking about going home. John Richards had pushed them to the limit. Their nerves were wrecked, stressed out listening to this little arrogant prick, strutting around in his Foreign Legion beret. The story slowly came out that John had been bullying everyone. He'd punished the JCs with physical exercise to the point at which some of them had actually puked up on the edge of the airstrip with exhaustion. But there was more. While I'd been away, a doctor and his two teenage daughters had arrived at Stoelman's Island. They'd run away from Paramaribo, and had made their way through the badlands to safety. John had mercilessly tormented the poor daughters. That was enough for me. I took him to a room and grabbed him by the throat; I was purple with rage. 'Believe me, John,' I told him, 'I am going to hurt you very badly soon. This time you have gone far too fucking far.'

He feigned innocence. 'Hang on Karl, I've been training those men.'

'You shit. You have nothing to say any more. From now on you will do exactly what I tell you. Do you understand me?'

'All right, all right.'

I must admit, it flashed through my mind to pull the Browning out and put the psychotic little twat out of his misery there and then. However, I decided instead to get

him out of the way for a week by sending him to the front
line to collect explosives and bring them back. There was
a stash of explosives at Stoelman's Island, but he didn't
know that.

'You're going to the front line John, get out of my sight.'

Psycho wasn't the only one who'd been throwing his
weight about. The Dutch lieutenant who hated white
mercs had not gone home; instead, he'd started ordering
my guys around. He'd come up with a suicidal plan to
blow up the concrete bridge at Moengo. I'd already
destroyed the Bailey bridge that sat on top of it. He'd
drawn a plan for his lunatic mission on the blackboard in
the guesthouse.

I'd had just about enough of him. 'Right boys, do you
know where he is at the moment?

'He'll be up at the radio station, he's always there.'

I pushed the radio station guards aside and burst
through the door. The bastard was sitting there with
Ronnie discussing something.

I pulled out the Browning, 'You speak English?

'Yes.'

'Listen shithead, you ever....'

Ronnie tried to interrupt.

'Wait a minute, Ronnie.' I pointed the gun at the
shithead lieutenant. 'You arsehole, you ever say one more
word to any of my men and I'll blow your fucking brains
out. Stay away from them, stay away from the guesthouse.
Draw on my blackboard again and I'll shoot you, do you
understand?'

He looked at me in shock. Prick. He was still shaking as I stormed out. Ronnie followed me. 'Karel, what's the problem?'

'Ronnie that man is no good, believe me,' I told him. 'Why do you think he wanted us out of here? He hasn't come to help you, he's come to overthrow you.' Room Sixteen had told me the lieutenant actually apparently worked for a man called Andre, a communist politician in exile who apparently had a particularly nasty reputation. 'Get rid of him, Ronnie, the man's trouble. I'm not saying he's a Bouterse man, but his interests are not the same as yours. He's a black man but he doesn't give a shit about the black people here.'

I didn't want to go into too much detail and have to reveal to Ronnie where my information came from. Thanks to Room Sixteen, I seemed to know more than Ronnie did at that stage. I knew for a fact that the Surinam army were biding their time, training up men ready for a big push. Eight hundred soldiers had been assembled at Moengo ready for the attack. Ronnie's men, who should have known this, didn't even bother to check out troop strengths. I also knew a lot about our friend Paco, the commandant at Langatabbetje. His intentions were the same as those of the Dutch lieutenant, to overthrow Ronnie but with the help of the CIA. Room Sixteen told me it would happen soon.

All I could do was carry on with the job and try to stay sane.

* * *

While John Richards was away collecting explosives from the front line, we set about testing the rockets. I put what explosive we had into the head of the rocket, along with a twelve-bore shotgun cartridge, safety dets and a charge that would go off inside the rocket on impact. We used gunpowder as a propellant. After a lot of messing, we got the rockets to work. Sometimes we'd get it right, other times it would all go wrong as we tried to find the correct mixture of powder for the propellant.

One of the rockets misfired. It went off with a big puff of smoke but the missile remained firmly in the launching tube. From behind me came a long, loud and exaggerated laugh. As I crouched down fiddling with the battery and ignition wires, I looked around to see the Dutch lieutenant. Everybody else watching the proceedings had seen successful rockets being fired; this joker only turned up when the misfire happened and tried to make a big deal out of it. That was it for me. Anger welled up inside. I jumped up off the ground, pulled my Browning out, cocked the hammer and took the safety off. I slowly walked towards him, the gun pointed directly at his face. 'Listen, you piece of shit,' I said, 'that's just what we need here isn't it, help like you.' I looked at all the men milling around and said, 'This is a man who's come to help you. This is how he helps, he stands here laughing and at night he goes back to his house and plays with his prick.' I snarled, 'Listen motherfucker, get off this airstrip now, get out of town. If I see you again I will kill you.' He literally ran off towards the hospital. I holstered the pistol and stood laughing with the boys. Half an hour later the Dutchman got his kit together and jumped in a boat, never to be seen again.

I planned to drop home-made napalm bombs from our plane onto Albina and Moengo, where the army were massing troops. We only had a Cessna, not a fighter-bomber, so we could only drop one bomb at each location. I'd make the bombs from large gas cylinders by taking out the valve from the top and screwing in a three-foot long extender fuse. On top I'd put in a T-connection with two pieces of pipe sticking out horizontally. Each pipe would have an elbow and two more sections of pipe. It would look like a candelabra, but instead of sticking in candles we'd put in shotgun cartridges. I'd take out the wadding and shot from the cartridges and replace it with two safety detonators. Then I'd tape det cord to these two safety dets and feed the cord down through the tubes into the bomb. I asked Ronnie to send some men to get hold of gas cylinders. We made drogue parachutes out of green nylon shower curtain.

Now, Ronnie liked the idea of having the bombs ready, but for some reason he didn't appear to be in any rush to use them. He didn't seem to want to antagonise the army. What was going on with the man? Ronnie's behaviour was becoming more and more worrying. The enemy was knocking on his door and what he doing about it? Playing video games in his house most of the time.

It didn't matter for the moment, because there wasn't any fuel for the plane. There was no avgas to spare in St

Laurent, so Ronnie sent men to Cayenne to find some. While we were waiting for fuel, the boys took me to see a gendarme called Pierre, who manned a small wooden fortress police station a few miles upriver on the French side at Grand Santi. Francois had told me that this was the man I should contact when I was at Stoelman's Island. Pierre wanted to have a look around Langatabbetje. Don't forget that, to all intents and purposes, Langatabettje belonged to the Surinam government, not the rebels. So for the French to go there it had to be highly unofficial. The solution we came up with was to organise a football match between his men and the Jungle Commandos. That way Pierre could stroll around the island and I'd show him whatever he needed to see.

We were still waiting for avgas when Patrick Chauvel arrived back on Stoelman's Island. This time he had brought with him the millionaire publisher of *Soldier of Fortune* magazine. Robert K. Brown is a giant of a man, not fat but heavy-duty, with legs and arms like barrels. I looked up at him and shook hands. Patrick introduced the man with Bob Brown as Derry Gallagher. Patrick managed to throw in that Derry had been an assassin in Vietnam. There was another guy there, Bob McKenzie. At that time, I didn't realise it, but Bob was a military hero. He was a soldier's soldier, severely wounded with the 101st Airborn in Vietnam and then went on to become a captain in the Rhodesian SAS. The last member of the party was Patrick's pretty blonde girlfriend, Delphine. They'd heard I was staying on a farm near St Laurent and had tracked the place down, but arrived a couple of days after I'd left. Later that night, I met up with them at the bar on Stoelman's Island. I say bar – it was really a couple of tables on the veranda of the general store.

Bob Brown had dressed up for the evening in uniform and boots. There was a real aura about him. If ever there was a genuine John Wayne living in the United States, this was the guy. He'd been a captain in the Green Berets and a member of the original A-teams that went into Vietnam early in the war. Now, as well as running *Soldier of Fortune* magazine, he owned a motel in Boulder, Colorado, where rootin', tootin' boys from all over the world went for an audience with Bob. The assassin was Bob's bodyguard – a nice enough bloke, but a terrible poser. He liked wearing Raybans even when it was dark. Bob McKenzie was quietly spoken and very unassuming.

I went back to the guesthouse for the boys. Charlie had been in the Rhodesian Grey Scouts. The conversation was so good we went through eighty bottles of beer that night. The next morning there was still no word from Psycho. No doubt he'd be in the badlands giving somebody a bad time. Bob Brown came down to the guesthouse with huge holdalls full of equipment he wanted to give us. There was thousands of dollars' worth of gear: uniforms, webbing, boots and a field hospital in a bag that was worth a couple of thousand dollars alone.

'There you go, Karl,' Bob said, throwing it all on the floor, 'that's yours.' Knives, compasses, bits of para cord, energy drinks, loads of stuff, it was unbelievable. There were even walkie-talkies and an armoured sniper scope. Then Bob told me that he wanted to present me with an Al Mar special forces survival escape resistance and evasion knife. It was like a Bowie knife, worth four hundred dollars and – unfortunately – no good to me. I'd already been given a pilot's survival knife by Bob McKenzie. That would do me just nice. But Mr. Brown insisted I stand with him and have my photograph taken being presented with this Al Mar knife. I couldn't say no under the circumstances.

Later on, I wandered over to their house. 'Hey you've arrived just in time,' Bob Brown told me. 'I've got something here for you.' It was a medal. They were going to present it to Ronnie, but they'd decided he was a lunatic and gave it to me instead. Without any pomp and circumstance, and thankfully with no more photographs for the magazine, he gave me the medal. The inscription read 'Soldier of Fortune Convention'. I walked back to the guesthouse wearing it and told the boys that I'd just been presented with the VNC.

'VNC?' they enquired.

'It stands for Very Nice Chap and I'm going to wear it from now on with great pride. Don't be jealous, boys.'

I actually wound up giving the VNC to my nephew, who is in a heavy metal band. He stuck it on his leather jacket with his other badges and wears it to this day when he's playing!

CHAPTER 12

Ronnie finally found some avgas but it was just enough for twenty minutes' flying time. Our leader wanted to take the Cessna for a joy ride. However, I diplomatically suggested the precious fuel might be better used for a couple of dummy bomb runs and to test out the drogue parachute. I had an idea to use the rockets as cluster bombs. I could put high explosive inside them with some more shrapnel and drop them ten at a time over Bouterse's troops. We did two bomb runs near Stoelman's Island, one with a heavy bomb and the second using the small cluster bombs. Ronnie wanted the journalists to see it, so when we dropped the heavy bomb, Bob McKenzie from *Soldier of Fortune* sat in the co-pilot's seat while I perched on top of the large bomb to launch it from the open doorway. I attached a piece of plastic pipe to the footstep in the cabin doorway. The drogue parachute was stuffed inside the plastic pipe and attached to the gas bottle bomb. When I pushed the bomb out, it would drag the drogue out of the plastic pipe and deploy. There wasn't a lot we could do with just twenty minutes' fuel, but the bombs worked. Just before the *Soldier of Fortune* guys pulled out, I asked Bob McKenzie if he fancied taking charge of our operation. He told me that I was already doing a good job, coming from a man like Bob McKenzie, that was a real feather in my cap. They left after a few days, promising to keep in touch.

All this waiting about was becoming frustrating. John L. and Charlie had been in Surinam for a month and had not even seen the front line. I had to get Ronnie away from his video games and have a serious talk with him. I finally managed to get Ronnie away from the TV screen long enough to have a chat to him about the way things were going. Ronnie believed all was well: 'We don't have to do any more Karel,' he told me, 'we don't have to take any chances.'

I was flabbergasted. 'We can't sit here indefinitely with the main road blocked. What are you going to achieve by sitting around?'

'What can the army do, Karel?'

'I'll tell you what the army can do. They can strengthen themselves up and while your boys are all sleeping and smoking dope up on the main road they'll come and take it back. I tell you now, if they do take the main road back it will be very difficult for us to reclaim it. We've got to do something, we can't just sit here.'

A lot of people had come out to Surinam to help Ronnie keep the war going to a final victory. I told him, 'Let's take Moengo and push on up towards the capital. Then we can say we really achieved something.'

My plan was to block off Paramaribo on both sides, shut the city's airport permanently and keep the capital in a state of siege, forcing the government to step down. I was sure it could be done.

Changing tack somewhat, Ronnie then started ranting on to me about Paco, the commandant at Langatabbetje. 'I've been finding out from my boys that Paco is making some monkey business behind my back,' he told me. 'That man is dangerous.'

I promised to go down river to Langatabbetje to find out what I could. I didn't want Ronnie's secret service going down there and fucking things up. From where I was sitting, Paco actually looked a lot more promising as a leader than Ronnie did. In fact, I knew from Room Sixteen exactly what Paco was up to. He was bringing in a bunch of Cubans from Miami to help us win the war. They were the expatriate Cubans who train in the Florida Everglades hoping to one day overthrow Fidel Castro. Once we'd defeated Bouterse, they were going to jump off from Surinam to invade Cuba. It all sounded good on paper. These things always do, but walking around with shoulder holsters and wearing Raybans doesn't get the job done. You've got to get your hands dirty; it's hard and it's dangerous. Now I understood Ronnie's paranoia. Believe it or not, I didn't want Ronnie hurt. Pushing him aside was one thing, but I didn't want them killing him.

I pressed Ronnie to tell me when the next delivery of fuel for the Cessna would be arriving, because I wanted to start dropping bombs for real. 'Karel,' he replied, 'I told you before, the gasoline is no panic. We don't need it right now.' Ronnie was playing for time for something, probably waiting to see what would transpire with Paco. That's why he was in no great rush to make any moves. But I was sick of biding my time. I told Ronnie I was going down to St Laurent. It was better than being sat on my arse in Stoelman's Island eating rice and shit. Then I said to him, 'By the way Mr. Baker's gone, do you know that? Mr. Baker ain't paying us any more, so how are you fixed for money to pay our wages?'

'Oh yeah, Karel, you know me. You don't worry.'

I grabbed a pencil and paper and wrote in big letters, 'When are you going to pay us?'

Ronnie looked hurt, he said with sincerity, 'Hey Karel, I get some money. I give you plenty money.' Hmmm, we'd see.

I went down river with John L., Charlie and Jean Le Bomb. Gary came with us to arrange credit with Robert at the Toucan Hotel, and to see his girlfriend. I was surprised Ronnie could spare Gary, his top bodyguard, because I'd noticed there were a lot more minders around now; Paco was obviously getting to him. When we arrived at Langatabbetje, Paco was in a meeting with three men from Holland. One was Paul, another was a Javanese bloke called Glen Chung and the third was a Hindustani, whose name I didn't catch. Paco looked nervous. He shook my hand and, with an exaggerated slap on my back, he said, 'How are you, my friend? How is it with Ronnie on Stoelman's?'

Armed with the information I had about Paco from Room Sixteen, I couldn't decide whether to make the first move or let Paco do the running. I'd offer him a carrot see if he went for it. 'I'll tell you how it is with Ronnie,' I said. 'I'm getting pissed off with him, he's not doing anything and he's beginning to get a bit paranoid as well.'

Paco didn't bite but he gave Paul a shifty glance.

'This thing is going nowhere,' I went on, 'so me and the boys are heading for St Laurent until Ronnie decides what he wants to do. Can you arrange a boat for me?'

Paul and his group were leaving on a boat that evening; we'd go with them. It seemed to me that Paul was in league with Paco. Why did a politician travel all this way from Holland and not go to see Ronnie, but instead spent his time chatting with one of Ronnie's underlings? When we stopped for a night in a village just above the Apatou rapids, I took Paul to one side and said, 'I'm very suspicious that you and Paco are up to something. Don't misunderstand me – I know that what you're doing is for the good. I'm behind you, I am not here fighting for Ronnie Brunswijk, I'm fighting for a cause – to get rid of Desi Bouterse – and I'll use any means to get rid of that bastard.'

Paul is a very pleasant, polite, educated man who speaks excellent English. But don't forget, he's also a politician. 'We don't mean any harm to Ronnie,' he told me. 'Ronnie's a good man. OK, he's lost his way a bit at the moment but he's OK. We don't want to harm him.'

Funny how he mentioned twice that they didn't want to harm Ronnie. That suggested to me that the plot was a bit deeper than Paul was making out. I suspected someone, somewhere would knock Ronnie off fairly soon. To my mind, Ronnie's paranoia was well founded. I'd noticed that Langatabbetje was buzzing with strange looks and people whispering. Plots were certainly afoot. Even the head man in the village had heard on the jungle drums that Ronnie's rebels were falling apart. While I'd been isolated at Stoelman's, farting about and dropping bombs, quite a bit of monkey business had been going on elsewhere. We had to keep a lid on it. An attempt on Ronnie's life would cause civil war among the rebels and that's when Bouterse would strike.

We arrived in St Laurent as human cargo under a tarpaulin sheet before nipping through the back streets to the safety of the Toucan. We weren't in too much danger; Jan was in Europe, trying to do a deal to sell the hijacked Twin Otter. I met with Francois in Room Sixteen at the Star Hotel. I knew Paul was going back to a big meeting in Holland to try and come up with a political solution for Ronnie to stand down. I also knew for a fact that Brunswijk was never going to stand down. Ronnie was king of the castle, and he'd remain king by hook or by crook. While the rebels were all deciding what to do, Room Sixteen thought it might be an idea for me to take my boys into the badlands and harass the army at Moengo, where 800 troops had assembled. Bouterse's men would then say, 'Hang on. Those bush negroes are supposed to be chopping each other to bits and pieces. How come they were up here giving us hell?' The French would add to the confusion by running a psy-ops campaign through their spies. I'd asked Paul whether it was true that the CIA would getting involved on our side. He looked taken aback but he did admit, 'Yes we have friends in the United States who are going to help supply us with weapons.' However, he warned it could take months. I'd been expecting couple of weeks, not the next few months. I didn't want to be hanging around for that long.

Next day we had a bit of a surprise. We were all sat on the terrace at the Toucan, watching out for any bad guys, when a bad guy in a cowboy hat wandered up. It was John Richards. He greeted us with that Cockney accent, 'Fucking hell, where've you been? I've been looking all over for you.'

Since I'd last seen him, I'd finally decided to get rid of John, and so I took him upstairs to give him the news. 'It ain't the first time you've behaved like that, is it John?' I told him. 'You're doing it all the time. You've lost it. What you need to do is go home and have a rest. In other words, fuck off.' John wasn't happy with that; he was going to make a big fuss and complain to Ronnie. Well, he could complain to whoever he liked – I knew no one would listen to him. What I didn't need him doing just now was shouting his mouth off in St Laurent. What was I going to do? I finally decided to play it cool for a while, then take him with me to the badlands and sack him once and for all there. Then he could travel back to St Laurent on his own and make as much noise as he liked; I wouldn't be around to take the flack.

Two white men sat on the pavement outside the Toucan hotel looking forlorn, pissed off and penniless. They kept staring at us as we sat on the veranda eating dinner. 'Those guys are looking for a job,' I said. We sent Psycho over to check them out. He brought the pair of them over. I'd been right. They were Belgian brothers, Patrick and Luke. They'd both served in the Belgian paras. They spoke excellent English and, compared to Psycho at least, were extremely intelligent. They'd seen us on TV in Belgium and had sold their car along with everything they possessed to raise the money for the air fare to see Surinam for themselves. Their return flight wasn't for a couple more weeks and they'd run out of money. They'd had nothing to eat and had been sleeping on the beach by the old jail for the last couple of nights. I could find some use for them. At the very least, they could make up our numbers on the trip to the front line. Psycho seemed to think I'd been bluffing about getting rid of him. I was happy enough about that for now, but I would certainly dump him when the time was right.

I treated Patrick and Luke to a slap-up meal. My God, they were starving. The pair of them each had a starter, a main course, dessert, coffee, Cognac and a cigar. Patrick in particular had impressed me during our conversation over their dinner; he would prove extremely useful as an interpreter.

As we set off by boat back to Langatabbetje, Psycho threw a tantrum about all the equipment we'd received from Bob Brown. We'd only saved him a piece of para a cord and couple of energy drinks. The way I figured it, there was no point of saving John anything as he was going anyway.

Back at Langatabbetje, Paco was looking even more worried. It turned out his real name was Erwin MacDonald, and our Erwin was becoming afraid for his life. It transpired that Ronnie now knew exactly what was going on. Instead of running, Paco was going to put his hands up and try to bluff his way out of it. Langatabbetje was again buzzing with rumour and suspicion. JCs kept asking me, 'Who are you going to be with, Paco or Ronnie?' I was walking a fine line, so I simply replied, 'I'm with Ronnie. He's the boss not Paco. Stop all this bullshit. Paco and Ronnie have no problems together. Paco's helping us.'

We weren't exactly well armed for a trip to the front line. I had a 556-calibre Beretta AR70 assault rifle, which I'd borrowed from Robert at the Toucan, and 400 rounds of ammunition for it – excellent by Jungle Commando standards. Charlie and John L. had no weapons at all; Psycho had a pistol. Paco had had no guns to spare. We'd pick some up at the front.

We arrived at the front line on a tractor pulling an old water bowser. The tractor stopped and we walked the last mile or so. Down the sloping hillside, I could see our roadblock beside a damaged bridge and a hole in the road. A mile and a half beyond that was the enemy. The boys had blown a section out of the bridge, but three-quarters of it was still intact. We made our way down the road to a small village and there was Yankie.

'Hey Karel, long time no see.'

'Yankie, I'm dying of thirst, give me something to drink.'

He sent one of his men running off. There were two loud shots and he came back with two coconuts. That coconut milk was the best drink I'd had in my life.

'I'm glad you've come Karel,' Yankie confided. It seemed the army up the road were getting braver. They'd send patrols in armoured cars who'd park up and watch through binoculars. Sometimes they'd fire mortars, sometimes a Cascavel would lob a couple of 90mm shells at the JCs.

'It's like they're testing us,' Yankie told me. It was plain to see that if the army threw a few sheets of steel across the gap in the bridge they could get a vehicle across, and troops could run over it. Yankie had informed Ronnie of this, but our leader thought the army were just bluffing. By pointlessly playing with his video games, Ronnie could lose this position at any minute.

Yankie reckoned they did not have enough explosive left to blow the bridge completely. I had a look myself. There was quite a bit of dynamite, but it had been left out in the sun and turned to a goo, that lookied like the middle of a Mars bar. At least I could salvage enough dynamite to do sufficient damage to make sure no vehicles would get across. I gathered together bits of det cord, detonators, wire and a battery. There was no time like the present.

'Be careful,' warned Yankie. 'The army are watching.'

'I'll fucking go with you,' said Psycho. This was a new one: John Richards trying to make himself useful. Yankie sent some of his boys out to alert the others who were in the firing positions that we were coming down. We checked the road out. No one there. Up where the road bends into Moengo, armoured vehicles had pulled off to one side of the road. Looking down through my binoculars, I could see men in uniforms milling around. We'd have to be extra careful now. I asked John to keep watch up the road and gave him the binos. 'John don't fuck around,' I told him. 'Let me know the minute you see anything untoward.'

I scrambled down the embankment to the river. My plan was to blast the legs out from under the bridge, one section at a time. Yankie hadn't been kidding – empty fifty-calibre cartridges were scattered all over the sides of the road. The army really had been going close to this bridge. I'd have to be quick. I lowered two different-sized charges into the water beside each leg. One was the demolition charge; the other, a smaller one, would create an air gap to blast the water out of the way. The air gap would make the leg weaker on one side than the other and help bring down the bridge. Sweat poured out of me as I worked away, constantly shouting to John, 'Is everything OK?' As I was wiped the sweat away, I got nitro on my hands from the leaking dynamite. It stung my eyes. Keep going, keep going, get it all linked up. Got to remember which one is which. I touched the battery to the first pair of wires, detonating the weaker charges, which blasted a hole in the water, creating the air gap. One second later, BOOM! The main charges went off with an ear-splitting bang. Plumes of water and chunks of debris spewed in the air as two great sections of the bridge crashed down into the river.

That would slow the bastards down. With a grin on my face, I jumped back to the side of the road shouting, 'Everybody back!' Yankie's men were still scrambling into the bunkers they'd dug out in the village when eighty-millimetre mortars started exploding all around us. Machine-gun fire opened up. Two shells from a Cascavel whistled right across us, one after the other, only to explode harmlessly 400 yards up the road beyond us. We sat in the bunkers, having a smoke, waiting until it all died down. Silence descended. The army hadn't come down the road. I was chuffed to bits.

The enemy would undoubtedly still be watching through binoculars. I wanted them to see a white man. There was only one way to do that – to walk out onto the road. There was a risk I'd be shot by a sniper or that they'd fire a 90mm shell at us. That was a risk I was prepared to take, to ram the message home to Bouterse that we were still here. 'Do you want to do it?' I asked John.

'Yeah, all right.'

The two of us strolled out to the centre of the road. It only took five or six seconds. I stood there praying I wouldn't be in sniper's sight, at the same time hoping somebody would see us and go, 'Fucking hell, mercenaries again.' Yankie was delighted. The bridge had gone and the enemy thought mercenaries were now holding the position.

Out of the back of the village came a nippy-looking sports car. It was a Datsun saloon with the roof sawn off, and all the doors and the windows taken out. Four or five of us jumped in and the car bent like a banana. 'Don't worry,' said Yankie. 'It's always like this.'

As we sped off up the road, every time we hit a bump the prop shaft would grind on the ground, sending sparks flying. Our Commando car looked as though it was rocket powered! I sat in the back with Yankie trying to talk above all the noise. It transpired that Yankie was beginning to despair of everything. Like many of the others, he was now hoping the rebels would be able to avoid a civil war among themselves.

* * *

Yankie wasn't the only one getting pissed off with the situation. I sat down with Charlie and the two Johns and we had a good chat about the situation we were in. We were no longer being paid, we were fed up of eating shit and now there was another problem: our tickets back to Europe had expired. Clearly, it was time to go home. We made our way back to Langatabbetje on the only transport that could be supplied, a tractor and trailer. It was a nightmare bashing along the road, down through the creeks where the bridges had been burned out, getting off every time and hauling the trailer up. We finally made it back to the Marowijne River. I fired several shots off in the air with my Beretta rifle, alerting the JCs on the island, and they sent a boat across to pick us up. Paco was still too scared to tell me what was really going on. In fact, he denied all knowledge of anything. I was beginning to worry about this guy as a potential leader. He had no balls at all. He may have been intelligent, but he had nerves of jelly.

While we were waiting for a boat out, Romeo Bravo sent a radio message asking me to go back to Stoelman's Island. I sent one back, telling him that if he wanted to talk to me, I'd be in the Toucan Hotel in St Laurent. Kilo Papa, out. Room Sixteen reckoned it would be months before the Yanks turned up with weapons; in the meantime there'd be nothing but bickering and backstabbing. I asked Room Sixteen to arrange our transport to England. That meant we'd have to be arrested and expelled back to the U.K.

Two days later, Ronnie turned up at the hotel.

'Karel where have you been? I heard you're going back to Europe.'

I told him straight. 'I can't hang around. You're doing fuck all. I don't know what you're playing at – that's your business – but I need money. If you want me to do something, pay me. I have to pay my rent just like everybody else.'

'OK,' Ronnie replied. 'You and John come and see me later.' Why did Ronnie want John when he'd already told me he wanted nothing more to do with him? Hmmm. That night, Gary took us to meet Ronnie at a house in the shanty town. His opening gambit was, 'Karel if you wait a few more days I will give you money. How much do you want?' I asked for two grand per man.

'I don't want all the group to stay,' said Ronnie. 'Just you, and you can bring John.'

'What about the other guys?' I asked.

'Fuck the other guys.'

There's loyalty for you. He saw the answer in my face: get stuffed. But he carried on regardless. 'Also Karel, we have to make more rockets.'

'How many more?'

'Same as before, we've got none left now. I shot them all training with the boys. Very good. Make more.'

So it came down to this. I'd been ducking and diving in St Laurent with Bouterse's men after me. All for what? So Ronnie could play silly fuckers. I'd guarantee that when he shot those rockets, sixty girls would have been standing there all clapping and cheering. The guy was amazing. Ronnie seemed to think he'd have loads of money soon, once Jan had done a deal on the Twin Otter. Somehow, I didn't share his optimism and I was sure there'd be no money. I was also sure I wouldn't be staying.

Eddie Dapp, the politician I'd met on that first canoe trip to Langatabbetje – the one who got an eyeful when Major Getback dropped his pants in the boat – was now in charge of refugees in St Laurent. Seven thousand refugees, who'd fled across the river from Surinam, were living at Mana, a town ten miles outside St Laurent. Ronnie seemed completely unconcerned about them. The French army were feeding and sheltering them. It was a French problem now. When Ronnie started this thing they used to call him the Robin Hood of Surinam; now he was just the robbing bastard of Surinam.

One hundred and fifty people were queuing outside Eddie's office waiting for cash handouts and assistance. Eddie wasn't there, but I found him at The Star Hotel. Eddie was very well-respected among the bush negroes, but his problem was that Ronnie had no respect for the elders. He was disappointed I was going home, but I told him I was one hundred per cent sure this would not be the end, I'd be coming back. Eddie gave me some money to take the boys for a meal. Downstairs, a white man and woman were sat in the bar. They were behaving so secretively that they were drawing attention to themselves. The woman nodded at me, and said, 'Hello how are you?' She claimed they were Belgian, told me her name was Inga, and added that her 'husband' didn't speak any English. I knew for a fact he was Cuban, spoke perfect English and lived in Miami. He was one of the Cuban spooks who'd come on a recce to start the ball rolling. Also sitting in the restaurant was a big, stocky white man and a younger guy – both suntanned with crew-cut hair. They were Dutch intelligence officers. They also thought I didn't know who they were. Nobody had approached me yet. Give them time. I dare say they were as confused as I was.

Jacques was back in touch. He'd invented and built a recoilless rocket launcher and wanted to show it to us on a shooting range outside St Laurent. Patrick Chauvel and his girlfriend came with us to video the launch. Jacques put a rocket into the barrel and fired it. Nothing happened, so he went over to it to sort it out. As he was right on top of the thing there was a massive bang, the launcher, which looked a bit like a recoilless rifle, flew back a few yards and the rocket almost took my nose off. It left me with burn marks on my cheek, which I still have today. Patrick swears he could see smoke coming from my hair. My eyes were burning, but I could see Jacques had hurt his elbow. He ended up with his arm in plaster from his shoulder to his wrist.

There had been no sign of Ronnie for days. The money obviously wasn't coming. Time to go, boys. I left the Browning with Henri; Robert would keep the night sight safe. The following afternoon, two cars arrived at the hotel. We four English guys were under arrest. The Belgians, Patrick and Luke, decided to stay.

We were put on a flight to the Caribbean island of Guadeloupe, four seats reserved at the back of the plane. I looked across and there was Inga, and her 'Belgian' husband. The look on their faces said it all. They were playing secret agents again. I explained to Inga – it was no good speaking to her husband, after all, he didn't speak English – that we were going home for a while, but we'd be back. I knew they were flying to Guadeloupe and then on to Santo Domingo, capital of the Caribbean island of the Dominican Republic, to see their big boss, a CIA man called Frank Castro.

On the flight to Paris, the stewardess asked why we were being expelled. 'Well, see that man there,' I said pointing to Charlie. 'He's in love with that man.' I pointed at John L. 'The problem is,' I went on, this time pointing at Psycho, 'That man there is also in love with him. I'm in love with him too and we've all been fighting among ourselves, so the police arrested us and here we are.' She looked at me like I was a lunatic, smiled politely and walked off. As we collected our passports from the captain after landing at Charles de Gaulle airport, the cabin crew were still wondering whether we really were homosexuals. We were met by PAF officials and then on we went to Heathrow, where a Special Branch man clocked us. John was going back to the Isle of Wight, the rest of us heading north. I noticed Charlie and John L. didn't even bother shaking hands with him. John strutted off to catch his bus and I was never to see him again.

A few days later, I was in a maisonette flat in the Maas Haven district of Rotterdam. Paul had brought me there to meet 'an important man'. This was getting more intriguing by the minute. It was pouring down outside as I opened the door to Paul and two white men. One must have been sixty, maybe a bit older. He was very stocky, with short-cropped grey hair. The other guy was probably about fifty.

'Karl, I'd like to introduce you to Raymond Westerling.'

Raymond was a bit guarded; he didn't smile. The other man was a friend who'd driven Raymond down from Amsterdam. Paul explained that Raymond was an ex-captain in Dutch Special Forces and a national hero in Holland. He had agreed to come out of retirement to work for Paul to travel to Surinam to advise the bush negroes and, particularly, Mr. Brunswijk. Apparently, both Ronnie and Bouterse knew all about Westerling. 'If Bouterse knows Westerling's in the country, he'll shit himself,' said Paul. This fellow must be something special, I thought.

I wasn't wrong. Raymond Westerling was an absolute gentleman, we hit it off together straight away. He was a highly experienced jungle fighter. During the war in Malaya, he'd taught jungle warfare to British Royal Marines and the Malayan Scouts, who later became the SAS. Raymond was no bullshitter and knew what he was talking about, though it had been a while since he'd been in combat. The last rifle he'd used was an M1 carbine – thankfully, there were plenty of them in Surinam. We chatted for hours and I told him how I'd crippled the country. I drew maps and sketches, detailing how we'd blocked the N1 and shut down SurAlco. He asked me about Mr. Brunswijk's overall plan. I had to explain to him that Mr. Brunswijk's overall plan involved girlfriends and video games. I explained to Raymond how I wanted to drop napalm bombs on Albina and high-explosive bombs on various army camps, to try to regain the momentum of our insurrection.

That was when Paul stepped in. 'We don't want you to drop bombs on Albina and set fire to the place,' he told me. 'Hindus from Nickerie side may be joining in with us in the war and some of those Hindus own a lot of property in Albina. If you set fire to Albina they will be very angry; we'll lose their support.' Maybe Ronnie had known all this, and that was why he wasn't in any hurry. Maybe he just wanted the bombs on standby for a rainy day. But if that was the case, then why hadn't he told me instead of fucking about?

Paul was going to send Raymond Westerling out to Surinam to unite the Jungle Commando and keep up the pressure on Bouterse. I was a bit concerned at this. Raymond had told me he hadn't been well lately and I was worried how he'd fare in the heat. Still, he was probably fit enough to go out to Surinam in an advisory role.

We drove to Amsterdam together and as we shook hands by the back entrance to Central Station, I told him, 'I'm looking forward to seeing you again, Raymond, in Surinam.'

'Karl, I haven't done anything for years,' he replied. 'I'm really looking forward to this so much. I'm pleased to have met you, you're a fantastic man.' Raymond Westerling, a national hero, telling me I'm a fantastic man. My feet never touched the ground as I walked through the station. Fired up, I went home, dialled John's number and told him over the phone that he was sacked.

A week later, I was back at Rochambo airport in Cayenne. It was dark inside the terminal building. I took off my sunglasses and squinted around. Francois was standing by the immigration desk. As my turn came to approach the desk, Francois stepped across to the officer and whispered in his ear. 'Passport, monsieur.' He gave my British passport a cursory glance and I walked straight through customs with Francois at my side. Outside in the car park I spotted Sharm, one of Ronnie's men. There was a woman with him. As Francois went off to find his car, she walked up to me and palmed something into my hand. It was a note, which read 'Do Not Speak To The Police.' I threw it away.

My first job was to find Ronnie and tell him that Raymond Westerling would be arriving fairly soon. I'd only been checked into the Toucan a short while when a guy called Pancho arrived to take me to see Paco. Paco and Pancho – they were like a pair of Mexican bandits.

Apparently, Paco didn't feel safe at Langatabbetje any more and had moved into The Star Hotel in St Laurent with fifteen of his men. How the hell could they afford that? I found out soon enough: all fifteen of them were dossing in one room! I had letters from Paul for both Paco and Ronnie. I handed one to Paco. He was obviously pleased with what he read.

Ronnie was still at Stoelman's Island playing video games. And there was still no fuel for the Cessna. I was buggered if I was going all that way up river to eat shit and watch Ronnie playing Space Invaders. Instead, Paco arranged for some of his men to take the three manila envelopes I'd been carrying up to Ronnie. Paco did have a bit of good news. Django, the rapist from Langatabbetje and Baku Gadu, the trouble-making voodoo man from Moengotapoe had got themselves killed. They and another bloke, Roy Botse, had got themselves into a trance at a voodoo ceremony. They'd got the power inside them, they put on their armbands to make themselves bulletproof, and marched into Carolina to steal an armoured car. The army were watching and shot them. Django and Roy died instantly but Baku Gadu was tortured. He actually appeared on TV looking very distressed, and later 'committed suicide'. I'd once warned him that he'd get other people killed. Behind God? He is now.

Pancho accompanied me back to the Toucan, via a little restaurant, 'Hello Henri, un Browning, s'il vous plaît... Merci beaucoup.' Then, translating through Pancho, I asked Robert for my night sight.

'Night sight? It's gone. I told Ronnie if he didn't pay me he wasn't getting the night sight back.' Ronnie had coughed up and taken the night sight away with him. A week went by and still I'd heard nothing from Ronnie.

There was a knock on the door of my room. It was Coolie Bob with four boys behind him carrying two black sacks of marijuana and a set of kitchen scales. The drugs stank to high heaven.

'Karel can we use your room? We have to cut this up and weigh it and measure it.'

'Cheeky bastards,' I told them, 'get out of here with that stuff.'

'Can it stay here for a couple of hours?'

'Jesus Christ, put it in the wardrobe there. If you're not back within two hours I'll throw it in the skip outside.'

Sure enough, Coolie Bob came back and when he'd sent his men away with the marijuana, I gave him a shopping list of things I needed: one large boat, a small canoe, six kilos of gunpowder, a small coil of wire, clothes pegs and a bell battery.

Back in Europe I'd met a spook – that's all I can say about him – who'd told me to keep the fire burning in Surinam. Things were about to hot up.

CHAPTER 13

C louds rolled in front of the moon, dulling the white sandy beach as I jumped out of the boat into knee-deep water. The outboard engine still spluttering, the boatman walked forward to the bow, pulling a primitive two-man canoe towards me. I dragged the wooden canoe up onto the beach. I held up my wrist watch and pointed to ten o'clock. He gave me the thumbs up. I took a roll of French money from my pocket. The boatman went to take the cash. I pulled my hand back – 'No, no, monsieur. Ten o'clock, money. Compris?' His face cracked into a smile. With a quizzical 'Bon chance', he slammed the boat into reverse and disappeared into the night.

It was six o'clock. I had an hour and a half to wait on this secluded beach at the northern end of Isle Portal. I opened my holdall bag and pulled out an extinguisher mine – I'd made it from a black cast-iron fire extinguisher I found just down the corridor from my room at the Toucan hotel. I'd taped all the gunpowder inside the neck of extinguisher. In my room, I'd made a detonator from sticky paper and wire. I tested one by putting it in the wardrobe and exploding it. It had gone off with a muffled bang, though fortunately no one heard it. I'd made another to the same specification. I took out the Beretta AR70 rifle Robert had lent me. I'd brought a hundred and fifty rounds of ammunition with me and five magazines for the rifle, but I wished I'd had the night sight.

I checked my webbing, then double-checked the contents of a carrier bag containing all the individuals items to detonate the extinguisher mine: the firing mechanism, the peg switch, wrapped in a plastic bag with an elastic band around it. The bell battery and wires were ready, the trip lines still on the roll because I didn't know what length they would have to be cut to. I'd made a circuit breaker from a piece of the plastic bottles the gunpowder had come in.

Then, I took off my civvies and put on French camouflage clothes, my boots and a bush hat. I could really have done with that night sight, but as it was I'd just have to rely on my eyes.

I lit a fag and looked across to the other side of the river. There were no S-Boats about. I went over the plan again in my head. A dirt road runs along the edge of the Marowijne River between Albina and Pappatam. The Surinam army drove up and down this road with impunity, supplying the garrison at Pappatam. I was going to paddle across from Isle Portal and plant a mine along the road, triggered by a trip line. I estimated it would take me an hour to cross the mile and a half of tidal water. I'd paddle most of the way but for the last quarter, I'd lie flat in the bottom of the canoe and let the boat drift with the tide. High water that night was at eight-thirty, and the tide would start to ebb at nine o'clock. If I'd calculated the tides right, leaving the beach at seven-thirty, I'd arrive on the other side at slack water, giving me half an hour to set the trap. In theory, I'd be back on the sandy beach at ten and with a bit of luck, I could be in the bar of the Toucan Hotel by eleven.

The lights of Pappatam twinkled in the distance. I'd reckoned it was mile and a half away upriver but it looked further, maybe two and a half miles. I was nervous and starting to sweat; it would wear off. I don't care what anyone says, operating alone is very difficult. It's nice to have a partner around at times like these – you give each other moral support. Working on your own behind enemy lines is not recommended.

I checked my watch. Still only quarter to seven. To ease the tension, I let my mind drift. In the days of the leper colony this place had been called Pigeon Island. It was here that Papillon bought a boat off the lepers and sailed down the Marowijne River, past St Laurent and Albina out into the Atlantic Ocean and freedom after years on Devil's Island.

I checked my webbing. Pilot's knife taped upside down on the left-hand side; ration packs Bob Brown had brought; vitamin drinks in the water bottles. If I got trapped on the other side, I'd have to wait twenty-four hours for the next night's tide. I pulled on the black special forces life jacket – another present from Bob Brown. I'd covered the shiny bright steel air bottle with black tape. As I rubbed cammo cream on my face, my stomach lurched. Control this, Karl. Are you going to do this or not? A little devil on my shoulder urged do it. On the other shoulder, a little angel whispered, 'Go back to the bar and have a drink, enjoy yourself.' This was ridiculous. I began to say to myself, 'You're a fool Karl, is this worth losing your life for?'

The man paying my wages, Paul, had no knowledge of what I was about, neither had Brunswijk nor Paco. Only Room Sixteen and Coolie Bob had any idea and I hadn't told them exactly what I was going to do. I stuffed my civilian clothes into the holdall, forced my way into the bush and hid the bag on the ground. I had to be able to find it again quickly, so I dragged a dead branch onto the beach and lay it on the sand, pointing at the spot where the bag was stashed.

I looked at my watch again. Time to go. My heart was in my mouth. Thoughts of giving up raced through my mind again. Stop it Karl, get in the boat. I paddled out into the river, the mine lying in the bottom on the boat, plastic bag beside it. I had the feel of the canoe, the rhythm of the paddle propelled me on into the darkness. Powerful strokes sent me out from the shadow of the island. Slow down! I was going to be fucked before I was halfway there at this rate! Check my watch. I'd only been going five minutes and I was well away from Portal. Take it easy! But if I rested too much, I'd drift too far. Nice and steady. Pray no S-Boats are going to loom out of the blackness. Any signs of a patrol boat with its sweeping arc lights and I'd be straight back.

Keep going. Now I was three-quarters of the way across. It was time to get my arse off the seat and lower my profile in the boat. I knelt down. With my backside resting on the mine, I crouched to paddle, but with each stroke I clunked the gunwhales.

I got braver and sat up a bit more. Any minute an S-Boat could come up around the bend from Albina. There were no lights on the other side. I paddled like hell now, towards a destination I still couldn't see. Fear gave me energy. Start drifting. It's good, don't flap Karl, you're doing fine, just fine.

At last I could make out the opposite bank, a sandy beach down to my left. Further upstream, there were overhanging branches. Stop paddling now. I grabbed a branch. Listen: just jungle noises and the sound of the water flowing. No S-Boat. I didn't really want to land on the sand. There could be huts here along the side of the road. I let go of the branch and very slowly drifted along the bank, looking for a place to land in safety. There it was: a big tree trunk growing out into the river with a clearing next to it. The boat's nose gently brushed the tree. A clunk, wobble a bit. I eased the boat along the trunk of the tree to the shore. Step out. I didn't pull the canoe right up. Take the rope out, tie it to a branch of the tree. Leave the mine in the boat. I could see the road ten yards ahead of me through the bushes, the sandy dirt light against the dark vegetation.

It was pitch-black, but occasionally moonlight would appear. I listened. Still just jungle noises. I looked at my watch. A few minutes after eight o'clock. I crouched in the bushes by the road, trying to get my heart out of my mouth and push it back down inside my chest. I checked my watch; it was just after eight. I'd paddled too fast. I now had nearly an hour to wait. I didn't want to leave until the tide turned at nine o'clock. It would only take five minutes to rig the mine and I didn't want to set it up just yet, in case a vehicle came past and detonated the thing before I could leave.

I took my bush hat off, shoved it in one of my leg pockets, and crawled out into the road. I was tempted to lay the mine at the side of the road but there was only one place for it: in the middle of the road right between the tyre tracks. The sand was quite soft. I propped the Beretta against a tree and took out an entrenching tool, another of Mr. Brown's gifts. The shovel blade clicked as I folded it out. I started digging a hole the length of a fire extinguisher and eighteen inches in depth; I didn't want it too deep. As I dug, I threw sand into the bushes, leaving just enough by the hole to cover the extinguisher. Back again into the bush to wait and listen. Get a grip, Karl, you're not surrounded by the enemy. Vehicles weren't a problem – I could hear them coming for miles. My main fear was getting a nasty surprise from men out hunting, armed with bows and arrows or twelve-bore shotguns. I didn't want to be paddling back across the river with an arrow through my head.

I picked up the mine and the plastic bag, moved into the road and placed the mine in the hole, the neck facing the river. As I took the tape off, a bit of gunpowder poured out; no problem. Feed in the detonator. The wires to the detonator were two feet long. I covered up the mine, leaving the two wires sticking up a bit. So far so good. Dare I risk a fag? I'll rig it up first and then have one.

I pulled a coil of two-strand wire from the plastic bag, connected it to the det wires and pushed them down into the soft sand. Hide the tracks. I nipped into the cover of the bush to study the ground. The disturbance was so slight it was almost impossible to spot. I rigged the wires to the peg switch and battery, leaving one wire disconnected to avoid an accident. Then, I tied one end of the roll of fishing line to a branch seven feet up a tree, on the other side of the road. I stretched the line across the road and secured it to another tree. This trip wire was for a military vehicle, I wasn't going to waste my time blowing up a civilian car, or even a man with a bow and arrow. Though, knowing my luck, some bastard with a long bow would touch the trip wire and set it off. It was now all rigged. I didn't connect it in case a vehicle did come past. I didn't mind losing the line, but I didn't want to detonate the bomb yet because I was not ready to leave. The relief. The fear had gone, to be replaced by elation. I lit a fag and I sat there with it cupped in my hand. I took a few drags, just enough to get nicotine inside me to calm my nerves. I buried the cigarette and checked my watch again. Forty-five minutes still to go. I was feeling cocky now. If anybody did come along with a bow and arrow or a shotgun, I was going to take him out. It was getting towards nine o'clock. The tide would be turning soon, time to go. I checked on the line again, connected the wires up and covered the battery pack with bits of vegetation.

Back in the canoe, I surged with nervous energy. Let's show these Olympic guys how to paddle properly! I was on a high, it was like I'd taken a drug. I powered the canoe towards Isle Portal. Fifteen minutes of paddling and I was safely in French territorial waters. Now, even if an S-Boat appeared, I was out of danger. As I paddled along against overhanging trees and mangroves on Isle Portal, I wondered if the ghosts of lepers were watching, thinking who's this crazy bastard? Round the bend to the beach, nose up onto the sand. As I pulled the canoe out of the water I heard a whistle. I jumped out of my skin and peered into the dark. It was the boatman. Brilliant. The boat was round the corner, its ten-foot long mooring rope pulled taught by the tidal run. He looked quite shocked seeing me in all my cammo kit. Last time he'd seen me I'd been in civvies.

'Un moment, monsieur, un moment.'

He gave me a flat-palm gesture that said take your time. I found the branch, disappeared into the bushes, emerged with the holdall and stripped off, stuffing my gear into the holdall. I noticed the boatman staring at the Beretta. I put my fingers to my lips: be quiet. He gestured to me to get into the big boat, started her up and went around to the other canoe. I leant forward, grabbed hold of the small canoe and pulled it back towards us. He grabbed the back end rope and tied it on. I secured the front end rope and we were off, heading for St Laurent. As we passed Saint-Jean, I gave him the money and shook hands. I jumped out of the boat among the huts of the shanty town and climbed up the embankment. Then I nipped alongside Papillon's jail and through a gateway into the jail itself. Gendarmerie never walked there. Past the old cell blocks inhabited by squatters. I walked through at a brisk pace, carrying the holdall and the rifle in a sack over my shoulder.

Up to the main gate of the jail; a quick squint around the corner. Nobody there. The Toucan was just two hundred yards away across the road. A brisk walk up to the end of the old hospital. I looked up and down the main road. This was the dangerous bit, where the gendarmerie normally patrolled. A few people mingled on the terrace of the Toucan; through the window, I could see Robert in the bar. I crossed the road, went through the side door of the hotel, headed upstairs, quickly entered the room and locked the door. I stashed the rifle and my cammo gear in the wardrobe. Thank God for that. I'd washed most of the cammo off with river water using a little mirror that I keep in my webbing. But when I looked in the bathroom mirror, I had a camouflage cream beard! It was all around my ears and my neck. After a quick wash I went downstairs for a drink and a quiet celebration. After a couple of beers with Robert, I went over to Henri's.

I was sitting in the restaurant drinking a large Ricard when Henri's son looked up, and asked 'What was that noise?' It sounded like a dull thud in the distance. Then it dawned on me. The mine must have gone off on the other side of the river. I wanted to check it out, but I couldn't give the game away. I finished my drink, paid the bill and ducked back to the Toucan. I went over to Robert and asked, 'Albina, explosion?'

'Oui, oui, explosion Albina,' he replied.

Next morning, I saw Paco over at the Star Hotel. 'Any news from Ronnie?' I asked him.

'Not yet Karel, but somebody blew up a YP last night.'

Looking poker faced, I tried to contain my excitement and asked, 'Oh what happened?'

'Don't know yet, the Surinam TV news said there was an explosion, some Jungle Commandos destroyed a YP close to Pappatam.' A YP is a Dutch-manufactured four-wheel armoured scout car that usually carries a driver and a gunner.

'Oh, so Ronnie's boys aren't lying around sleeping. That's good,' I replied.

'According to the news report, the government are very angry,' added Paco.

'Oh right.' I changed the subject before my excitement got the better of me. 'What's happening with Ronnie?'

'He'll be here soon,' replied Paco. I told him that hanging around, ducking and diving, was getting too much for me. I'd decided to go up to Cayenne and stay in a safe house.

'Sure, Karel, if he comes we'll tell him where you are and he can go and see you.'

I was packing my gear at the Toucan when Robert knocked on the door. He had a white guy with him who wanted to talk to me. The man introduced himself as Jack W from the U.S. State Department and he'd been talking to politicians from Surinam. He wanted to ask me a load of questions. I didn't have to answer the questions of course, but being the friendly bloke I am, I gave him the overall picture. I certainly didn't tell him I'd just blown up an armoured car. At the end of our chat he gave me a post office box number through which to contact him. No phone number, just a P.O. box.

That afternoon I was sitting on the terrace at the Toucan when Robert came over with two more white men. They had South African accents; this operation was turning into the League of Nations. One of them introduced himself as Peter and he was, in fact, a Brit. 'I believe you know Bob McKenzie,' he said to me. The pair of them claimed they were freelance journalists working for Omega Press and were going up to Cayenne the next day on the same truck as me. It transpired that Peter was in fact Peter Cole, a former captain in the Rhodesian SAS, and he'd been one of Bob McKenzie's men.

The truck took me to the safe house in Cayenne. It was the place owned by Robbie Cassie that we'd been on our way to when we were arrested by the French frontier police. When I met Cassie at the bungalow he told me to be careful because a man who worked at the Surinam

Consulate in Cayenne lived over the back. What a place to have a safe house! Apparently, the man from the Consulate had moved in after Robbie had bought the place.

Robbie told me Raymond Westerling was in hospital and was having tests on a stomach complaint, so there would be a delay. He also told me an American mercenary called Doctor John would be arriving soon.

The next day I spoke to Paul in Holland. Raymond was out of hospital and should be fit to travel in a week, he assured me. I settled down in the safe house to wait for Raymond and, of course, Ronbo. I spent hours just sitting on a hammock on the veranda, hidden from the road by sheets on a clothes line. One of Ronnie's men would sit at the end of the sheets, casually keeping an eye on the road.

One afternoon, a white saloon pulled up in the street outside. The four coloured men in the car sat and stared at the house. A JC called Sharm hissed, 'Karel, look.' I peered round the side of the sheets. I was damn sure these were bad guys. Sharm thought he knew one of them from the Surinam Consulate. Hidden from view by the sheets, Joey slipped back into the house and came out with a .22 semi-automatic rifle, which they call a pif, paf. He stood casually in the doorway while I eased myself out of the hammock, stepped inside the kitchen and cocked the Browning. The Consulate were bound to know all about this safe house. Let's face it, why else did the man from the Consulate move in at the back? Sharm picked up Robbie

Cassie's three-inch Magnum shotgun. From that range we could have peppered the car. However, five minutes later they drove off. They were there to intimidate us. Once you have been compromised, you get out. Unfortunately, we had nowhere else to go except St Laurent and they were looking for us there. People from the Consulate had never been to this house before, so I had to conclude they were looking for me. Someone must have told them I was there. When Robbie Cassie returned I told him what had happened. He went as white as a sheet. Robbie Cassie was a rice dealer. The house was full of sacks of rice, so I piled some of them up near the French widows to make a little sangar. If the car turned up again, we could get down behind the rice sacks and shoot the shit out of the Consul's men.

Robbie had two little dogs that ran around the house. The following day, one of the dogs disappeared and the other became extremely ill, heaving up all over the place. The day after, we found the missing dog decomposing rapidly in the heat. Its body had been hidden under a corrugated metal sheet. Putting two and two together, we guessed the dogs had been poisoned, more than likely by the blokes in the car.

One night, Robbie went up to the airport and brought three Americans to the safe house. One was a big, tough-looking bastard. This was Doctor John, the famous mercenary. Nice enough bloke, don't get me wrong, but I think he'd watched a few too many movies. What these American mercs do is ring up magazines like *Soldier of*

Fortune and ask, 'If I go to this place and that place and take lots of photographs, will you be interested in buying them off me?' If the magazines say yes to an article about their escapades, then these guys go down there and offer assistance to train the local soldiers – and I emphasise that word 'train'. Generally they do not take part in the action. The other two were a cameraman and a film producer, brought by Doctor John to film his exploits. It turned out Doctor John was actually a doctor of psychology. The film crew wanted to hear how we'd been under fire from fifty-calibre weapons. I told them how I was so close I could feel the muzzle blast. The producer said, 'I want to feel that muzzle blast.' Jesus Christ.

The film crew were going down to Stoelman's Island to see Ronnie and make a movie of Doctor John running around firing the Korean Daewoo 556 rifle he'd brought with him. They went and we idled away a few more days. Westerling was still in hospital.

A few days later, a fat, ugly guy in Jewish dreadlocks and wearing a powder-blue all-in-one jumpsuit arrived. He wore training shoes, huge amounts of cheap jewellery around his neck and on every finger. He had two watches on one wrist and bracelets on the other. This vision of sartorial elegance was Mr. Fritz Hirshland, a record producer from Holland. He claimed to have been the producer of the hit record 'Rock Me Amadeus'. He was also a friend of Johnny Camperfane, a Dutch DJ whose father had been executed by Bouterse. Mr. Camperfane Senior's crime had been to run Surinam national radio. Fritz sat down and waffled for hours, he even suggested raising money for the organisation by getting the Jungle Commandos to make a record. This guy was such an outrageous head case, I was seriously thinking about giving him to Doctor John the psychologist to sort out. We all laughed as he left the safe house. We were laughing on the other sides of our faces when Ronnie made him his public relations man. Hirshland had promised to make Ronnie famous.

Another message from Holland: Westerling was out of hospital but he had to rest. Another day passed and a car pulled up outside the house. A bodyguard got out, followed by a woman who looked like the singer Randy Crawford. Turned out that it wasn't a woman – it was Ronnie, with long nylon dreadlocks pinned to his head! Seven thousand refugees had crossed the river when I closed the main road and even more fled after the Mooiwana massacre happened, poverty was biting deeply into them. Unfortunately all their hopes were pinned on a man who had disguised himself as Randy Crawford.

Ronnie stepped into the house. 'Karel, how long have you been here?'

I told him and asked him if he'd received my message from Paco's boys.

'I've got no message. I heard nothing from Paco,' he replied.

'What about the letters from Paul?' I asked.

'I never got any letters,' he said. All was becoming as clear as mud. There was dirty business going on here. I told Ronnie about the letters.

Ronnie exploded. 'I'm going to kill that motherfucker.'

'Ronnie slow down, hang on. Before you start killing anybody, maybe there's some misunderstanding,' I said, and started filling him in on a few things. When I told him about Raymond Westerling, his eyes came out on springs.

Ronnie told me he was in Cayenne to discuss some business. I knew what his business was. Room Sixteen had told me Ronnie was holding ceasefire negotiations with Desi Bouterse. It seemed Bouterse had been in contact with Ronnie. The dictator couldn't beat the Jungle Commandos by military means but he might be able to fuck them with subterfuge. The dictator was handing out carrots and in return Ronnie had promised there'd be no action against the army. No wonder the government had been angry when I blew up the armoured car.

I didn't tell Ronnie everything I knew, but I did warn him, 'Bouterse is playing games with you. You're like a monkey on an elastic band to that man. Don't fall for it, Ronnie; he's playing games.'

'I know Bouterse,' Ronnie countered. 'I used to be his bodyguard. He's a very smart man, but I too am smart.'

'Sure you are, Ronnie. I agree you are very smart, but don't fall for it. Believe me, Ronnie, cut the man off.' Even as I said the words, though, I doubted very much that Ronnie was taking them in. After failing to persuade me to go with him to Stoelman's Island, he left.

Raymond Westerling was back in hospital again. I'd been at the safe house for three weeks; it was time to return to Europe. This time I had a valid ticket and didn't need to be expelled. Room Sixteen would see me safely onto the plane. Robbie Cassie wanted to take me to the airport two hours before the flight. The place was bound to be crawling with spies. An hour would have been more than enough but Robbie insisted, explaining that he had to meet some people at the same time. I checked in and went over to the bar to have a drink with Pierre from Room Sixteen. Francois was away trying to find out what Bouterse was up to. Robbie was with us, looking extremely nervous about something. At one point he said he was going to the toilet and walked off. He returned looking pale. Following thirty yards behind him, mingling with other passengers, was a small group of men from the Surinam Consulate.

Robbie was extremely agitated, but he tried to hide it by giving me a smile. Among the men in mirrored sunglasses and suits was a short, stocky coffee-coloured bloke. Pierre looked amazed. He said, 'That's Antonius.' I'd heard all about him. He was the chief of the Surinam Consulate's dirty tricks department. He'd been sent to Cayenne from Paramaribo. 'He's a dangerous piece of shit,' said Pierre. So what was Robbie Cassie doing taking a couple of beers over to them? Robbie came back still looking pale and nervous. He said, in a low voice, 'Karel can you come and talk to these people? There's no trouble, they just want to speak with you for a moment.' Pierre looked at me and shook his head. I turned to Robbie, 'Tell those men to fuck off, I've nothing to say to them. If I speak to them it will be on their own territory in Surinam.'

Pierre pulled Robbie to one side and had a quiet talk in his ear. I didn't hear what was said. Robbie stood there like a schoolboy, trying to look at me appealingly. He seemed to be under some serious obligation to these people. Finally, I decided something had to be done. 'I'll tell you what I'll do,' I told him, and stood up.

I quickly walked across and snatched the two beers back. 'You ain't fucking getting them boys, that's all I have to say to you.' I walked back with the beers, put them on the bar and told the barmaid to dump them. It was just a flash of anger, a stupid move, but I did it. Robbie suddenly decided he had to leave. 'I think you better had,' I agreed. Pierre asked me to walk to the other end of the bar, where he could make a telephone call. As soon as he hit the phone, the Surinamese vanished.

The plane landed at Orly airport, south of Paris. I had to be careful now. Who had Antonius called? I dare say Pierre had me under surveillance too. I took a taxi to the Gare du Nord and then a train from there to Paul's office above the video shop in Rotterdam. Raymond Westerling was now very ill. Paul warned me against visiting him in hospital. My face was now well known in Holland and a mercenary visiting a national war hero might be picked up on. Paul thought it best that I return to the U.K. When I got home there was a message from George Baker.

I phoned him straight away. 'Karl, some very interesting people have been into my bar,' he told me. 'They are Austrian mercenaries. They have a lot of experience, know a lot about Surinam and they want to talk with you.

They're going to help us, Karl. They're going to buy weapons, supply a ship, land them off the coast and they're going to pay for it all, too.'

'How old are they?' I asked.

'They're only young, all early to mid-twenties.'

And they were all 'very experienced mercenaries'? It just didn't ring true. 'Listen George,' I told him, 'be very careful, because they don't sound right to me. They're either dreamers or they're up to no good. If I were you, I'd forget about them. Get rid of them.' George told me he was going to talk with them again and he'd let me know more.

I'd changed my telephone number because John Richards had been calling me up demanding to know why I hadn't taken him with me back to Surinam. Then I learned he'd recruited a group of ex-Legionnaires and former Royal Marines to work for him there. A telemessage arrived at my house asking me to phone John on a number in the Isle of Wight. I called him from a phone box. I couldn't believe what he was telling me. 'I've been over to Holland and seen a man called Antonio,' he revealed. 'He's a really nice guy and he said the Surinamese government will pay us to kill Ronnie.'

'Oh, right John,' I replied, unenthusiastically. He obviously meant Antonius.

Ignoring my indifference, he blundered on, 'I've made arrangements, we're going to go back over there – me, you and my boys. The army's going to be waiting for us on a river bank near Albina and they're going to hand us weapons and we'll go and kill Ronnie. They'll give us a load of money.'

'Oh, really? John, are you completely fucking insane? I'm having nothing to do with that. It's entirely up to you but I'm telling you now, I strongly advise that you don't do it. Don't trust Antonius, the man is a piece of shit.'

John was having none of it. 'You don't know. I've been in that consulate a few times with him; he always gives me a nice cup of coffee. I tell you what, he opened a drawer and there was a gun in it.'

'He'd probably open up another drawer and there'd be a tape recorder there too.'

'No, they hate Ronnie, they're all right. I trust them.' By this point, I was thinking, 'I'm glad I got rid of you John.' The man was a walking liability. That's when he hit me with it.

'Karl, they want to see you. Go over to Holland, they'll pay your ticket – he's told me to tell you that. They'll give you money. You're in no danger, Karl, they won't ambush you. They just want to talk to you.'

I contacted my spook and Room Sixteen. They were sure Antonius wanted to ambush me. I phoned John back again a few days later. 'This is my last word on the matter,' I told him. 'I'll have nothing to do with it and I strongly advise you do not do it.'

John was very disappointed. But there was no way I was taking the bait: apart from my reservations about John himself, and Antonius, I was also concerned about the English guys that John had recruited. My fears would turn out to be well founded.

CHAPTER 14

The next couple of months were a very busy time for me, running backwards and forwards to Europe for various meetings with men in suits and people from the Surinam community. On one trip I discovered Paco had brought in a boffin from Holland to deal with the S-Boats. This scientist had built a remote control torpedo to destroy an S-Boat at Albina. On a test run at Langatabbetje, the torpedo shot out over the river and sank without trace. Apparently, that escapade cost $10,000.

Meanwhile, Mr. Bouterse was reported to have bought six Siai Marchetti aircraft, little single-engine propeller-driven planes, which he was going to convert into ground-attack aircraft. These planes flew from Italy, up through Scandinavia across to Iceland, Greenland, Canada and down the eastern seaboard of the United States. They got as far as New York, where the Yanks confiscated them. There was more good news. At one time, Bouterse had threatened to clear our island bases. Using assault troops would have been too difficult, so he planned instead to fire phosphorous rockets from a helicopter on to Stoelman's Island and Langatabbetje.

However, I was told that the Dutch had impounded a large consignment of phosphorous rockets at Rotterdam docks.

Another piece of news: Desi Bouterse had been in Brazil with a gang of his bodyguards in a hotel. They were carrying holdalls full of cash and had had whores in their room. When they'd finished, the whores told the police they had just been with a gang of bank robbers. The Brazilian cops raided the hotel room and found holdalls stuffed with many thousands of dollars in cash. They arrested Bouterse and took him away, with him protesting all the while, 'I'm the President of Surinam.' Eventually it was all cleared up. Bouterse asked for an official apology, but received none. It later transpired Bouterse had been in Brazil to buy a large consignment of ether, which was to be used for the manufacture of cocaine.

My activities had put Surinam in such a vice-like grip that eventually Bouterse was forced to reach a settlement with Ronnie Brunswijk to end the stalemate. The deal, brokered by the French, was grandly named the Kourou Agreement. Bouterse would step down in a few months making way for free elections to take place. I'm not sure of all the finer points, but part of the agreement stipulated that the bush negroes would be given land and reparations would be made to the dispossessed. Ronnie hailed it as great victory. He and his bodyguard Gary arrived at Kourou in sunglasses and dressed in U.S. Army combat gear, including brand-new American webbing – with nothing in it – and sporting red berets. Ronnie had his Randy Crawford dreadlocks on again – look cool man, look cool. Sad to say, all was not what it seemed. The Kourou Agreement was a sham that covered up the fact that Bouterse and Ronnie were doing drug deals together that were a damn sight more lucrative than waging war.

It wasn't just me and the guys in suits who were cynical about the whole thing. Thousands of refugees in French Guiana also decided not to trust the pair of them, and refused to move back into Surinam. There are a few thousand to this day in French Guiana, still at the refugee camp in Mana too afraid to go back. I remember people in Holland patting me on the back and congratulating me on a job well done. But in all honesty, I couldn't stand there satisfied that the job was well done, because I knew for a fact that the job was far from finished. Meanwhile, Mr. Bouterse was arming the Toucayana Indians, the indigenous people of that region, with RPGs, MAG machine guns, FN rifles and Kalashnikovs. This was Bouterse's way of keeping control, by using the Toucayanas to start the war off again.

Paul called me at home to tell me that Raymond Westerling had died in hospital. It was a very sad day for me. I wasn't sad because Westerling hadn't gone to Surinam; I was simply sad that the man had died. He was a gentleman and it had been a privilege to meet him. One day I'm going to try and look up his family and go and visit the grave. When I told Ronnie the news, he didn't seem to care.

Shortly after Ronnie signed the Kourou Agreement, the Cuban exiles started arriving in Surinam. At this point, the men in suits suggested I distance myself from events. This was supposed to be a top-secret operation, although it seemed half the world knew about it. Frank Castro and his Cuban exiles, known as Alpha 66, flew in Dakotas from Santo Domingo to Surinam, via Aruba, a tiny Dutch-held island off the coast of Venezuela. Alpha 66 had made a deal that instead of their normal training in the Florida Everglades, they would set up a training camp in Surinam with the eventual purpose of invading Cuba. Frank had been involved in the abortive Bay of Pigs operation in April 1961, when 1,500 Cuban exiles opposed to communist dictator Fidel Castro tried to invade Cuba. The invasion was financed and directed by the U.S. government. Now Alpha 66 planned to stage a similar operation, but they were going to kick off from Surinam. Frank would come in, help Ronnie and in return Alpha 66 would be allowed to train up and assemble an army to invade Cuba. Quite a few of the Alpha 66 men were veterans from the Bay of Pigs operation. Maybe they wanted to speed things up before they ended up in a graveyard along with Fidel Castro.

Why, I don't know, but Ronnie sent Fritz Hirshland up to Santo Domingo to fly back with one of Frank Castro's cargo planes. Stopping off at Aruba for refuelling, the Dakota was seized and the cargo of guns confiscated. The pilots were locked up. The finger was pointed at Mr. Hirshland. He'd started to play amateur secret agents but denied he had anything to do with snitching on everybody. However, he'd tipped off a number of journalists about the flight and once the story got out, the authorities were left with no choice but to seize the plane. Nice one, Fritz. Later, Mr. Hirshland was to write a book in which he told all about the CIA operation.

At one stage during the Alpha 66 operation, Bouterse gave up Moengo. With the SurAlco bauxite mine closed there was nothing to be gained by holding the town any more, so the army pulled out and Ronnie walked in. It was party time. Ronnie and his American friends strutted around Moengo with their shoulder holsters and mirrored sunglasses. Unfortunately, for some strange reason, Bouterse changed his mind again and attacked Moengo. The army came down the main road, stopped well short of Ronnie's roadblocks, disappeared off into the jungle, flanked Moengo and then attacked it. Ronnie and the JCs, along with Frank Castro and his men, all legged it. They ran so fast they had to leave a couple of aircraft on the airfield at Moengo, which were destroyed by the army.

According to Hirshland's book, during the time Ronnie and Frank were in Moengo an aircraft flew in from Colombia carrying 2,000 kilograms of cocaine and £4 million in counterfeit one hundred-dollar bills with five different serial numbers. Apparently this was to be used in a CIA sting to destabilise the government of Surinam. Unfortunately, the airfield that had been designated to land in was too short for the plane, an Australian-made GAF Nomad. The airfield needed a plane with short take-off and landing (STOL) capability. The GAF Nomad didn't have STOL ability. The pilot took out the air charts and looked for the next suitable airstrip – somewhere covert away from Paramaribo. On the map, Moengo looked very good and that's where they landed, right behind Ronnie's front line. The two occupants of the plane were dragged out. One, a Colombian, was beaten up. There was something odd about the other pilot. He turned out to be an officer from the United States Drug Enforcement Agency (DEA) in disguise, pretending to be a Colombian drug baron's personal pilot. Very amateur. Even I could have planned a better operation than that. Far from being saviours, the Cuban exiles were a circus sideshow.

Paul called to tell me the organisation was having serious financial problems. Frank Castro and his boys were not coming free of charge. Ronnie was handing out money hand over fist. Plane loads of fancy chrome-plated gangster guns like Mach 11 sub-machine pistols kept arriving, and they all had to be paid for. Things were beginning to look desperate.

'Karl,' Paul asked me, 'can you find any backers?'

I told him I could talk to a couple of people. My instructions had been to keep the ball rolling, so I wasn't going to say no. At the same time, I didn't want to be mixed up in money raising. I'd done this sort of thing before and it always ends in grief.

First, I went to George Baker. He continued to go on to me about the Austrians. They were still planning to buy weapons, arrange a ship and land off the coast of Surinam with a group of mercenaries to go to Ronnie's aid. There was one problem: they wanted me on that boat because they needed loads of up-to-the-minute information. I still smelled a rat and told George to forget it. I called Room Sixteen and warned them to look out for a group of Austrian mercenaries. Later on, Legionnaires and a gendarme arrested six Austrians on a boat on the French side of the Marowijne River. They were taken to St Laurent for questioning and when the French cops opened these guys' passports they went apeshit. They had immigration stamps for Lebanon, Cuba, Hungary, Libya... in fact, they'd been in and out of every bad place on the planet you could think of. Their leader was Hans Jorg Shimanek; his sidekick was called Rada. The French concluded they were neo-Nazi terrorists hired by Bouterse, via Libya's Colonel Gaddafi. At first it was thought they'd entered Surinam through British Guyana. It later transpired they'd flown to Paramaribo, where, because of the covert nature of the operation they were on, their passports had not been stamped. Later, the pair of them went on trial in Austria for neo-Nazi activities, not connected with Surinam, and were both jailed for ten years.

The phone rang. It was Frank Castro in Santo Domingo telling me John Richards and a group of English mercenaries were being held in a cell at Cayenne airport. During the time Frank had been going backwards and forwards between Santo Domingo and Surinam, Paco had returned to Holland. It turned out John Richards had been to see Paco and got money to fund him and his group to go out and kill Ronnie. John also went to see George Baker, who told him to piss off. Then he went to Eric Micheletti at *Raids* magazine, who put John in touch with a film-maker who also funded the trip. There was a suggestion that Antonius from the Surinam Consulate paid him as well. The French allowed John and his boys to go in to Surinam because they had wind that he was going to kill Ronnie. Their view was that it might not be a bad idea. With Ronnie out of the way, that would leave the door open for Paco to step in if John pulled it off. If he didn't manage to kill Ronnie, things would remain the same.

Richards had promised each one of his men £30,000 to go to Surinam for three months to help the Hindustanis from the Nickerie side train up a guerrilla army and then attack Bouterse. What a laugh, who was going to give Richards that sort of money? Psycho's team consisted of French film-maker Eric Deroo and a colleague, Brits Simon Shaw, Pat Baker, Alan Boydel and Neil Finnighan plus Bill Oakey, an Irishman living in London. A Norwegian, Palle Christensen, was also recruited. Most of them were ex-Legionnaires. Boydel and Finnighan had been in the Royal Marines.

Soon after Richards and his mercenaries landed in Surinam, the two French journalists became unnerved by the men's behaviour, especially once they had guns in their hands. So they quit. Pat Baker, who'd served in the

Queen's Irish Hussars, a tank regiment, had difficulty agreeing with the others and he also went home. The group split into two factions: Psycho, Shaw and Christensen from the French Foreign Legion paratroop division, the Deuxième REP on one side; Boydel, Finnighan, known as Finney, and Legionnaire infantryman Oakey on the other. Boydel and his team thought the Legionnaire paratroopers were reckless. They made their way to Brunswijk's headquarters in Moengo, where Ronnie was perplexed and suspicious. At that time an agreed ceasefire was in place. John didn't know about the truce. Ronnie certainly knew from various sources that John was up to no good, yet he still allowed them to stay on and train the Jungle Commandos.

As usual, the mercs fell out among themselves. Richards had apparently been recorded discussing a personal bank account in Holland, where the mercenaries' pay of over £210,000 had been deposited.

Somehow Ronnie found out about John Richards's assassination plot. Brunswijk seemed to believe that Boydel, Finnighan and Oakey were not part of the assassination plot. Ronnie announced he was going to kill Richards.

The paratroopers claimed to have killed seven government soldiers and wounded fourteen others in an early-morning attack on an army base. When the jubilant ex-Legionnaires arrived back at camp, Boydel, Finnighan, Oakey and an unsuspecting Simon Shaw captured John Richards in his hut. They jumped him, disarmed him and

Simon gave him a rifle butt in the head a couple of times. Richards was dragged to the centre of the town and handed over to Ronnie.

Boydel claimed the other three Legionnaires were disarmed, escorted to the river and sent back to French Guiana. John Richards was taken into the jungle and executed. In a confession, secretly filmed by ITV's *The Cook Report* and broadcast in 1995, Boydel admitted, 'When they took him to the jungle, I felt terrible but he deserved it. They tied him to a tree and he asked, "What's going to happen to me?" Bill just said, "You're going to get bitten by mosquitoes and then Ronnie is going to question you." Finney had a Mossberg shotgun, Bill had a FAL rifle and I had a Mossberg. I said I couldn't do it. Then I heard John scream "No!" Then bang, bang, bang.

'Bill's gun jammed, so he cocked it again and Finney was pumping shots into John. I saw Bill throw it down and swear. He grabbed the shotgun off Finney and I saw the shells hitting him and he was twisting around. All his chest was gone. I walked over and said, "Yeah he's dead." But as I walked away I heard this voice saying, "Why are you doing this to me?" so I turned round and put the barrel to his head and went boom. I was sick after I'd done that. I was a bit upset that night, but Finney said he deserved it because he was trying to get us killed. John had every intention of ripping us off and he deserved to die for that. If you are in a mercenary operation the rule is "Don't muck the boys around, you are going to get killed." It's an unwritten rule. He was whacked and his body was torn apart. We dragged his body into the bush. I asked if we were going to bury him but Bill and Finney said, "No, leave him for the animals."'

After the killing, the three left the jungle and were arrested by French government forces. They were deported the following day but they still had time to watch the government-run TV station display John Richards's blood-splattered body. Officials claimed Surinam troops had ambushed the mercenary leader, who was shown with half his head blown away.

Simon Shaw was later reported to have said, 'Alan confessed to me that he killed John. He was the one that contacted me and told me John was dead and I asked him straight away... who did it? He said, "We did", obviously meaning himself, Finney and Bill. He then explained to me exactly how it happened.'

Pat Baker revealed that he'd had a telephone call from Boydel and Finnighan. He said, 'They were still in Surinam. Alan said to me, "We've done the bastard. John's dead." Also at the same time, Finney was shouting down the phone, "We've killed the bastard! We've killed the bastard!"

The news of John's death spread like wildfire. Within four hours of him being tied to that tree and shot, I knew he was dead. I received a call from a good friend in Holland, Mike Stift, who told me how John had been topped near Moengo and that three Englishmen were being held for it. Mike had no other details. When I'd heard John had gone back out to Surinam, I'd predicted to Mike that he and his men would end up being killed. I'm afraid to say mercenary work attracts psychos like bees to a honey pot. Makes you proud to be British, doesn't it? Scotland Yard became interested in John Richards's death but later Boydel was told no charges were pending and the matter was dropped. It was said £210,000 for the mercenaries' wages still remains in a bank account in Holland, though I don't believe it for one second.

Sad news, but I had a few priorities of my own to face, namely fund-raising. I called David Tompkins. David had been a mercenary in Angola and he'd just come back from Colombia, where he'd been trying to assassinate world-famous drug baron Pablo Escobar, leader of the ruthless Medellin Cartel. David knows a lot of people but the only name he could come up with was a man I've known for years. For legal reasons I can't name him, but we'll call him Mr Slimeball. 'You've got to be careful with him,' he admitted. 'He's a little bastard but it's surprising who he could introduce you to.'

I phoned Mr Slimeball, and from the first words I had with him he started fucking about. 'Is that xxxx xxxx?' I asked. 'This is Karl, the guy in Surinam.'

'All right my son, can you hang on? I'm just on another line here to New York.' For all I know he may have cupped his hand over the phone at that point and simply pretended to tell someone he was busy and would call them back later in New York. Mr S. came back on the phone to me: 'All right my son, how's it going?'

Next day I met him at the Adelphi Hotel in Liverpool. He was accompanied by his wife and a minder, an ex-cop. Kidd sent his wife into Lewis's store with his credit card to get her out of the way. I explained how we were looking for backers. 'Do you know anybody?' I asked.

'I know loads of people, don't worry about that, I'll find the money,' he assured me. 'I know about this job. I've read about it in intelligence reports.' Oh right. He continued, 'Let me think now, I've got to see Mr. Suharto of Indonesia' – that was Kidd for you, ever one for throwing names around. We chatted for a while longer and agreed that he'd be in touch in a day or so. For a bit of security, I told him my phone had been cut off and I gave him a friend's number to call. He said he would get back to me in a day or so. Three hours later he was back in touch with my pal Steve H., another ex-Rhodesian army guy. From a payphone up the road from my house, I called him in his car. By now he was somewhere near Lincoln.

The voice crackled. 'I've raised two million pounds already and we can probably get some more. What we need is a trip over to Holland to see your people. When can you do it?'

'As soon as you like, Mr Slime,' I told him.

Later I called Mike Stift in Holland and Ab Hoffman, a former instructor in the Dutch navy, who'd been seconded to train the Surinam navy on how to use S-Boats. Thanks Ab! I also put in a call to another of Mike's friends, Eddie, who was one of Europe's top ophthalmic surgeons. We were going to set up a little sting to see what Mr. Kidd was up to. If he was genuine, no harm done. I certainly wasn't going to take him to see Eddie Dapp or anybody like that. If his heart was in the right place I'd introduce him to the right people later. Mike, Ab and Eddie the surgeon were going to be big shots in the Surinam political world and I was going to introduce him to them. Mr Slimeball arranged an airline ticket for me from Manchester. He was flying from Hull and we'd meet at Schiphol airport.

I watched him arrive with his bodyguard and his girlfriend who worked in the travel agents where he'd bought the tickets. My three 'politicians' were waiting in the Rembrandt Hotel in Amsterdam. Mr Slime opened his briefcase and pulled out a questionnaire to fill in. You give him all the information about yourselves and your little army, he copies it up into a report and then sells it to the enemy. The 'politicians' filled the questionnaire with crap.

Kidd pulled out a map of Surinam. He'd come up with a massive plan; we had to attack Paramaribo with Chinese hand-portable rocket launchers. 'This is going to win friends and influence people in the capital' I thought to myself – 'we'll bombard it first and kill some civilians.' I knew it had been a complete waste of time, but on the bright side, Mr S had paid my ticket and I was sitting in Amsterdam in a nice hotel, eating and drinking at his expense and meeting old friends. The 'politicians' took full advantage of Mr Slime's hospitality – the three of them went home well pissed that night.

When I arrived back in the U.K., I contacted Mike Stift. We laughed and joked on the phone about what had happened with our 'friend'. Now we had to sit tight and wait to hear from him. A couple of days later I was walking back to my flat from a local supermarket when I noticed a white Ford Fiesta car parked up on the right-hand side of the road, the side I was walking on. As I got closer to the car I noticed that there was a coloured man in it. Now I live in a very quiet residential area and it's a fact that no coloured people live there. We have one or two Asian doctors but it's very unusual to see a coloured person and so this guy caught my eye. There was also a white man in the front of the car. As I got a bit closer, I realised that the coloured man was Antonius, the head of dirty tricks at the Surinam Consulate. What the fuck was he doing here? Mr Slimeball immediately flashed through my mind. I was almost up to the car; I had to make a decision. Do I jump into a garden and make my way through the garden and over the back? Are they going to shoot me? Then I thought, 'No, just keep going.'" I was about ten yards from the car when Antonius looked up and recognised me. He slid back down behind the steering wheel a little and looked the other way. He put a hand up as if to scratch his head, so I couldn't see his face. Too late, of course – I'd already clocked him. The white man was about thirty years old, wearing gold-rimmed glasses. He looked down as if he was searching for something in the glove compartment. These guys weren't going to shoot me if they were doing that. I walked past the car, took a left round a corner and quickened my pace. After all, I was only armed with two cartons of milk and a newspaper. I could hear them reversing the car at high speed. When I looked around, they'd shot up past the road where I'd taken a left. They screamed up to the top, did a left, left again and by the time I reached my road they were coming down it at high speed. As I walked towards my flat I could see a skip full of branches in the road a few yards ahead. This would be my cover. As the car came down the road, I walked with the skip blocking their view of me. As the car came past, Antonius's friend tried to take photographs of me. Well now, Mr Slimeball, what are you up to now?

A few days later, Ab Hoffman found out. Ab was able to go in and out of the Surinam Consulate in Amsterdam without arousing suspicion, so I used to use him to spy for me. He discovered that as soon as I had flown back to Manchester, Kidd had turned round and gone to the Surinam Consulate to tell them he was into our group at a very high level and that he had access to a lot of information about us. When Antonius saw some of the information Mr. Kidd had taken from his questionnaire he told Lenny he'd been taken for a ride. So then, I'm informed, Mr Slimeball offered to kill me for a fee of around $50,000. 'Okay,' Antonius told him, 'you kill him and then we'll pay you.' So Slimeball travelled back to the U.K., spent a little time at home, probably kicking himself. Then he flew back to the Consulate in Amsterdam and told Antonius the job had been done – I was dead.

Antonius said he needed a little time to get the money together. Slimeball stayed at a hotel in Amsterdam, again at his own expense, while he was waiting for the money. That was when Antonius turned up and took the photographs of me. Mr S. went around to the Consulate, where he was shown photographs of me alive and well. There you go Mr Slimeball, never misjudge people by their accents. Antonius was later expelled from Holland for activities 'not in line with his diplomatic status'. Couldn't have happened to a nicer guy.

CHAPTER 15

The Kourou Agreement was in tatters. The Cuban exiles had gone back to Florida. Moengo was back in army hands. The Jungle Commandos still held the main road. Who should phone me but George Baker asking me to go with him to Surinam to find a way to end the stalemate. George promised to pay wages for myself and Steve H., who'd helped me out with Mr Slimeball. Steve is ex-Rhodesian Light Infantry, he'd been in Fire Force and was a good lad. The money from Paul had dried up, so it was nice to be employed again and not just sitting in the background watching. It was good to be going back. I was refreshed and feeling quite fit, although I still couldn't stop coughing all the time. I was now using asthma inhalers. I phoned Room Sixteen and told them when we would be arriving.

As we picked up our luggage from the carousel at Cayenne airport, three white men stepped out of the crowd and grabbed each of us by the arm: 'Excuse me, messieurs, please come with us.' We went into an office and they asked us to go into the cell. 'Is there a problem?' I asked.

'Yes, there's a problem.'

Fucking hell what's up this time? 'You cannot come in,' one of the policemen told me, 'You must go back.'

By now I was seriously hacked off. Pierre from Room Sixteen was on his way from St Laurent to explain everything. Half an hour later, he arrived and told me, 'Karl, there's been a diplomatic complaint. The Surinam Consulate knew you were on the way and they complained to Paris. I'm afraid Paris has had to give us instructions to kick you out.'

'Is there any way out of this?' I asked him.

'No, there's no way out. You've got to go back,' he assured me.

This was my third trip with George and each time it had culminated in virtual disaster! George was in a foul temper, blaming me for the fuck up, whereas it was actually nobody's fault but his. What did he expect when he bought his airline tickets in a Surinamese travel agency in Amsterdam? Eventually, George calmed down and handed a wad of money to Pierre. It was for Tommy Dennely, an American mercenary – a genuine one, too – who'd been waiting for us in Surinam. I hadn't met the man myself, but people who know what they are talking about said Tommy was a totally trustworthy guy. He was up at Stoelman's Island with Ronbo.

Back to Heathrow and some heartening news: Lloyd's of London had paid Ronnie £400,000 in cash for the Twin Otter. A new one would have cost them a couple of million pounds, so rather than pay out they offered Ronnie four hundred grand to give plane back. A mechanic and a pilot flew out from London, successfully started the Twin Otter, refuelled it and flew it to Paramaribo. Ronnie got all the money, and I did not receive a cent. I believe Ronnie bought himself a nice new minibus to run his boys about in French Guiana – that made sense. He also bought a huge video camera for making movies of himself – that didn't make sense, but that's Ronbo for you. Ronnie also threw a few lavish parties to celebrate his success as guerrilla leader.

It seemed I wasn't the only one pissed off with Ronnie; other people had also been getting fed up of him. Two of the bush negro village leaders, Om Bodo and Asi Bonet, both of them real gentlemen, were tired of their people having to live on the river as refugees. I'd met them the time I went downriver with Paul and Glen Chung. The head men went looking for Ronnie to try and get some action. By this time Ronnie was at Stoelman's Island with all the good guys and all the shiny new guns the Cuban exiles had left.

The only people still remaining at Langatbbetje were the absolute scum. Om Bodo got into an argument with the commandant at Langatabbetje, who shot dead the village head man. Asi Bonnot arrived a short while later, when news got out, and he too was shot and killed. The following day, Asi Bonnot's son arrived on Langatabbetje to plead for the bodies. He was told that not only could he not have the bodies back, but he could actually join them and the psychopath shot him dead too. Ronnie backed his commandant.

More news. Ronnie was coming to Holland to meet a number of politicians and wanted to see me. I met Ronnie in a council house in Tilburg, a town near the Dutch border with Belgium. He put his arms around me and started all the 'Hey, my friend,' nonsense, but behind that front, I could tell that he was seriously nervous. He still held the N1 road and claimed he had groups of JCs prowling around keeping an eye on the army. I knew for a fact they were prowling around, stealing and smuggling. Without any mercenaries or Frank Castro's mob, Ronnie was feeling a bit exposed. And when Ronnie felt vulnerable, he always turned to me.

'Can you bring some boys over?' he asked. 'Maybe something will happen.' He'd got to say that, simply to get me interested, but in truth he just wanted me there as a deterrent. I'm not showing off, but every time I wasn't there, the army jumped on Ronnie and gave him a pasting, as they did at Moengo. I tackled Ronnie about Om Bodo and Asi Bonnot. His answer was, 'I've got no control of the situation, how can I be on Langatbbetje and Stoelman's Island at the same time?'

'Of course you can't Ronnie,' I retorted, 'but it's quite simple: you don't leave a madman in charge of Langatabbetje. That's where the fault lies with you.' But at the end of the day, he simply didn't give a shit. Since he'd started dealing in cocaine with Bouterse, he'd become arrogant. He thought I didn't know about it, although by then half the world knew. Ronnie no longer had any shame.

'Anyway, can you bring some men out? he pleaded again.

Ronnie wanted six or seven guys, but in the end he could afford just five. I went home and recruited Steve Conway, an ex-British army lad and three of his mates. We arrived at Victoria station in London, but before I bought tickets for us all on the boat train, I called Tilburg, just to make sure everything was going ahead as planned. I discovered that Ronnie had done a bunk and gone back to Surinam. No one knew what was happening, so I aborted the mission there and then.

A couple of weeks went by and the spooks in suits were getting agitated. They wanted to know what was going on. Arrangements were made for me to see Eddie Dapp and Ronnie's younger brother, Leo Brunswijk. Leo was at college in Holland training to be a flight engineer. I flew to Amsterdam with a big Jewish guy called Ritchie. He'd been in the Israeli army and trained as a bodyguard; a handy guy to have around. I contacted Leo and told him I was in Amsterdam. We arranged to meet the day after next. Leo finally turned up *ten* days later. The spooks were now very jittery and I was very pissed off. Profuse apologies from Leo – he'd been to Surinam to see Ronnie who wanted me to go out there with just one man in two weeks' time. Back to the U.K.

Invisible hands were at my back, pushing me to get the war going again. They had news about why Ronnie was so eager to have me out there once more. Ronnie had gone to Paramaribo, taking with him a young boy called Stuart who worshipped him, and a commandant named Duchy, who'd been promoted to bodyguard. They'd gone to Paramaribo to chat with Desi Bouterse about the plane load of cocaine and dollars. I distinctly remember warning Stuart not to let Bouterse's men see him.

As they got out of the vehicles, Stuart and Duchy were bundled into a room and told to wait for Ronnie. As they reached the doorway, Bouterse's men opened fire, killing them both – shot in the back. Ronnie was tied up, taken to a cell and beaten. I dare say Bouterse threatened that unless Ronnie gave him what was owed, he and the JCs would be chased from Stoelman's Island. Ronnie got back in one piece, shocked but still alive – unlike the other two. That's what you get when you think your boss is bulletproof. Ronnie later burned the coke on national TV in front of officials from Holland and Surinam. Some people say it was just flour.

I made a phone call to French Guiana to let Room Sixteen know that my arrival was imminent but when I called the Star Hotel, Room Sixteen had checked out. I rang up the office to be told that Francois and Pierre were no longer working there. Something strange was going on. I'd have to watch myself. Word came through Leo for me to go back to Surinam. I still hadn't heard from the French. It could have been a set up, so I rigged Ritchie out as a journalist – I even gave him a camera tripod – and sent him on ahead at his own expense. He wasn't wanted in French Guiana and would be able to travel without any problems. He would travel to St Laurent and take a boat 'upstairs' to see Ronnie at Stoelman's. When he returned to St Laurent, Ritchie was to call me, but not from the Toucan Hotel.

Two weeks later, Ritchie phoned me from a call box in St Laurent. He'd been in hospital suffering from malaria. Things were OK, though. He'd seen Ronnie and there'd be no problems for me going through Cayenne. I asked Ritchie to tell Jacques we were coming back. Ritchie called back – Jacques didn't live there any more, he'd gone to Belgium. Everybody was pissing off, and I couldn't say I blamed them. Steve H. and I travelled to Holland, where Leo bought us tickets to Cayenne.

Things had changed in Surinam while I'd been away. The main road was now open for traffic, though Ronnie still had a grip on the area. Little groups of his men kept an eye on things. Langatabbetje now belonged to Desi and the army were in control of the island. Ronnie held Stoelman's Island, which was out of bounds to Bouterse's men. To see Ronnie, we would have to pass Langatabbetje on the French side of the river. As we sat on the terrace of the Toucan, a small crowd spilled out onto the street from the small cinema across the road. Among them was Oki. I noticed a shaven patch on the back of his head. He'd been shot in the head as he ran away. He'd ducked his head down and the bullet struck him just above the nape of his neck, hitting his skull and making a rivulet under the scalp before coming out.

He spotted me and greeted me warmly: 'Hey Karel, how are you my friend?'

It seemed Oki was out of favour with Ronnie and he'd left the Jungle Commandos. As we chatted to Oki, Robert led three black guys to a table close by. They sat there furtively looking across at us as Robert muttered to them.

'Robert can we have another beer please?' I asked. As he brought over the drinks, I nodded my head in the direction of the three guys. 'Who are they?'

'Surinam police,' said Robert putting a finger to his eye as if to say watch out for them. Jesus – he'd told them who we all were! We had to get down to the river as quickly as possible. It was unsafe to travel on the river at night, but at the crack of dawn we were being driven towards the river at Saint-Jean, where a boat was waiting. Hammering along a dirt road on the outskirts of St Laurent, two gendarmes in a police car pulled alongside and signalled our driver to stop. A giant French cop climbed out of the car and pointed at us. 'Karl Penta, Stephen H. and Ritchie B. follow me.'

We followed his car back into St Laurent, past the Toucan Hotel and up to the gendarmerie barracks. Inside the grim concrete walls I felt more than a bit jittery and the other two weren't looking too happy either. Something was seriously wrong here. It turned out it was me that was wrong.

'Come in. Café monsieur?' the policemen asked. Over steaming cups of coffee, he said, 'We're glad we caught you before you left; we have some things to tell you.' I asked where Francois and Pierre had gone. They'd both been moved to another country. It looked to me like the

French were shutting down the operation. Anyway, the policeman shown me photostat copies of one hundred-dollar bills with certain serial numbers. 'Don't take any of these off Brunswijk for payment,' he warned me, 'because if they are found on you they will be confiscated.' Right. He then showed me photographs of all the boys who were now trafficking in cocaine. He pointed to a picture of Fritz Hirshland and said 'merde' (shit). Dead right on that one, monsieur. And he had one final piece of advice: 'Don't come back into St Laurent, because you will be arrested and chased out. Off you go and good luck.'

As we landed at the Jungle Commando camp below Langatabbetje, Om Leo was waiting for us. 'Karel my friend. What you bring for me?' Fuck all, pal. Back onto the boat. On we went past the barracks, past the army camp there, past the lookout post. We saw some of Ronnie's boys on the rocks on the other side, and gave them a wave as we went past. Approaching Langatabbetje we hid under the tarpaulin as the boat veered to the French side. At Stoelman's Island, Jungle Commandos wearing Military Police badges milled around a customs post. It all looked very organised. The Number One MP stepped forward. It was Dino, the guy from Amsterdam who'd tried to do the iffy arms deal with me in Belgium. He looked a bit nervous because he knew I was onto him. I wasn't going to say anything, though – not at this moment, anyhow.

'How are you doing, Dino?'

He was all over me. 'Karel it's great to see you my friend. I didn't know you were coming back, this is fantastic.' His eyes almost pleaded 'Please don't snitch on me.' They would take us to see Ronnie. Things had certainly changed since I'd been away: it was all procedures now. Visitors had to wait at the old customs house, which had become a military police post. We were halfway there when Ronbo came running down the track. There was the usual kissing nonsense, and then we sat down to talk.

'Did you hear about Duchy and Stuart?' he asked me.

'Yes, Ronnie I heard, about it. A fucking stupid move on your part.'

'Oh no, Karel, I was doing business with Bouterse. We had this cocaine and the dollars. The bastard wanted it back from me so I went to do a deal with him and that's when they killed the boys.' As I said, smart move Ronnie. He told me he'd now done a deal whereby if he left Bouterse alone, the dictator would ignore him in return.

'Oh right,' I said, 'he'll leave you alone here on Stoelman's Island because he's got everything else.'

'Yeah, but I don't need the rest.' *What?*

'But what about the people that matter, Ronnie?' I asked. 'There must be something like fifteen thousand refugees living along the Marowijne River. What about all the thousands who ran off to Holland? They all want to return.'

'Yeah, that's going to take time, we need more negotiation with Bouterse.'

I couldn't say anything at the time, but I knew all about Ronnie's cocaine deals with Bouterse. Cocaine was being bought very cheaply in Paramaribo and shipped across the river into French Guiana. The river was now crawling with French troops. They weren't expecting war to break out; they were looking for cocaine traffickers. So the rebel leader had degenerated into a drug baron. I was feeling pretty sick at that. However, I didn't have too much time to dwell on Ronnie's loss of scruples. I had work to do: I still had to gee the guy up, find out if there was any possibility of starting the war again. 'If you're not going to fight,' I asked him, 'why am I here?'

'To train the boys.'

'Why do they need to be trained if the war is finished?'

'I don't trust that Bouterse,' he replied. 'Maybe soon something's going to happen.'

'Like what? Spell it out to me; put me in the picture. I don't like walking around in the dark.'

'I don't have big evidence,' he said. 'But I think something will happen.'

Ronnie, what the fucking hell are you up to now? Was I going to end up like Stuart and Duchy? No chance. I figured that when Ronnie did the dirty on the dictator, or vice versa, Bouterse's men were going to come down and chase him from Stoelman's Island. That's why I was there. Ronnie went on to tell me about the army attack on Langatabbetje. A helicopter gunship arrived and fired rockets. They were the same rockets that had been seized at Rotterdam docks, but somehow they'd mysteriously disappeared only to turn up in Surinam. A couple of the boys died in that rocket attack. One of the men was actually killed when he stood behind a tree. Both of his hands were ripped off and he died from blood loss.

A couple of days later, Ronnie come running up to me. 'Karel, my radio is on fire.'

'Well, throw a bucket of water over it,' I replied.

'No, no, fire is from messages I have from Paramaribo, they call me plenty. They know you are here and they want to speak with you.'

'Who's *they*, Ronnie?'

'The Surinam army want to send some officers to come and speak with you.'

'What do they want to talk about?'

'They think you come here and make plenty trouble again in Surinam.'

It turned out that two officers and a pilot wanted to fly in to Stoelman's Island that afternoon to talk to me. This would be the first enemy aircraft that had landed on our territory in the whole damn war. It was also the first time any army officers had come to negotiate on our territory. That's how much they trusted Ronnie. The meeting would be held in the old customs house. All the weapons came out: MAGs, Minimees, they even had a fifty-calibre mounted on an observation tower up at the airfield. All the boys looked the part in uniforms with jungle boots and webbing full of ammunition, all courtesy of Frank Castro.

Ronnie found a tablecloth from somewhere and put it on a table in the police post. He also arranged a few chairs. As he stood back to admire his handiwork, he told me, 'Karel, I'm going to speak with them first and you're going to hide over there in the next room with your two friends. Then I'll send for you and we'll give them a fright.'

'Ronnie you mustn't take these men too seriously,' I cautioned him. 'They're gangsters with military uniforms on, that's all.' I had a damn good idea why they were really coming. They were going to ask Ronnie to hand me over. I explained my fears to Steve H. and Ritchie B. Ronnie was insisting there'd be no weapons in the room during negotiations. I had a snub-nose .38 Smith & Wesson air-weight, six-shot revolver, which I decided to hide on me. If Ronnie was mental enough to hand me over, I'd make an escape attempt in the aircraft with my .38. If they handcuffed me and the revolver was discovered, I was seriously considering suicide. I did not want to arrive alive in Paramaribo in a pair of handcuffs. Anyway, let's not panic yet, boys. The JCs ran around, getting in their positions to look as effective as they could. The little party on the aircraft were about to be met by about fifteen of Ronnie's men, fully armed. Another fifteen, armed with MAGs, would be lying in strategic positions around the police post. They were all going to be seen purely for effect, of course.

Fritz Hirshland, who'd grown a beard and now looked like a cross between Che Guevara and Fidel Castro, arrived. He was wearing full camouflage uniform and sported two cardboard epaulettes with his rank drawn on in Biro! The guy was getting more wacky by the minute.

Hirshland was going be the interpreter for the meeting. I
wasn't happy about that, but Ronnie wanted his publicity
man there. Shortly before two o'clock, a camouflaged
Defender flew low over the airstrip, flashing its landing
lights. From behind the cover of the building, we watched
the barrels being moved off the strip ready for landing.
We disappeared out of sight as Ronnie and Bouterse's men
went in to the police post. Four of Ronnie's bodyguards
stood outside the office where the meeting was held. The
door was ajar. I squinted through to see a white Air Force
pilot wearing a pair of mirrored sunglasses. A clip-on
holster with a semi-automatic pistol was perched on his
lap, in full view of everybody. Two coloured army men,
one old, the other about forty, sat in front of Ronnie.
They all looked distinctly pale and nervous. A shiny Mac
11 submachine pistol gleamed on the desk in front of
Ronnie. There was no question anybody was going to
start shooting. These guys weren't suicide cases.

They chattered for about forty-five minutes, in Taki
Taki. Ronnie's chief bodyguard, Pablo, standing outside in
his uniform, leant back towards me in the doorway,
whispering to me what was being said. He hissed, 'They're
asking that you go to Paramaribo with them for
questioning.' I decided there and then to play my ace card.
When I'd finished with these men there was no way that
Ronnie would hand me over. A few more minutes passed
before a guard summoned me, Ritchie and Steve. As the
three of us walked in Ronnie, feigning innocence said,
'These three men want to speak with you Karel. Sit down.'

Three empty chairs were waiting. They'd brought a camera to take my photograph. Hirshland turned to me and asked, 'What is your name?'

I said, 'Are you joking? Tell these officers if they don't know my name they can ask their friend Antonius. He'll give them my name, address and photographs of me. For the record, my name's Donald Duck.' Ritchie gave a false name, too. Steve told them he was Philip Windsor; the older army bloke wrote down the Duke of Edinburgh's name.

'Can we have your addresses and date of birth?' Hirshland, sat there in his cardboard epaulettes, was loving it. Time to play my little ace card. 'Fritz, shut up! Enough of all this bullshit,' I snapped. Pointing at the three men across the table, I went on, 'I know you three comedians speak English, I know that very well.' They blanched. 'You know my name.' Then, stabbing a finger at Ritchie and Steve, I continued, 'The names of these two men are none of your fucking damn business. I have no respect for you. The three of you come here masquerading as army officers. You're all gangsters and friends with Mr. Bouterse.'

Now pointing towards Ronnie, I said, 'I know what you've come here for... to ask this man to hand me over. Well, let me tell you something. If it wasn't for this man's concern, you three would never leave this island. Do you understand me? The only way you would leave this island is in plastic bags, so don't come here giving shit out about handing me over. You can forget that. And what are you doing with that pistol on your lap? You were told no weapons in the room.'

His voice trembling, the pilot said – in perfect English – 'Ronnie said it would be OK as long as I just put it there out of the way.'

'You're lucky I don't take it off you and shove it up your arse, you shithead.' By now I was shouting like I was mentally unstable, to put the fear of God into the three of them. We weren't here for an intellectual debate, so I went on, 'Listen. Go back to Paramaribo and tell Desi from me, I don't have a problem with the Surinam people; I don't really have a problem with the Surinam army. My problem is with that piece of shit Bouterse. I don't know what part you scumbags play in the whole sordid business, but you tell him from me that if I catch up with that man, I will fucking kill him.' Waving my arms towards Ronnie's boys I said, 'All of these men standing around here, where are their families? They're in fucking refugee camps because of you shower of pricks!' By now I was shouting loudly so all the boys outside could hear. 'I'm telling you now, the game is up for you lot. Do you know why I'm here? Because I've got forty men on standby in England. There are aircraft waiting now in Santo Domingo with weapons. It takes just one phone call and next time we're coming to Paramaribo. No more fucking around up on the main road, next time it's Paramaribo. You can tell Desi all of these things. I'm sick and tired of you animals!'

Silence from them. Their hands were shaking, their faces pale. Eventually the pilot said, 'I know what you mean, Bouterse's the main trouble maker.' He was trying to pass the buck. I verbally abused him a bit more then I said to Ronnie, 'I've got better things to do. I don't have time to talk to these three fucking jokers I'm leaving this room.' Ronnie was trying to hide the big smile on his face. He stood, gave me a salute and I stormed out with Ritchie and Steve slamming the door behind us. As we walked off, I smiled and said, 'Let's go and have a beer, boys.'

That night, Ronnie threw a huge party. As we waited for the band to finish setting up, Ronnie sat on an oil barrel lying on its side. He banged on the barrel, 'Karel, come sit here with me.' I went over and sat beside him. 'You done very good for me today, Karel,' he told me, smiling.

'That's what I'm here for Ronnie. You think about what's happening in Paramaribo now. Bouterse is very afraid. He thinks you can just pick the phone up and forty men will come, weapons, everything. He's very nervous now, I'm sure of that. *If* he swallows it.' The chances of him swallowing it were pretty high.

The group was deafening, blaring out salsa music. Ritchie put up with it for about five minutes and disappeared. Ronnie decided he was a pop star, grabbed the microphone off the singer and started braying like a donkey. 'Course, nobody could laugh without fear of retribution. Next morning, I'd expected Ronnie to be nursing a hangover but he'd been on the radio talking to Desi Bouterse instead. It seemed the Great Dictator was angry I hadn't been handed over.

Steve was feeling under the weather. He was becoming quite delirious; sometimes he didn't know where he was. We therefore decided to head back to French Guiana. At Om Leo's camp on the way downriver, I heard a story on the BBC Caribbean Service about a British mercenary who was wanted by the Surinam government. Apparently, he had last been seen on Stoelman's Island with the rebel leader Ronnie Brunswijk. This mercenary who was destroying their country was supposed to be hiding out in the jungle somewhere.

Ronnie sent a boat and we travelled down to Saint-Jean. Our great leader had been having meetings with the French authorities. It seemed everybody was looking for me. Bouterse was very angry and he'd talked with the French government in Paris.

'There's a lot of problems,' Ronnie told me.

'I know that,' I replied. 'I've done my job by warning Bouterse what will happen if he continues. The rest is down to you. I'm going home with the boys; if you need me, you know where to call me. Try to get your act together and think about all of these people here.' Time to go boys, back to the Toucan Hotel to get arrested. We'd only been there an hour when eight gendarmes arrived to nick us. The TV cameras were waiting at Cayenne when we were officially kicked out. The French had to cover their own arses, but I didn't feel too disgruntled; I know the way the game is played. Back to Heathrow. Three singles to Liverpool Lime Street, please.

The next day, Steve was in a hospital isolation unit. He had a terrible bout of malaria and something was growing in his leg. Eventually a big grub that had grown inside his ankle popped out. A little live souvenir from Surinam.

Spooks in suits visited me again. I told them what had gone on. Apparently, we could congratulate ourselves on a job well done, but now it was time to sit and wait. I was also seeing people from the exiled Surinam community. They'd completely lost it with Ronnie and wanted to try and start a new rebel group. However, there was a slight problem: no money left, they'd invested it all in Ronbo – who was politically and geographically back at square one.

In a desperate attempt to get things moving again, I went on an obvious non-starter to Santa Domingo with David Tomkins who brought along an annoying fucker who called himself Phil Stevenson. I knew that wasn't his real name. He was, in fact, called Phil Sesserego. He spent the whole of that unpleasant week talking about the SAS and dropping the names of blokes in the Regiment into the conversation. He gave the impression that he'd been a member of the SAS, but I knew that was a load of bollocks.

One day, not long after I returned from Santa Domingo, Eddie Dapp phoned me with a warning. Apparently, Desi Bouterse had got an Obia man to put a voodoo curse on me. I laughed down the phone at him. 'OK, Eddie.' But within twenty-four hours I was seriously ill. For days on end my life seemed to be ebbing away, but no one could work out why. Samples of my blood were sent to the School of Tropical Medicine for analysis. To this day, no one knows why I was so ill. It may have been the power of the Obia men. It may just have been coincidence. I'm still not sure.

One thing's for certain. Ronnie Brunswijk believed in voodoo and was afraid of the Obia men. I could never understand why the Obia men didn't force him to stand down. Maybe Ronnie looked after them with money. At the end of the day, Ronnie was a coward. Apart from that one time at Albina, when he ran so fast he would have put an Olympic runner to shame, Brunswijk didn't fight anywhere while I was in Surinam. Maybe it will take another war to oust him.

Bouterse once said that Ronnie had a lot of horsepower but no horse sense, which was quite true. An example: one day I drove past the Efterling theme park in Holland with Ronnie. He spotted a hotel made to look like a castle and told me, 'One day, I'm going to have a castle like that in the jungle.' The monster Eddie Dapp created was out of control. It's easy to say with hindsight that Ronnie should never have been put in such a position of power, but he should have seen the thing through for the sake of his people and not come to some shady compromise with Bouterse. He chose the easy route.

I reckon one of the bush negroes must stand up and do something. All those boys who sit on the river bank in their despair, all the ones who fought while Brunswijk skulked, should get up and get rid of him. Deal with Brunswijk first, then deal with Bouterse. They called Bouterse Mr. Super Plus; I made him look like Mr. Tractor Oil. And if I can do that once, someone else can do it again.

EPILOGUE

As I write this in the autumn of 2001, it is now fifteen years since I first went to Surinam. You might like to know what has happened in those intervening years:

DESI BOUTERSE eventually did stand down as dictator, allowing a properly elected government to take control in 1989. He hasn't given up politics, though, and is now an MP in Surinam. However, if he ever steps out outside Surinam he will be jailed. In his absence, a court in the Netherlands found him guilty of drug trafficking and sentenced him to twenty years. He cannot be extradited from Surinam, but if he travels to a country where Interpol holds sway, he will be brought to Holland to serve his time. Even if he stays in Paramaribo, he may find himself in prison. Investigations are still going on into the allegations that Bouterse ordered rival politicians to be executed.

RONNIE BRUNSWIJK became rich trading in timber, gold and cocaine. Indeed, it is believed that he combined his interests sometimes, using timber shipments to hide cocaine consignments. He still lives in Surinam and he, too, faces a jail sentence in Holland after also being convicted in his absence of drug trafficking and sentenced to seven years. Ronnie enjoys complete freedom to travel around in Surinam, although he has had a few scares. He's been locked up once or twice, he's been poisoned in jail and there have been a few attempts on his life. But I think it's a case of better the devil you know....

PACO paid the ultimate price. Death squads began operating in Surinam. One group of six Jungle Commandos was foolish enough to walk into a bar in Paramaribo during the 'ceasefire'. They were shot in cold blood by Bouterse's Death Squad. Paco suffered a worse fate at their hands. He and his bodyguard Frankie were on a boat on Brokopondo Lake when the two of them mysteriously disappeared. When Paco's body was eventually recovered, there was nothing left of it but bits of meat and a few rags. His corpse had been fed to the dogs and then set alight; his ID card was the only means of telling that it was him. Frankie was also murdered.

The ever-trustworthy FRITZ HIRSHLAND thrived on the oxygen of publicity. It could have come as a surprise to no one, then, when he published a book in Holland detailing Frank Castro's dealings. Fritz made a huge fuss, claiming he was working for Dutch Intelligence; Frank Castro was very pissed off about it. However, Fritz must have had a whole bunch of demons no one knew about, because one day he booked himself into the Krasnapolski Hotel in Amsterdam and killed himself with a drugs overdose – in the very room he'd been conceived in. That was the same hotel where Schimanek and Rada amused guests by turning up for breakfast wearing U.S. Army tiger-stripe uniforms.

Talking of untrustworthy people, ROBBIE CASSIE, suffered six heart attacks as a result of the pressures of dealing with both sides in Surinam. His last heart attack was fatal.

Another double-dealer, KOYKU, managed to persuade Ronnie to let him become an Obia man. But all the time he was planning to escape. One day he stole a car near Moengo and made a break for it. The boys stopped him at the roadblock with a hail of bullets; Ronnie could not allow him to escape because he knew too much about the Jungle Commandos. One bullet went through the upright by the door and hit Koyku in the head. It was a serious wound, but he survived. However, Koyku subsequently went off his nut anyway, and spent much of his time wearing a woman's dress. He was caught one day staring directly at the sun and they let him go home.

DRED – the cook who kicked Koyku in the face at the airstrip and whom I had to punch in the mouth – well, he's dead now too. He drowned in the rapids near Apatou.

MAX, who flew with us to hijack the Twin Otter lost his wife, his home and his mind through following Ronnie. He was jailed in French Guiana for cocaine trafficking. On his release he declared himself to be a prophet. He is now in Amsterdam, preaching to anyone who will listen to him. Poor Max.

I told you that ANTONIUS was booted out of Holland. Well, he returned to Surinam and I understand he got into trouble trading in hooky passports during the takeover of Hong Kong. By the way, did you ever wonder how Antonius got my address in Liverpool? John Richards gave it to him.

I bumped into ALAN BOYDEL in a street in Zagreb, Croatia. 'You're Karl,' he greeted me, 'I recognise you from the photographs of John Richards in Surinam.' We went for a drink in a bar and he told me his version of John Richards's demise. He claimed John had been shot by Ronnie's bodyguards, because he had been ripping everybody off. Sure Alan, sure.

Sadly, BOB McKENZIE, the ex-Rhodesian SAS man from *Soldier of Fortune* magazine was killed in an operation in Sierra Leone.

Not everyone in this story has died, gone to jail or gone round the twist, though.

GEORGE BAKER renamed his bar, in Oud Hoogstrat near Amsterdam's red-light district, the Karel Apple Bar. George now lives in Surinam after admitting on TV that Bouterse had been right all along!

DR MENGELE and his sidekick Didier are now practising medicine in Paris. I met Patrick Chauvel in Paris not too long ago. I dare say my appearance surprised him: he thought I'd been killed in Surinam.

PAUL also went to Surinam and got his wish. He is a minister in the government there.

EDDIE DAPP, the man who created the monster that became Ronnie Brunswijk, retired from refugee work and is now a lay preacher in Holland. I still keep in touch with Eddie to this day.

I next saw closet SAS man PHIL SESSEREGO on TV punching a camera in the BBC after being exposed. Sesserego wrote a book undr the name Tom Carew in which he claimed to be an ex-Regiment trooper who fought in Afghanistan.

On my last trip to Stoelman's Island, I read a newspaper article which revealed that John the Twin Otter pilot was fit and well and had returned to work. That was very good news.

I have never seen MAJOR GETBACK, the combat cook, since. I don't want to either. I did see KEITH a couple of times – we had a drink together but subsequently lost touch. HENK went to Holland and disappeared without trace.

I told you how Keith liked a drink. Well, I took to drink for twelve months as a result of stress.

* * *

Anyway, that's my story. There was certainly more action I could tell you about – such as the time I ran out of ammunition and had to fight my attackers off with my knife, fork and spoon! Many things have been left out of this story – some deliberately, some because of the constraints of the size of the book. Still, many blushes have been spared.

But the story still goes on. Just a few months ago a plane landed near Albina on 'some business'. Six Brazilians on board were shot dead, as was Shorty, one of Ronnie's boys.

Never ends, does it?